New Comparisons in World Literature

Series Editors
Upamanyu Pablo Mukherjee
Department of English Comparative Literary Studies
University of Warwick
Coventry, UK

Sharae Deckard
School of English, Drama & Film Studies
University College Dublin
Dublin, Ireland

New Comparisons in World Literature offers a fresh perspective on one of the most exciting current debates in humanities by approaching 'world literature' not in terms of particular kinds of reading but as a particular kind of writing. We take 'world literature' to be that body of writing that registers in various ways, at the levels of form and content, the historical experience of capitalist modernity. We aim to publish works that take up the challenge of understanding how literature registers both the global extension of 'modern' social forms and relations and the peculiar new modes of existence and experience that are engendered as a result. Our particular interest lies in studies that analyse the registration of this decisive historical process in literary consciousness and affect. We welcome proposals for monographs, edited collections and Palgrave Pivots (short works of 25,000-50,000 words).

Editorial board
Dr Nicholas Brown, University of Illinois, USA; Dr Bo G. Ekelund, University of Stockholm, Sweden
Dr Dorota Kolodziejczyk, Wroclaw University, Poland
Professor Paulo de Medeiros, University of Warwick, UK
Dr Robert Spencer, University of Manchester, UK
Professor Imre Szeman, University of Alberta, Canada
Professor Peter Hitchcock, Baruch College, USA
Dr Ericka Beckman, University of Illinois at Urbana-Champaign, USA
Dr Sarah Brouillette, Carleton University, Canada
Professor Supriya Chaudhury, Jadavpur University, India
Professor Stephen Shapiro, University of Warwick, UK

Tavid Mulder

Modernism in the Peripheral Metropolis

Form, Crisis and the City in Latin America

Tavid Mulder
Emerson College
Boston, MA, USA

ISSN 2634-6095 ISSN 2634-6109 (electronic)
New Comparisons in World Literature
ISBN 978-3-031-34054-3 ISBN 978-3-031-34055-0 (eBook)
https://doi.org/10.1007/978-3-031-34055-0

© The Editor(s) (if applicable) and The Author(s), under exclusive licence to Springer Nature Switzerland AG 2023
This work is subject to copyright. All rights are solely and exclusively licensed by the Publisher, whether the whole or part of the material is concerned, specifically the rights of translation, reprinting, reuse of illustrations, recitation, broadcasting, reproduction on microfilms or in any other physical way, and transmission or information storage and retrieval, electronic adaptation, computer software, or by similar or dissimilar methodology now known or hereafter developed.
The use of general descriptive names, registered names, trademarks, service marks, etc. in this publication does not imply, even in the absence of a specific statement, that such names are exempt from the relevant protective laws and regulations and therefore free for general use.
The publisher, the authors, and the editors are safe to assume that the advice and information in this book are believed to be true and accurate at the date of publication. Neither the publisher nor the authors or the editors give a warranty, expressed or implied, with respect to the material contained herein or for any errors or omissions that may have been made. The publisher remains neutral with regard to jurisdictional claims in published maps and institutional affiliations.

Cover illustration: Sinisa Kukic/Getty Images

This Palgrave Macmillan imprint is published by the registered company Springer Nature Switzerland AG.
The registered company address is: Gewerbestrasse 11, 6330 Cham, Switzerland

ACKNOWLEDGMENTS

Above all, I am most grateful to Karen, my wife, for the support and encouragement she has given me over many years of research, writing, and re-writing. Teddy, my son, has always put things in perspective, and I cherish the distractions that his inexhaustible energy has provided.

Michelle Clayton has offered invaluable feedback on the project from the very beginning and she remains a crucial source of support. She has consistently pushed my thinking in new directions, and the comparative and interdisciplinary dimensions of the project follow directly from our conversations. Emilio Sauri has read (and re-read) more of the book than anyone else, always helping me to identify what is at stake and the most compelling points in the argument. Emilio has been a model of intellectual rigor, not to mention a good friend. Ericka Beckman has been incredibly generous with her support, and she has inspired me through her scholarship.

I have had some of my most intellectually stimulating conversations with Matt Gannon, Alex Moskowitz, and Jaime Acosta Gonzalez. But most importantly, I am immensely fortunate to count on their friendship.

I would like to thank the Warwick Research Collective, especially Sharae Deckard and Pablo Mukherjee, for embracing me in Utrecht, for shaping my perspective on world literature, and for their editorial direction. I am also grateful to the following people for their intellectual contributions and friendship: Esther Whitfield, Stephanie Merrim, Timothy Bewes, Mariano Siskind, Neil Larsen, Paul Stasi, Bret Benjamin, Nicholas Brown, Robert Kaufman, Sarah Wells, Silvia López, Cynthia Steele, Marshall Brown,

José Antonio Lucero, Will Arighi, Liz Gray, Michelle Rada, Pavel Andrade, Anna Björk Enarsdóttir.

My family's support is beyond measure. Most fundamentally, I am grateful to my parents, Lois and Andy. I also want to thank all my loving brothers, sisters, nieces, nephews, and in-laws.

A version of a section in Chap. 1 is reprinted with the permission of Penn State University Press and appeared in my article "Nonself-Contemporaneity: José Carlos Mariátegui and the Question of Peripheral Modernism" (*Comparative Literature Studies* 58, no. 2 [2021]: 383–387, https://doi.org/10.5325/complitstudies.58.2.0371). Chapter 2 is a revised and expanded version of an article that has been reprinted with permission by the journal *A Contracorriente*: "The Torn Halves of Mexican Modernism: Maples Arce, O'Gorman and Modotti," *A Contracorriente* 19, no. 3 (2022): 260–290.

Contents

1 Album or Book?: Form and Content of the Peripheral Metropolis — 1

2 "Outline of Civilization": Maples Arce, O'Gorman, Modotti, and the Limits of the Mexican Revolution — 49

3 "Facet by Facet": José Carlos Mariátegui's Politics of the Modernist Essay — 81

4 "The Century of Phrases": Roberto Arlt's Negative Dialectic of Belief and Distrust — 119

5 "There's Only One Crisis. The Sexual Crisis": Modernist Dissociation and the Reserve Army in Patrícia Galvão's *Parque Industrial* — 175

6 Conclusion: The Peripheralization of the Metropolis — 213

Index — 221

CHAPTER 1

Album or Book?: Form and Content of the Peripheral Metropolis

> That things are 'status quo' *is* the catastrophe.
> —Walter Benjamin, *The Arcades Project*

In *La cabeza de Goliat: Microscopía de Buenos Aires* (Goliath's Head: Microscopy of Buenos Aires, 1940) the Argentine essayist Ezequiel Martínez Estrada asks if "the aesthetic of the city corresponds more to the album or to the book?" (88).[1] That is, does the city embody a dis-

---

[1] "La estética de la ciudad, ¿corresponderá al álbum más que al libro?" My reading of this passage owes a great deal to Laura Demaría's discussion in *Buenos Aires y las provincias: Relatos para desarmar.* Demaría critiques the way Silvia Rosman gives priority to the album over the book in her account of Martínez Estrada's work. Demaría, by contrast, insists on the ambivalence, complementarity, and ultimately unresolved character of the Question. She articulates the dilemma nicely: "Por la primera mirada, la ciudad sí queda cartografiada en el fragmento del álbum de fotografías que destaca Rosman y con esta lectura concuerdo; pero, si se acepta la inscripción en el ensayo de una segunda mirada que acaricia voluptuosamente a la ciudad, el álbum ya no puede narrarla. La mirada que muestra ya no es una ciudad ensimismada sino en relación con las provincias, necesita del libro para construir una 'gran narrativa' que una los fragmentos y dibuje los contornos de esa Buenos Aires que les da la espalda a las provincias. Desde esta seguna mirada centrífuga, la fragmentación del 'álbum' es reemplazada por la continuidad del 'libro.' En consecuencia, la supuesta disyunción de la pregunta da paso a una complementariedad entre 'álbum' y 'libro,' en una narrativa paradójica que conjuga en tensión los dos elementos" (73).

© The Author(s), under exclusive license to Springer Nature Switzerland AG 2023
T. Mulder, *Modernism in the Peripheral Metropolis*, New Comparisons in World Literature,
https://Doi.org/10.1007/978-3-031-34055-0_1

continuous series of photographic images or a continuous narrative? On the one hand, Martínez Estrada recognizes that the experience of the city demands a form of fragmentation, an approach that "sees it from all sides," as in analytic cubism (24).[2] On the other hand, he feels compelled to construct a coherent story that would weave together the history of Buenos Aires. In the spirit of the "album," Martínez Estrada constructs his account through brief, essayistic sections that rapidly change focus and develop points more suggestively than exhaustively, but, in agreement with the demands of the "book," *La cabeza de Goliat* is an extended meditation on Buenos Aires. The Argentine essayist thus answers the question not by selecting one option over the other but by articulating a relation between continuity and discontinuity, between apparently opposed formal structures, while preserving their mutual tension.

Martínez Estrada poses this question to himself in *La cabeza de Goliat* because he is searching for a form that is adequate to its content, a content that is not simply the unmediated experience of Buenos Aires or its physical reality, but also a specific interpretation of the meaning of the city. Historically, Buenos Aires was supposed to represent the forces of "civilization" in the struggle against the threat of "barbarism" emanating from the *pampa*, from nature and the rural countryside. In the nineteenth century, this is how Domingo Faustino Sarmiento, the Argentine intellectual and politician, formulated the challenge facing Latin American nations in his immensely influential *Facundo: Civilización y Barbarie* (1845). By the beginning of the twentieth century, it appeared that this struggle had been decided decisively in favor of urban civilization. Latin American nations had been integrated into the world market, and the state was consolidating its authority after decades of intermittent civil wars between centralists and regionalists.

Martínez Estrada, the consummate pessimist, rejects such an idea of historical progress. In *Radiografía de la pampa* (X-Ray of the Pampa, 1933), he recasts Domingo Sarmiento's "civilization or barbarism" not by inverting the formula, privileging nature and rural life over urban society, but rather by insisting on their underlying identity: "What Sarmiento did not see is that civilization and barbarism were the same thing, like

---

[2] "Así se lo desgaja de su real situación, y aunque para muchos sea ésa la manera normal de mirar la metrópoli, conviene verla por todos los lados."

centripetal and centrifugal forces of a system in equilibrium. He did not see that the city was like the country and that within the new bodies were reincarnated the souls of the dead" (256).[3] The city may have triumphed over the country, but the vanquished enemy would persist in modern Buenos Aires because civilization carries barbarism within itself. Between civilization and barbarism, city and country, there is more continuity than discontinuity, but not the sort of continuity that implies an organic whole. Instead, Martínez Estrada evocatively compares Buenos Aires to Goliath's head. "[A] phenomenally large head usually indicates mental excellence," but in the case of Buenos Aires, "We start to realize that the head was not too big, but that the entire body was malnourished and poorly developed. The head sucked the blood out of the body" (*La cabeza de Goliat* 30).[4] Or, as Martínez Estrada phrases it later in the book, "The formation of Buenos Aires has been produced from a centripetal, not an expansionary, movement" (64).[5] In Martínez Estrada's account, the disproportionate size of Buenos Aires derives not primarily from its own dynamic forces but rather from a parasitical relationship with the provinces, draining the *pampa* of its vital energy. Instead of a healthy organism, whose parts perform specific roles in the reproduction of the whole, Buenos Aires grows at the expense of the parts on which it depends, and this asymmetrical relationship ultimately develops into a crisis in which the city breaks with and turns away from the rest of the country. At this point of rupture, Goliath's oversized head has been "decapitated" but it goes on "living" (*Radiografía* 37). In short, the initial discontinuity (civilization or barbarism) proves to be an underlying continuity, but due to the contradictory character of this continuity, the result is discontinuity. Martínez Estrada thus presents Buenos Aires as a city torn asunder in two

---

[3] "Lo que Sarmiento no vio es que civilización y barbarie eran una misma cosa, como fuerzas centrífugas y centrípetas de un sistema en equilibrio. No vio que la ciudad era como el campo y que dentro de los cuerpos nuevos reencarnaban las almas de los muertos."
[4] "Antes el problema no nos inquietaba y más bien era motivo de recóndito orgullo; porque tener una cabeza fenomenalmente grande suele ser indicio de excelencia mental, para el que calcula por metros ... Empezamos a darnos cuenta de que no era la cabeza demasiado grande, sino el cuerpo entero mal nutrido y peor desarrollado. La cabeza se chupaba la sangre del cuerpo."
[5] "La formación de Buenos Aires se ha producido por un movimiento centrípeto y no de expansión."

directions. Focusing on the west, for instance, where "the houses of Buenos Aires spill over into the pampa" (74),[6] the city bleeds into the countryside, the two becoming almost indistinguishable. But focusing on the east, the city's port, Buenos Aires appears eminently modern and urban, oriented toward Europe and cut off from the provinces of the interior. Buenos Aires is a city that is at once rural and urban, continuous and discontinuous with the rest of the nation. Stated in such a manner, Martínez Estrada's claims about Buenos Aires may seem incoherent. But when presented in the adequate form, one that mediates the principles of a book and an album, these claims become persuasive and compel conviction about the nature of the forces driving the development of the city. In effect, Martínez Estrada suggests that Buenos Aires constitutes a peripheral metropolis, a social space that is simultaneously a periphery relates to the centers of global capitalism and a center relative to the region's vast, underdeveloped hinterlands.[7]

---

[6] "El oeste sigue siendo la más rural de las zonas metropolitanas, o la más cívica de las zonas del llano, según se considere que Buenos Aires desborda sus casas hacia la pampa, o que ésta entra, por el subsuelo, hasta el estuario. Es una franja de sutura del país con la urbe."

[7] I conceive of the "peripheral metropolis" as an urban manifestation of the concept of the semiperiphery. As simultaneously peripheral relative to the core of the capitalist world-system and core in relation to the periphery, the "peripheral metropolis" highlights that these concepts refer not to territorial spaces as such but to relational processes. By conceiving of Latin American cities in this way, I aim to grasp how the uneven and combined development of capitalism does not neatly correspond to national boundaries. We can only meaningfully understand a country like Argentina, for instance, if we grasp the relation between the pampa, its agricultural zones, and the commercial function of Buenos Aires, and this relation in turn only becomes fully intelligible in terms of Argentina's position in the international division of labor. Even "Urban settings," as Sharae Deckard and Stephen Shapiro write, "have their own class-differentiated regions from the peripheral slums inhabited by manual labor forces and reserve armies of the unemployed, to the core sectors where elite classes live and work" (10). Ultimately, they continue, "the semiperipheries are the zones where political economy receives its greatest cultural inflection, where socioeconomic and socio-ecological contradictions are amplified and mediated through new cultural innovations" (11). Along these lines, as I will elaborate later in this chapter, I also claim that Latin American city in this historical moment dramatically displays the crisis of the region's dominant economic model.

1 ALBUM OR BOOK?: FORM AND CONTENT OF THE PERIPHERAL... 5

Martínez Estrada's essayistic reflections allow us to identify the central line of thought running through *Modernism in the Peripheral Metropolis*.[8] In the 1920s and 1930s, a crisis emerged in Latin America, indicating that urbanization in the region was assuming shapes and posing problems not anticipated by models in Europe and the United States. This book deals with writers and artists who, situated within this crisis and thus unable to know how it would unfold, produced works that elaborate this intuition about the shifting character of the Latin American city as a peripheral metropolis—as a social space whose specific shape only becomes fully intelligible in the context of global capitalism. I argue that these writers and artists draw on modernist forms and techniques in order to raise questions about how to make sense of a discordant content, namely, the experience of the city in this historical moment of crisis. *La cabeza de Goliat*, as we have seen, makes a claim not only about *what* has happened to Buenos Aires but also *how* we should conceive what has happened, and the persuasiveness of this claim cannot be separated from the dissonant form of an essay that is at once book and album, continuous and discontinuous. In various other ways, the works of writers and artists examined here—Roberto Arlt, José Carlos Mariátegui, Patrícia Galvão, Manuel Maples Arce, Juan O'Gorman, and Tina Modotti—give compelling accounts of the shape of the historical transformation appearing in Latin American cities not only by depicting aspects of the situation in the content of their work, but also, and more crucially, by producing formal arrangements that make the crisis sensible and intelligible as the unity of

---

[8] I use the term "modernism" not without reservations. *Modernismo*, the cognate in Spanish, refers to a turn-of-the-century literary style associated most prominently with the poet Rubén Darío. My work deals with a later generation of artists who were also confronting a different set of social and aesthetic issues. Latin Americanist literary critics typically refer to the art and literature of the 1920s and 1930s as *las vanguardias*. Therefore, I could have chosen the title *The Avant-Gardes in the Peripheral Metropolis*. However, while some of the artists examined here, Manuel Maples Arce in particular, could be considered avant-garde, the term, at least with its connotations in English, would appear inadequate for other artists and writers. An additional complication. In Brazil, *modernismo* designates a loose collection of writers and artists who came on the scene with the Modern Art Week of February 1922. The term can also be applied more broadly in Brazil to an artistic tendency throughout the twentieth century that traces its roots back to this foundational moment. Ultimately, I opt for "modernism." Even if it may evoke a different historical moment and style for those familiar with Spanish-speaking Latin American literary history, it captures in English the sort of aesthetic techniques and commitments examined here more effectively than "avant-garde."

apparently independent social phenomena. A crisis is normally experienced as the fragmentation and breakdown of the existing system, but these writers and artists also suggest that a crisis reveals the interdependence of the parts of a form of social life. These modernists thus insist that the duality of Latin American societies—the split between rural and urban, modern and traditional, national-popular and cosmopolitan—should be understood not as unrelated phenomena but as aspects of a unified and contradictory historical process. They do not defend one pole of the duality against the other or articulate a cultural identity based on the contrast; rather, they grasp formally the movement whereby incompatible principles coexist by passing into their opposite and giving rise to forms of integration that affirm what should be overcome. These inversions, which in this historical moment appear most palpably in the city, are given a compelling expression through the dissonant formal configuration of the works discussed in *Modernism in the Peripheral Metropolis*. With modernist techniques and forms that simultaneously foreground unity and disunity, these artists and writers suggest that the crisis does not amount to a momentary disturbance after which a stable social order reinstitutes itself. Rather, they conceive of social relations in Latin America as constituted in and through an ongoing, unresolved crisis. Dwelling in the contradictions animating the crisis, these modernists grasp how this crisis does not precipitate a historical transformation but generates specific issues, problems that have become increasingly urgent as Latin American has become the most urbanized region in the world: indigenous migration, surplus populations, inequality, and anomie.

Before elaborating on my argument in this introduction, we should briefly look at two more examples because, as I have just asserted, artistic and literary form mediates how we make sense of content. The theoretical and historical claims I advance in *Modernism in the Peripheral Metropolis* derive from the interpretation of modernist works in the sense that they are made possible by attending to the formal dynamics that make such claims persuasive and compelling. The first example comes from the Argentine Horacio Coppola, a "straight" photographer who learned modernist principles of composition at the Bauhaus. In 1936, Coppola was commissioned to produce a collection of photographs for the fourth centenary of the foundation of Buenos Aires.[9]

---

[9] Indeed, Martínez Estrada's use of the term "album" is likely an allusion to Coppola's work. The entirety of *La cabeza de Goliat* could be considered a pessimistic alternative to the celebrations of Buenos Aires in 1936.

I. Desde Avenida del Trabajo y Lacarra (1936), © Archivo Horacio Coppola

II. *Nocturno* (1936), © Archivo Horacio Coppola

Coppola's images established the modernity of the city. They offered "the first modern gaze on" the city, presenting "a modern Buenos Aires that still today has the capacity to appear contemporary to us" (Gorelik, "Images" 109). Through chiaroscuro and the geometric shape of the jagged skyline, "Nocturno" presents a city that could easily be mistaken for Manhattan in the 1920s. But in other photographs, Coppola turns his camera on the edges of the city, on the "orillas" that Jorge Luis Borges explores in his early poetry. In "Desde Avenida del Trabajo y Lacarra," for instance, the *pampa* appears integrated into an expanding city of geometric, modern housing. These images present seemingly incommensurable spaces, and yet at the same time they are both photographs of Buenos Aires for Coppola. The ultra-modern skyscraper and the simple home in the outskirts become representations of Buenos Aires not simply because of their indexical relation to the physical city but because their juxtaposition grasps the tension at the heart of the city in its contradictory relationship to the rural hinterlands and the core of the world economy, the way, in Martínez Estrada's account, it simultaneously faces the east and the west.[10]

Paralleling in many ways the relation between Buenos Aires and the *pampa*, the social situation in Peru at the beginning of the twentieth century was largely defined by a split between the coast and the sierra, between urban Lima and the largely indigenous highlands.[11] And like Martínez Estrada and Coppola, the Peruvian poet Carlos Oquendo de Amat insists on the capacity of modernist form to make sense of the meaning of this split. His *5 metros de poemas* (5 Meters of Poems, 1927) is assembled in the form of an accordion: each page, excluding the first and last, is attached to another page on each side, making the work into one long, folded, continuous strip. In this way, *5 metros de poemas* evokes cinematic montage.[12] Additionally, the work contains various calligrams, betraying the influence of Apollinaire. And yet, alongside the proliferation of modernist experiments, Oquendo de Amat includes verse forms that evoke tradition: rural settings, domesticity, natural symbols. For instance, the first poem, "aldeanita" (little village girl):

---

[10] As Adrián Gorelik has argued, Coppola's photographic project was informed by a classicism that insisted on an "essential order," allowing "him to portray the traditional houses as if they were modern objects and the most modern and thriving parts of the city as if time never touched them" ("Images" 112). I would add that this classicism turns into its opposite in Coppola's photographs. The commitment to an "essential order" led him to capture both "modern" and "traditional" aspects of Buenos Aires, rather than one or the other, but the effect is to highlight the tension at the heart of the city, not its underlying harmony.

[11] The following discussion of Carlos Oquendo de Amat's *5 metros de poemas* has been taken from my article "Nonself-Contemporaneity: José Carlos Mariátegui and the Question of Peripheral Modernism." In that article, I show that for Mariátegui the meaning of modernist and avant-garde art in the periphery depends on its relationship to contemporaneity. For the full article in *Comparative Literature Studies*, see https://doi.org/10.5325/complitstudies.58.2.0371.

[12] This affinity with film is further reinforced by the inclusion of a ten-minute "intermission."

1 ALBUM OR BOOK?: FORM AND CONTENT OF THE PERIPHERAL... 9

>   Silk village girl
> I'll tie my heart
>   to your braids like a ribbon
> Because in this fragile cardboard morning
> (to a fine emotional wanderer)
> You gave the water glass of your body
> and the two coins of your new eyes.[13]

Many of the poems in *5 metros de poemas* follow the pattern of "aldeanita" in their orientation toward tranquil, pastoral moods.[14] At the other thematic extreme of *5 metros*, "new york" embodies a chaotic urban scene.

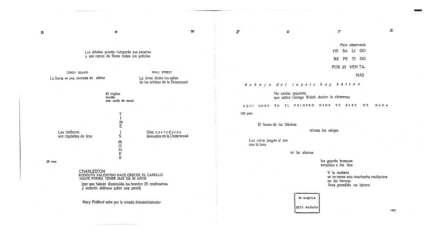

The poem presents the quintessential expression of capitalism's temporal regime of domination—"TIME IS MONEY"—and thus stands in stark

---

[13] Aldeanita de seda / ataré mi corazón / como una cinta a tus trenzas / Porque en una mañanita de carton / (a este bueno aventurero de emociones) / Le diste el vaso de agua de tu cuerpo / y los dos reales de tus ojos nuevos. Carlos Oquendo de Amat. *5 metros de poemas*, trans. Joshua Beckman & Alejandro de Acosta (Brooklyn: Ugly Duckling Presse, 2010).

[14] These poems carry titles like "madre" (mother), "campo" (countryside), "jardín" (garden), and they return to images of the moon and the sky.

contrast with the serene rural setting in "aldeanita." Moreover, Oquendo uses the calligram to graphically represent advertisements, skyscrapers, and other tangible features of the metropolis. With these calligrams and its peculiar layout, 5 *metros de poemas* constitutes a veritable laboratory of avant-garde techniques.

One might be tempted to dismiss these experiments, claiming that they exhibit not an overarching vision of Peruvian social reality but merely an interest in modernist techniques for their own sake.[15] The hyper-modern "new york" poem, in particular, seems to have no connection to an underdeveloped nation in South America. But, as Michelle Clayton argues, "there is little in the collection that justifies taking the 'local' poems as more *authentic* than those that focus on modern cities or on foreign views" ("Modes of Transport" 105). Because of its "very form, which unfolds like a filmstrip and thereby tethers together its disparate contents," 5 *metros* insists that "the Andean idyll subsists" within "a broader experience of modernity, and that to separate them out is to do violence to the reality of a context increasingly organized by and within global" capitalism (105). The point is not to locate a space outside the world economy, a space that contains a putatively pure expression of Peruvian culture. Rather, the juxtaposition of urban and rural settings serves to make visible the dissonant forces shaping Peru in that moment. 5 *metros* thus offers a persuasive interpretation of Peru's peripheral situation precisely through, not in spite of, its experiments in modernist form.

The socio-aesthetic problem of 5 *metros de poemas*, in other words, lies in the question of how to relate apparently incompatible elements. Jorge Coronado proposes one answer with the idea that the poetic subject here is a "migrant" who "finds himself trapped in the agon between the ubiquitous representatives of … two powerful, though unequal forces— traditional culture and modernization—whose fate is indistinguishable from his very own" (84). By framing Oquendo de Amat's work in terms of the figure of the migrant, Coronado accurately identifies a crucial aspect of the work's historical context. Migration from the *sierra* to Lima increased rapidly in the early decades of the twentieth century. Oquendo himself moved to Lima from Puno, in the extreme southwest of Peru, when he was a child. But the figure of the migrant raises certain

---

[15] José Carlos Mariátegui and César Vallejo made such a critique. I discuss Mariátegui's reception of peripheral modernism in relation to the contemporaneity of the non-contemporaneous in "Nonself Contemporaneity: José Carlos Mariátegui and the Question of Peripheral Modernism."

implications that ultimately misconstrue the formal character of 5 *metros*. The migrant implies a sequential narrative revolving around the biography of an individual moving from one location to another. Along these lines, Coronado argues that by the end of the poem the "cultural components" find themselves in a state of "total separation" (88), as the migrant nostalgically longs for the world he has left behind. But Oquendo does not suggest that urban and rural are independent social spaces or that the development of the former has no connection to the latter. The sequential character of the migrant's experience is belied by the structural simultaneity foregrounded in the poem's use of montage and calligrams.[16] This "total separation" appears in 5 *metros* as a *result* of simultaneity, of the work's total organization or formal structure.[17]

We get a glimpse of how this peculiar simultaneity works in 5 *metros* when we turn to its enigmatic first line: "open the book like pealing a fruit."[18] But what kind of fruit? If it were, for instance, an apple, then the skin would be removed with a knife in one more or less continuous piece. Other fruits, like an orange, cannot be pealed in this manner; the skin is removed piece by piece, in fragments. By not specifying which type of fruit, Oquendo de Amat forces us to consider both options simultaneously. Ultimately, this statement about pealing a fruit sets up a framework for understanding the rest of the work since 5 *metros* itself follows the same structure: it is both a continuous strip and discrete pieces of paper.

This sort of structure also comes to the fore in the way the city poems take the form of calligrams. Because of their simultaneity, calligrams are inherently difficult to read, confounding the standard movement from left to right, from top to bottom. In "new york" and "amberes" this difficulty is compounded because the titles stretch across two pages, prompting an additional question: is the poem a single calligram or two? Do we read the verso first, the recto second, or both at the same time? As with the idea of pealing a fruit, it seems we must do both simultaneously.

---

[16] Coronado's impulse to narrativize the poems can be seen in his brief summary of the work: "5 *metros* insists, in a first instance, on the lament in the face of modernization (this being a form of modernity itself), then attempts to create a hybrid, and finally opts for a total separation of the cultural components in question" (88).

[17] Clayton similarly argues that the attempt to make 5 *metros* "cohere into a kind of Bildungsroman" assumes that "the Andean space remains effectively untouched by modernity" and that "there is no cross-contamination between the poems on domestic and on modern themes" ("Modes" 111–12).

[18] "abra el libro como quien pela una fruta."

Extending beyond the city poems to the work as a whole, we can now see that urban and rural exist simultaneously even as each term defines itself negatively in relation to the other. In other words, *5 metros* is a work about the "simultaneity of the non-simultaneous,"[19] the uneven and combined development of capitalism. Through a contradictory simultaneity, Oquendo gives a compelling formal articulation of the claim that, in the words of the Warwick Research Collective, "capitalist development does not smooth away but rather *produces* unevenness, systematically and as a matter of course" (12).[20] *5 metros* suggests that unevenness—the split between urban Lima and indigenous highlands, and the tension within these spaces—is the result of a unified, albeit contradictory, historical process. Migration, accordingly, appears as an essential aspect of the peripheral metropolis, as a specific issue in Peru that cannot be separated from the global forces of capitalism.

LATIN AMERICAN MODERNISM IN THE CONTEXT OF A "COLLAPSING SOCIAL EDIFICE"

Insofar as the peripheral metropolis points simultaneously toward the centers of global capitalism and to the vast, underdeveloped countryside, it embodies the duality at the heart of Latin American social formations. Paulo Arantes calls it a "dual allegiance," citing the formulation of the historian of Brazilian cinema Paulo Emílio Salles Gomes: "We are neither Europeans nor North Americans. Lacking an original culture, nothing is foreign to us because everything is. The painful construction of ourselves develops within the rarefied dialectic of not being and being someone else" (Arantes, *Sentimento* 15). In accounts of Latin American modernism, the 1920s and 1930s mark a moment in which this duality appears alternatively as a problem, as an obstacle to modernization, and as solution, as the basis of a specifically national-popular identity. However, I would

---

[19] I discuss Ernst Bloch's concept of the "simultaneity of the non-simultaneous," or "the contemporaneity of the non-contemporaneous," in "Nonself Contemporaneity: José Carlos Mariátegui and the Question of Peripheral Modernism."

[20] The quote continues: "Combined *and* uneven: the face of modernity is not worn exclusively by the 'futuristic' skyline of the Pudong District in Shanghai or the Shard and Gherkin buildings in London; just as emblematic of modernity as these are the favelas of Rocinha and Jacerezinho in Rio and the slums of Dharavi in Bombay and Makoko in Lagos, the ship graveyards of Nouadhibou and the Aral Sea, the vast, deindustrialized wastelands north, east, south and west, and the impoverished and exhausted rural hinterlands" (WReC 12–13).

argue that critics of Latin American modernism often take this duality as a given because they discount questions of aesthetic and literary form. In *Modernism in the Peripheral Metropolis*, by contrast, everything hinges on *how* the duality is conceived, on the *form* of articulation of apparently incompatible phenomena. I insist that the modernists examined here do not identify with one pole of the duality against the other or strive to formulate a cultural identity based on the contrast. Rather, through the assertion of a critical distance from the duality, they are able to take it seriously, thereby grasping the truth of the disunity—namely, that it is the peculiar expression of a social formation that can only reproduce itself through crisis because of its position in the international division of labor. In this section, I outline the crucial differences between my account of Latin American modernism and prevailing tendencies in the field by discussing the Argentine novelist Roberto Arlt (1900–1942). Arlt's work, I argue, does not take the duality of national-popular and cosmopolitan tendencies as a given; instead, the duality is mediated by a formal organization in which the tension between dissonance and autonomy makes the disunity appear as something intelligible that, nonetheless, should not be.

The tendency to interpret Latin American modernism in terms of the stubborn opposition between cosmopolitan and national-popular orientations finds perhaps its most influential articulation in Ángel Rama's essay "Las dos vanguardias latinoamericanas" (The Two Latin American Avant-Gardes, 1973). Starting from the premise of a disjuncture between the particular social reality of Latin America and universal artistic forms, Rama argues that national-popular modernists attempt to calibrate these universal forms to national situations, whereas cosmopolitan modernists seek an "abrupt rupture with the past" ("Las dos" 62). If the former aspires to communicate with "a social community," often by drawing on indigenous cultures and the language of popular sectors, the latter "intensified their link with the structure of the European avant-gardes" (62).[21] On one side, we would find Diego Rivera and the Mexican muralists who constructed historical narratives synthesizing indigenous, colonial and revolutionary elements for a largely illiterate public. On the other side

---

[21] "un sector del vanguardismo, más allá del rechazo de la tradición realista en su aspecto formal, aspira a recoger de ella su vocación de adentramiento en una comunidad social, con lo cual se religa a las ideologías regionalistas; otro sector, para mantener su formulación vanguardista, que implica abrupta con el pasado y remisión a una inexistente realidad que les espera en el futuro, intensifica su vinculación con la estructura del vanguardismo europeo, esto lo forzará a crear un posible ámbito común para las creaciones artísticas de uno y otro lado del Atlántico, lo que obligadamente pasa por la postulación de un universalismo."

stands a figure like Vicente Huidobro, the Chilean poet who wrote in French and Spanish and collaborated with cubists and Dadaists. Rama concludes the essay by situating the Argentine novelist Roberto Arlt in relation to this account of the Latin American literary field. For Rama, Arlt does not identify with the European avant-gardes; instead, he draws on realist traditions to approach his local context, to "renew literary forms to adjust them to the new reality"—namely, that of the rising urban petite bourgeoisie in Buenos Aires—and to thereby "secure ongoing communication with a public" (63). In short, Latin American modernists seemingly face a choice between mutually exclusive options: either technical, formal innovation or popular accessibility; either participate in the formal experiments of the artistic avant-gardes and ignore the traditions and issues relevant to Latin Americans, or address the Latin American public by subordinating artistic form to the demands of local reality.

The terms of Ángel Rama's work on Latin American modernism continue to shape scholarship on the topic.[22] It is not hard to see why this sort of interpretation has proven so influential. For instance, decolonial theory, with its emphasis on de-linking from Western epistemologies, radicalizes the spirit of the national-popular orientation in Latin American modernism. Decolonial critics have deepened Rama's insights into how certain artists reject the formalist impulses of the European avant-gardes and engage in projects to vindicate indigenous cultures and marginalized worldviews. The cosmopolitan impulse in contemporary Latin American literary studies,

[22] Given Rama's influence on the development of Latin American literary criticism in the past fifty years, it would not be an exaggeration to say that his work is not simply representative of the direction of current work on Latin American modernism but is partially responsible for the direction it has taken. For instance, George Yúdice evokes Rama when he writes: "Latin American literary histories explain that the period between the two world wars saw the development in Latin America of two tendencies: on the one hand, a cosmopolitan vanguardist accommodation to the 'esprit nouveau' of the European avant-gardes, and, on the other, an amalgam of *mundonovismo* (Latin and/or Indo-Americanism or New Worldism) and the call to forge new national literatures based on the worldview of (indigenous or Afro-Latin American) subaltern cultures" (53). Yúdice does not fundamentally challenge Rama's account; rather, he adds to it by insisting on the context of imperialism, in which the peripheral avant-gardes can appear as a global struggle to mobilize popular cultures in Latin America to challenge the institution of art. Vicky Unruh owes a different, but nonetheless significant, debt to Rama in her path-breaking *Latin American Vanguards*. She argues that Latin American artists engaged in a project of "rehumanizing" art, rather than "dehumanizing" it, as the European avant-gardes did, in order to bring art closer to Latin American social reality and to establish "encounters" with the public in the national context.

by contrast, continues to show how modernists, inspired by what Mariano Siskind calls a "desire for the world," had their fingers on the pulse of contemporary developments in the global political and artistic scene.[23] Cosmopolitanism, these critics suggest, does not necessarily entail ignorance of specifically Latin American questions; rather, it establishes global connections and offers ways of understanding local issues in a broader context.

In this way, the cosmopolitan direction in Latin American literary criticism dovetails with the expansionary impulse of "new modernist studies,"[24] which has not only reconceived modernism along broader spatial and temporal lines but has also challenged the "great divide" between high and low culture that previously seemed to be one of modernism's most distinctive features. Where modernism once seemed preoccupied with limits—its distance from an emerging culture industry, its connection to only the most advanced, urban settings in the industrial world—it now appears as a global, planetary movement that circulates across national borders.

Because Rama's account encompasses both national-popular and cosmopolitan tendencies (or, to use today's jargon, the decolonial turn and new modernist studies), I will focus in what remains of this section on explicating how my account departs from that offered in "Las dos vanguardias." As I mentioned above, Rama takes Roberto Arlt to exemplify the national-popular orientation in Latin American modernism, but I will argue that Arlt's work indicates the limitations of Rama's account. My point is not that Arlt is more cosmopolitan than Rama suggests. Rather, I turn to Arlt to outline a conception of modernism as embodying a specifically artistic "way of rendering intelligible and compelling" (Pippin 2–3) implicit aspects of and tensions within social life, especially in a crisis when the possibility of shareable meaning itself becomes an issue for this form of social life.

In his account of Arlt, Rama echoes a standard mid-century interpretation, namely, that Arlt represents the realist and populist counter-tendency to the cosmopolitan, "art for art's sake" attitude associated with Jorge Luis Borges. In Argentine literary history, Arlt and Borges have often been seen as representing two competing literary circles: Boedo and Florida,

---

[23] See Siskind, *Cosmopolitan Desires: Global Modernity and World Literature in Latin America*.
[24] For the programmatic statement on the trope of "expansion" in the "new modernist studies," see Mao and Walkowitz.

respectively.[25] Critics now recognize that such a confrontation was primarily rhetorical, since many writers, including Arlt, moved in both circles. And yet, we should acknowledge the kernel of truth contained in this split. Most Boedo writers were children of immigrants who grew up in popular neighborhoods or *barrios* (Boedo being the name of one of those *barrios*), whereas the Florida writers shared surnames with major figures in Argentine national history. With this polemic in mind, Beatriz Sarlo identifies "two types of writer": "those who were 'Argentines without effort,' because they did not need to disguise a foreign accent, and those who by their origin and their language could not claim to be part of any long national tradition" (*Borges* 102).[26] Arlt mocks these "Argentines without effort" in the preface to his novel *Los lanzallamas* (The Flamethrowers, 1931). Arlt recognizes the impression among this literary elite that he writes "poorly": "It's possible. Either way, I wouldn't have any trouble naming numerous people who write well and are read only by polite members of their own families" (*LSL/LL* 285).[27] The "Argentines without effort," Arlt suggests, constitute themselves as a group through their distance from the popular masses. Arlt points out the hypocrisy that they have embraced James Joyce for the provocative "spiritual delight" Bloom takes in the bathroom at the beginning of *Ulysses*, but they denounce Arlt's works for their "brutality" (285–6). What underlies this judgment is an obsession with Joyce because he is, in Arlt's words, "English" (286).[28] He adds: "Once James Joyce is within the reach of everyone's wallets, society columns will invent for themselves a new idol read by no more than half a dozen initiates" (286). Arlt seems to denounce the cosmopolitan attitude of the "Argentines without effort." But it is telling that he does not articulate this critique in strictly cultural terms. The problem is not that the literary elite follow developments in the European avant-

---

[25] For critical accounts of the writers associated with Boedo and Florida, see Masiello and Leland.

[26] In a country that had experienced a massive influx of immigrants in recent decades, second only to the United States in the early twentieth century, the question of accent betrayed social anxieties that went far beyond literary orientations.

[27] "Se dice de mí que escribo mal. Es posible. De cualquier manera, no tendría dificultad en citar a una numerosa gente que escribe bien y a quienes únicamente leen correctos miembros de sus familias." For an excellent account of Arlt's "poor" writing and "illegibility" more broadly in Latin American literature, see Julio Prieto, *La escritura errante*.

[28] This could be taken as a sign of Arlt's ignorance, but I would like to think that Arlt is subtly alluding to the way the Argentine literary elite had downplayed the colonial question of Joyce being an Irish writer.

gardes at the expense of the national context. Instead, Arlt suggests that it is ultimately an issue of inequality, of a disunity that is at once cultural, social, and economic.

Antonio Candido reminds us that a fundamental aspect of inequality in Latin America has been illiteracy, the "basic feature of underdevelopment in the cultural area" (38).[29] If Latin American writers cannot rely on a popular domestic audience, because of illiteracy and a more general "cultural weakness: lack of the means of communication and diffusion" (Candido 38), then it should come as no surprise that the "Argentines without effort," among others, primarily address each other or a foreign reading public. Given these underlying circumstances and constraints, it cannot simply be a matter of one's attitude toward national-popular sectors. The separation between elite and popular culture is not the result of the former imitating European forms and developments; rather, and here is the crucial point, the split between cosmopolitan and national-popular orientation can only be made fully intelligible when it is taken as a consequence of what Roberto Schwarz calls "forms of inequality so brutal that they lack the minimal reciprocity ... without which modern society can only appear artificial and 'imported'" (*Misplaced* 15). These "forms of inequality," which I take to be the constitutive dissonance of the peripheral situation, impede the achievement of a social synthesis, the mutuality of relations whereby society becomes a cohesive whole, and this dissonance, as I will argue below, manifests themselves most palpably in the city at this historical moment. In the absence of "minimal reciprocity," an immense burden weighs on the possibility of shareable meaning, including the ability of the writer to communicate with an audience. Brutal inequality undercuts the formation of a tradition or stable social context in which individuals can make sense of themselves and each other as sharing a normative framework of interpretations and expectations.

Arlt acknowledges that his works cannot overcome this problem on their own and somehow communicate directly with the reader. Unlike the literary elite he mocks in the preface, Arlt shares a background with the popular sectors in Buenos Aires. And yet, he insists that he cannot understand himself as sharing a form of social life with these popular

---

[29] Illiteracy levels were, by Latin American standards at the time, relatively low in Buenos Aires, but I raise this point because of its relevance for other Latin American contexts. And the broader point I am trying to make about the relationship to the public still stands in the context of Buenos Aires, even if illiteracy wasn't a major problem.

sectors, as sharing the sort of framework of beliefs and actions on which mutuality depends: "In fact, we don't know what to think of the people. If they are idiots in earnest, or if they take to heart the crude comedy they perform every hour of the day and night" (*LSL/LL* 286).[30] This typical modernist disdain for the public could, in a text written by, say, T. S. Eliot, be taken as a sign of elitism, but given Arlt's previous comments, something else seems to be at stake. The context Arlt describes is not fundamentally a social world divided between cosmopolitan elites and popular masses. Rather, he suggests that he does not share a form of life with the popular sectors because this social context itself, lacking the reciprocity that should characterize a modern society, does not form a coherent whole. In such a context, Arlt cannot rely on conventions, a tradition of shared meanings. This is the situation described by Clement Greenberg in "Avant-Garde and Kitsch" (1939). When a society, Greenberg notes, becomes increasingly unable "to justify the inevitability of its particular forms," the materials on which artists depend "for communication with their audiences" disintegrate and "It becomes difficult to assume anything" (3–4).

For Arlt, this problem, the inability to assume anything, follows from the way that the crisis has emptied traditional forms of their credibility and given rise to issues that cannot be solved within the available framework of practices and interpretations. "[T]oday," Arlt writes, "amidst the noise of an inevitably collapsing social edifice" (Arlt, *LSL/LL* 285), the norms that were once taken for granted become a problem and no longer provide a stable background for shareable meaning. But Arlt also indicates that a stable social context vanishes to the extent that everything, including literary works, has been turned into a commodity. This is what is at issue when Arlt distinguishes between the "Argentines without effort," who write only for the "polite members of their families," and his own position as a writer for a people about which one does "not know what to think." The "Argentines without effort," we could say, attempt to disavow the modern social situation of art by holding onto the idea of writing for the salon. Arlt, by contrast, fully acknowledges the demands placed on him by this social situation, namely, that he must write for a market. And yet he attempts to neutralize the demands of the commodity. Perhaps more clearly than any of his Latin American contemporaries, Arlt recognizes the fact that his books were commodities to be sold on the market, but he also

[30] "En realidad, uno no sabe qué pensar de la gente. Si son idiotas en serio, o si se toman a pecho la burda comedia que representan todas las horas de sus días y sus noches."

knew that his novels could succeed as literary works only if they successfully suspended their commodity status, if they somehow refused to be subordinated to the demands of an inscrutable market.

Returning to Ángel Rama we can now see the double disavowal on which his account rests. By invoking a national-popular community to whom the artist could address his or her works, Rama inadequately accounts for the peripheral forms of inequality that impede the formation of social synthesis or cohesive collectivity. And, in assuming that the meaning of the artwork ultimately depends on its relationship to the public, Rama overlooks that communication for the modernist is not a solution but a problem. In the modernist situation, artists cannot "assume anything" in their relationship to an audience—which, by now, has become a market—and instead must somehow attempt to suspend the determination of the work by the commodity.

It is precisely in neutralizing the demands of the commodity, in asserting its autonomy, that the modernist work compels conviction and absorbs its audience. Art has lost its immediate role in social reproduction, but it remains significant by recognizing and appropriating the autonomy (or alienation) that has been imposed on it. In Rama's account, the national-popular modernist indeed recognizes this alienation, but he or she also misrecognizes it insofar as it appears as the disjuncture between universal, European forms and Latin American content. To the extent that this modernist believes that alienation can be overcome within art, often by drawing on pre-modern styles and forms, Rama fails to grasp the underlying social basis of this alienation.[31] Art cannot immediately recuperate its lost audience. Rather than paper over this loss, modernism must sustain it, by, in Theodor Adorno's words, "portray[ing] within its own structure the social antinomies which are also responsible for its isolation" (Adorno, "Social Situation" 130). And in so doing, modernist art gains "the power of far-reaching sublimation of drives and the cogent and binding

---

[31] I have in mind here Theodor Adorno's critique of Stravinsky. For Adorno, Stravinsky "recognizes the fact of alienation" but believes that his musical compositions can overcome this alienation by drawing on "stylistic forms of the past," forms that were embedded in a more integrated society. Adorno opposes Stravinsky to Schoenberg, an artist who "out of indifference towards" the social situation of music, represents social contradictions as immanent problems of form. Adorno also outlines a third type of music. As represented by Kurt Weil, this option recognizes the social character of alienation, thus avoiding the "positive solution" in which the second type was trapped. Its role is thus fundamentally negative. A fourth type refers to the attempt "to break through alienation from within itself" by producing immediately useful music ("On the Social Situation of Music" 132–133).

expression of humanity" (130). On first approximation, this "binding expression of humanity" does not seem to be on the table for Roberto Arlt. Although he longs to produce a masterpiece like the novels of Flaubert, Arlt recognizes that "style requires time" and money (Arlt, *LSL/LL* 285), but he must write in "raucous editorial offices" where he is "hounded by the obligation of [his] daily column" for the newspaper *El Mundo* (*LSL/LL* 285).[32] Arlt thus identifies that the demands of artistic unity are at odds with an antagonistic reality. And yet, the artwork, if it is to compel conviction, must draw its materials from this very reality. We might say that Arlt's material conditions—writing for a living, working in "raucous editorial offices"—impose external constraints on his artistic aspirations, that they are perhaps explanations for his "poor" writing. But what makes Arlt's novel compelling is "the fact that precisely those external circumstances are actively taken up by [the work] in ways that are irreducibly normative" (Brown, *Autonomy* 30). Arlt's notorious grammatical mistakes do not simply reflect the fact that Arlt had to rush to finish the novel. Rather, his "poor writing" becomes a moment of dissonance within the novel, its self-consciousness of the failure to make a coherent whole out of materials shaped by brutal forms of inequality in the periphery. It is not that dissonance reduces the artwork to mute materiality, to a mere index of historical conditions. Rather, dissonance and autonomy reciprocally determine one another. Dissonance, as the disintegration of autonomy, discloses the artwork's contradictory social context, the possibility of the collapse of shareable meaning, or what Arlt calls "a collapsing social edifice" (*LSL/LL* 285). At the same time, the autonomy of the literary work makes the historical contradictions intelligible. Insofar as the work asserts its independence from the immediacy and confusion of experience, these historical forces crystallize into a determinate shape. Moreover, autonomy, as the unity highlighted negatively by the disintegrating force of dissonance, preserves the potential of what could be if it were not for these forms of inequality. Through this dialectical relationship of autonomy and dissonance, Arlt give a compelling expression to humanity's needs in the present, producing "books that," in a typically violent Arltian metaphor, "contain the violence of a 'cross' to the jaw"

---

[32] "Escribí siempre en redacciones estrepitosas, acosado por la obligación de la columna cotidiana."

(*LSL/LL* 286).[33] More than modernist "shock" or empty provocation, this "cross" is an expression of historical suffering, of what ought not to be. It is precisely through artistic presentation that Arlt is able to give expression to the dissonance of a "collapsing social edifice," that he is able to elaborate the intuition of urgent tensions in social life into an intelligible and sensible form.[34]

The (Peripheral) Metropolis, the (Uneven) Seat of the Money Economy

This dialectical relationship between autonomy and dissonance grasps the contradictory character of the peripheral metropolis.[35] In Martínez Estrada's terms, it is precisely the relationship between book and album that expresses the specificity of Buenos Aires insofar as it simultaneously faces East and West, toward the *pampa* and the centers of global capitalism. This duality or "dual allegiance," to use Paulo Arantes's phrase once again, represents a significant shift away from expectations about

---

[33] "Crearemos nuestra literatura, no conversando continuamente de literatura, sino escribiendo en orgullosa soledad libros que encierran la violence de un 'cross' a la mandíbula."

[34] The discussion of dissonance here and elsewhere has been inspired by Theodor Adorno. See *Aesthetic Theory*, especially the section "Semblance and Expression," pp. 100–118. I also owe a debt to Jensen Suther's discussion of dissonance in "Black as the New Dissonance: Heidegger, Adorno, and Truth in the Work of Art."

[35] The Argentine literary critic Beatriz Sarlo uses the term "peripheral metropolis" in her rich cultural history of Buenos Aires in the 1920s and 1930s. Through close readings of literary works and archival research, Sarlo draws attention to the fact that economic modernization in Argentina was carried out by the nation's oligarchy, meaning that new technologies and capitalist social relations often coexisted and fused with traditional cultural patterns. The paradoxical combination of "defensive and residual elements, alongside progressive programs" (Sarlo, *Una modernidad* 23), which intensified with massive immigration and migration from the countryside, gave rise to what Sarlo calls a "culture of mixture" (32). In this book, I build on Beatriz Sarlo's impressive account of Buenos Aires not only by examining other urban centers in Latin America (Lima, Mexico City, and São Paulo) but also by explicitly articulating the "peripheral metropolis" as a key concept for thinking through the contradictory forces that drove the development of the Latin American city and structured the relation between the core and periphery. See *Una modernidad periférica: Buenos Aires 1920 y 1930*. It should be noted that Sarlo's central concept is not the "peripheral metropolis" but "peripheral modernity," which she adapts from Marshall Berman's *All That Is Solid Melts into Air*. She uses "the peripheral metropolis" explicitly in the title "The Modern City: Buenos Aires, the Peripheral Metropolis," a chapter in English that offers a snapshot of certain themes from *Una modernidad periférica*. For this chapter, see the edited collection *Through the Kaleidoscope: The Experience of Modernity in Latin America*, ed. Vivian Schelling.

urbanization. The "metropolis" typically describes, as the historian of São Paulo Richard Morse writes, "an urban order which overflows its 'city limits' to rearrange the institutions of the whole countryside," making "the wider hinterland an economic tributary" (xxi). Martínez Estrada palpably expresses the sense that Buenos Aires has overflowed its "city limits" in the image of Goliath's hypertrophied head. But when Martínez Estrada asks the question about form, he also indicates that the growth of the city, the characteristic feature of the metropolis, has not in Latin America established a coherent, self-reproducing relationship in which the countryside becomes subordinate to the authority of the city. Richard Morse, writing in the middle of the twentieth century, would note that the growth of Latin American cities has been "of a compressed, haphazard nature," with the effect that no "rural-urban equilibrium has been established" (200–201). As the twentieth century continued to unfold, it would reveal in increasingly stark terms the intuition of Martínez Estrada, along with the other modernists discussed in this book, that urbanization in Latin America was assuming a shape unlike that of the metropolis in Europe and the United States. To grasp the specificity of the peripheral metropolis, the modernists distinguish it from, for instance, Paris and London, but they also recognize the inseparability of its development from the forces of global capitalism. In this section, I discuss how expectations about urbanization in Latin America began to unravel as the crisis of the 1920s and 1930s brought about a reorganization of the international division of labor. In effect, this historical moment constitutes a hinge between two historical periods in Latin America: in the nineteenth century, integration into the world economy based on exports; in the mid-twentieth century, inward-looking development and industrialization. And yet, we will see that the "collapsing social edifice" disclosed in Arlt's moment will prove to be not a temporary condition in a historical transition but an ongoing feature of the peripheral situation, of a social formation that reproduces itself through disunity and the integration of incompatible normative commitments.

In the works of certain Latin American modernists, we can identify the outlines of a concept of the peripheral metropolis. This notion emerges as artists and intellectuals in the 1920s and 1930s work through the intuition that as urbanization in the region followed the expected patterns of cities in Europe and the United States, it was also generating unforeseen issues. Accordingly, we start with the concept of the metropolis before elaborating on its peripheral form. The metropolis, as we saw above, overflows its city limits, thereby bringing about a new relationship between urban and rural. The metropolis, therefore, does not simply designate a large city; it becomes a center of the economic and political relations that compose the capitalist world-system. With regard to the latter, Raymond Williams offers characteristically illuminating comments. In "Metropolitan Perceptions and the Emergence of Modernism" (1989), Williams traces modernism's formal innovations to the position of artists in the metropolis. He relates the development of the metropolis to imperialism, to the formation of a truly global capitalism in the late nineteenth and early twentieth century. In the age of imperialism, the metropolis names a social space "beyond both city and nation in their older senses" insofar as it has been constituted by "the magnetic concentration of wealth and power in imperial capitals and the simultaneous cosmopolitan access to a wide variety of subordinate capitals" (44).[36] To the extent that wealth and culture accumulate in this social space, the metropolis appears as a center of the capitalist world-system. But the fact that the metropolis exists as a center does not entail that it is self-contained, that it crystallizes out of a process unfolding in the city alone. In *The Country and the City* (1973), Williams foregrounds how the metropolis is mediated by the city's relationship to the global countryside. As Williams memorably writes, "one of the last models of 'city and country' is the system we now know as imperialism" (279). Imperialism, in other words, does not overcome the antithesis of city and country; it universalizes it. The imperial context, Williams insists, makes sense of the metropolis not only as a rapidly growing urban space but also as a social formation whose significance extends beyond the city and the nation in virtue of its position as a magnetic pole in such a political and economic system, insofar as it rearranges the international division of labor. Of course, the peripheral metropoles in Latin America, unlike Paris, New York, or London, cannot legitimately claim to be the center of an imperial system, but they do possess something of the character of the imperial metropole in being, to return to Ezequiel Martínez Estrada's

---

[36] For an excellent account of metropolitan modernism that builds on this observation, see Paul Stasi, *Modernism, Imperialism and the Historical Sense*. In a certain sense, my project takes up Williams's suggestion that an account of modernism and the metropolis "involves looking, from time to time, from outside the metropolis: from the deprived hinterlands, where different forces are moving, and from the poor world which has always been peripheral to the metropolitan systems" ("Metropolitan" 47). But instead of examining the "hinterlands" proper, the putative outside of the metropolis, I focus on the peripheral metropolis for the way it embodies the inherent unevenness of capitalist modernity.

metaphor, an oversized head in relation to the malnourished body that is the countryside. I return to the international significance of the relation between the city and the countryside in my discussion of José Carlos Mariátegui in Chap. 3.

In addition to regarding the city in terms of this international division of labor, the writers and artists discussed in *Modernism in the Peripheral Metropolis* hold that the city represents a specific form of social life, namely, a shape of sociality mediated by capitalism. In this way, they would agree with Georg Simmel's famous statement in "The Metropolis and Mental Life" (1903)[37] that the metropolis "has always been the seat of money economy" (411). In the context of modernist studies, critics often point to Simmel's comments on the "intensification of nervous stimulation which results from the swift and uninterrupted change of outer and inner stimuli" (410). But I would argue that what is most compelling about this essay is Simmel's articulation of an account of capitalism not simply as an economic system but also as a form of social life.[38] The metropolis, in his analysis, embodies the profound social consequences of the shift from what Marx calls in the *Grundrisse* "[r]elations of personal dependence" to "personal independence founded on *objective* dependence" (158).[39] For Simmel, "relations of personal dependence" predominate in rural communities and (pre-capitalist) towns through "deeply felt and emotional relationships" and "the steady rhythm of uninterrupted habituations" (410). In such communities, where the division of labor is socially

---

[37] Simmel's essay was written as a lecture for the 1903 German Metropolitan Exhibition in Dresden. For a detailed analysis of Simmel's work on the metropolis, see Frisby, *Cityscapes of Modernity*, pp. 100–158.

[38] In "Homo Palpitans: Balzac's Novels and Urban Personality," Franco Moretti similarly challenges the association of shock with the metropolis. Referencing Walter Benjamin's work on Baudelaire, which draws heavily on Simmel, Moretti claims that the experience of shock rests on "an extremely rigid and poor system of expectations" that is typical in villages, whereas "city life mitigates extremes and extends the range of intermediate possibilities: it arms itself against catastrophe by adopting ever more pliant and provisional attitudes" (*Signs* 117). Since city life puts a premium on coordination, it must develop flexible systems of interdependence.

[39] Cunningham holds that "the metropolis appears in two significantly different ways in Simmel's account: as both its 'seat' and as that which is itself 'dominated' by its form. In the first case, the metropolis is understood as something like the 'material support' of monetary exchange, the primary space 'in' which exchange happens (takes place). In the second, the metropolis designates the general processes by which *space itself* is formed or produced by exchange (in a way which *takes* 'place,' 'hollows out' its 'specific [use] values' and 'incomparability')" (*"The Concept of the Metropolis"* 20).

organized, production and consumption are held together by traditional values and relations of domination. By contrast, the metropolis disarticulates production and consumption. Pre-capitalist social arrangements in which "the producer and consumer are acquainted" give way to "production for the market, that is, for entirely unknown purchasers" (411). This reorganization of social interdependence thus gives rise, according to Simmel, to an intellectual and calculating orientation, a purely "matter-of-fact attitude in dealing with men and things" (411).[40] This attitude expresses the form of independence founded on objective dependence characteristic of capitalism because social relations come to be mediated by things, namely, money. And money, for Simmel, is "the most frightful leveler (414). "[W]ith all its colorlessness and indifference," it "becomes the common denominator of all values; irreparably it hollows out the core of things, their individuality, their specific value, and their incomparability. All things float with equal specific gravity in the constantly moving stream of money" (414). Indeed, the independence one putatively gains in the capitalist city, in the metropolis, would perhaps "more correctly [be] called indifference" (Marx, *Grundrisse* 163) insofar as it leads to an attitude of "reserve" toward unknown others (Simmel 418).[41] This indifference and reserve appears most prominently in the metropolis, but its ultimate roots lie in capitalism's dissociated or asocial form of sociality. I return to these aspects of the city in Chap. 4 when I discuss distrust and cynicism in Roberto Arlt's *Los siete locos* and *Los lanzallamas*.

Insofar as the metropolis is the seat of the money economy, it embodies in stark terms one of the intractable contradictions of capitalism, namely, inequality. In the peripheral metropolis, as we will see in more detail below, this inequality assumes such a brutal shape that, to return to Roberto Schwarz's brilliant comment cited previously, it makes the reciprocity

---

[40] David Cunningham, drawing on the works of Simmel and Massimo Cacciari, emphasizes this aspect of the metropolis when he argues that it should be understood in terms of "uprooting." As the "determinate negation of *the city* as a historically specific form of the urban," the metropolis cancels not only the form of the rural community but also the sort of "dwelling" characteristic of the pre-capitalist city ("The Concept of the Metropolis" 15–16).

[41] Simmel modifies this sense of indifference in a way that will be important for the chapter on Roberto Arlt: "For the reciprocal reserve and indifference and the intellectual life conditions of large circles are never felt more strongly by the individual in their impact upon his independence than in the thickest crowd of the big city. This is because the bodily proximity and narrowness of space makes the mental distance only the more visible. It is obviously only the obverse of this freedom if, under certain circumstances, one nowhere feels as lonely and lost as in the metropolitan crowd" (418).

posited by modern society appear artificial and imported. And yet, this inequality follows necessarily from the structuring principles of modern society. Hegel captures the nature of this dialectical reversal in his brief comments on poverty in *The Philosophy of Right* (1820). Although he formulated these thoughts before the full development of the modern metropolis, his notes have arguably become more compelling in the twentieth century and surprisingly relevant for peripheral cities. Hegel shows how the poverty resulting from wage-labor contradicts the normative commitments of bourgeois civil society and the state to freedom and equality. In capitalism, the individual's relation to the means of subsistence and to social recognition is mediated by work, by exchanging his or her labor power for a wage, but when unemployment increases in a crisis, masses of people are barred from participating in wage-labor. Poverty, for Hegel, represents a crisis in bourgeois civil society because its existing practices prove inadequate to solve this problem. Poverty is a consequence of overproduction, so putting the poor to work "would increase the volume of production" and "merely exacerbate" the problem (267). In a wonderfully dialectical formulation, Hegel writes: "despite an *excess of wealth*, civil society is *not wealthy enough*—i.e., its own distinct resources are not sufficient—to prevent an excess of poverty and the formation of a rabble" (267).[42] For Hegel, the formation of the notorious

---

[42] Hegel also insists that charity is not an adequate remedy for poverty because receiving an income "without the mediation of work ... would be contrary to the principle of civil society and the feeling of self-sufficiency and honor among its individual members" (267). Hegel also rules out what he calls corporations as institutions that could possibly resolve the problem of modern poverty. This has led a number of commentators to claim that poverty is the one problem that Hegel cannot solve. I would follow Matt Whitt's argument that "Hegel offers no remedy for poverty because the persistence of poverty is essential to the development, rather than the dissolution, of the particular ethical community that he theorizes" (259). Identifying without solving the problem of poverty, Hegel discloses "the internal limits" of this ethical community in the sense that "freedom cannot be actualized within the ethical community except through ongoing opposition to the rabble's disordered unfreedom" (275–6).

rabble[43] does not simply index an absolute drop in living standards; rather, it derives from the tension between the wealth generated in civil society and the failure of the institution of wage-labor to work as it should. It is not only that people starve because they cannot obtain goods by participating in the institution of wage-labor. They also cannot be socially recognized as having inherent value because, in being unemployed, they have been marked as worthless.[44] Hegel highlights the normative dimension of this crisis when he insists that the rabble is constituted by a specific "mentality," an "inward rebellion against the rich, against society, the government, etc." (266). The poor thus become a rabble because, unable to participate in the institutions that should provide social recognition and the means to lead one's life, they cannot recognize the demands of society as their own and instead see it as an alien other that is indifferent to their needs and freedom. In short, Hegel does not present poverty as a contingent problem that will be overcome as civil society becomes sufficiently wealthy. Rather, insofar as poverty designates a self-generated, intractable problem for modern society, it gives rise to a condition of anomie that especially characterizes the peripheral metropolis.[45]

In Latin American cities, inequality becomes an acute problem and generates systematic anomie in what the Argentine historian José Luis Romero calls the shift from the "bourgeois city" to the "massified city." More broadly, this shift expresses a transformation of Latin America's

---

[43] It has often been suggested that Hegel's notion of the rabble (der Pöbel) was the inspiration for Marx's proletariat. Frank Ruda, in *Hegel's Rabble*, offers the most comprehensive analysis of this term in Hegel's political writings. Beyond the link with the proletariat, Ruda also elaborates on Hegel's suggestion that there is a rabble-mentality of the "rich man [who] thinks that he can buy anything" (Hegel 454). For Hegel's comments on poverty and the rabble, see also Whitt and Mann 144–162.

[44] On the "functional" and "normative" character of the problem of poverty in Hegel's analysis, see Jaeggi, *Critique*, pp. 153–162.

[45] Interestingly, Hegel recognizes the international significance of poverty. If the crisis of poverty results from overproduction, Hegel anticipates that civil society will be driven "to go beyond its own confines and look for consumers" in order to prevent the formation of the rabble (267). In other words, civil society will turn to colonialism. According to this solution, excess commodities and capital would find profitable outlets in semi-colonial economies and the unemployed would migrate from the core to the periphery of the capitalist world-system. But in the peripheral metropolis this "solution," which in reality only displaces the problem, proves to be untenable. With the unemployed coming from the imperial core and peasants fleeing the countryside in the wake of collapsing export markets, the peripheral metropolis in the early twentieth century becomes a global depository for the poor who have nowhere else to go.

relation to global capitalism. From approximately 1850 to 1914, Latin American economies underwent a phase of expansion based on exports.[46] The "massified city," as we will see below, emerges out of the crisis of the export paradigm and in the midst of inward-looking development projects.

In the second half of the nineteenth century, Latin America entered the international division of labor by exporting foodstuffs for consumption and raw materials for industrial production in the capitalist core. The rise of "bourgeois city," in Romero's account, reflects how "certain substantial transformations ... in the economic structure of almost all the Latin American nations ... reverberated specifically across the capitals, the ports, across the cities that concentrated and oriented the production of some products in high demand in the world market" (247).[47] Cities play a crucial role in this period because the commercial activities therein coordinate Latin America's production of agricultural goods for the consumption of increasingly urban populations in the core of the world-system and the export of raw materials for industrial production. Since the city looks toward the world market, the physical transformations of Latin American cities in this era often borrow from European urban centers. Every nation had its "Haussmann," an urbanist dedicated to modernizing the "historical center, both to widen its streets and to establish smooth communication with recently built areas," and to constructing "monumental public buildings ... extensive parks, grand avenues, modern public services" (274). Mexico City's Paseo de la Reforma, for instance, was conspicuously modeled on the Champs-Élysées in Paris.[48] During moments when the

---

[46] Historians periodize the export phase differently. Some emphasize 1914 as the endpoint, whereas others highlight 1929. In very simplified terms, we could say that 1914 constitutes the *economic* end of the period of export-led growth, since Latin America's export markets were dramatically disrupted by WWI. The year 1929, despite being associated with the stock market crash, marks the *political* end of this period because of the number of military coups that took place in that year.

[47] As this quote intimates, the export paradigm meant that the port held a key function in the social structure of Latin American nations. In the case of Argentina, Buenos Aires is both the capital and the port, but in Peru and Mexico the capital and main port do not coincide: Lima vs. Callao, in the case of Peru; Mexico City vs. Veracruz, in the case of Mexico. Although this project is not focused specifically on this disjuncture of political and economic power, I will address at certain moments how this disjuncture generates peculiar problems that are related to the idea of "urbanization without industrialization."

[48] The Paseo de la Reforma was designed and initially constructed during the French invasion of Emperor Maximiliano. It is noteworthy that the Paseo de la Reforma project was not abandoned after the French occupation. In fact, Porfirio Díaz continued to develop the boulevard, making it into a sort of linear reconstruction of Mexican history for the anniversary of Mexican independence in 1910. On this history, see Tenorio-Trillo 3–42.

global economy was growing rapidly and demand for raw materials was high, a burgeoning middle class emerged alongside the development of domestic markets and industries. Latin American "economies grew more rapidly than ever before," but it was a volatile arrangement, as Tulio Halperín Donghi insists, since "they also experienced crises of increasing intensity" (158). Moreover, this pattern of growth was relatively isolated within each nation. Romero writes, "The economic expansion fueled from outside was reflected in the centers that maintained contact with the outside, and it accentuated the difference that already existed between them and the rest of the cities. It was as if two worlds were growing apart, one modern and the other colonial, but these worlds also coexisted" (282). Although the system relied on agricultural production in the countryside, the gains from such an arrangement were largely confined to the cities, to the zones in which commercial activities were concentrated.

The breakdown of export-led growth did not take place over night; rather, it unfolded gradually, passing through moments of apparent revival and phases of distressing uncertainty. The slow unraveling of the economic and political system began around the time of WWI. "Any way we measure it," Hobsbawm writes, "the integration of the world economy stagnated or regressed" (88) in the interwar period, an unwelcome prospect for economies, like those of Latin American nations, that depended vitally on trade. The world market for primary goods remained weak throughout the period, even during the speculative boom of the 1920s.[49] When the stock market crashed in 1929, it represented not the sudden collapse of the system but, in Tulio Halperín Donghi's words, "a rude anticlimax to half a century of economic expansion composed of discrete local cycles of boom and bust (many of which had reached the end of their prosperity well before 1930)" (169). From the perspective of Latin America, the crash did not abruptly throw into question a system that had been functioning normally. Instead, it definitively confirmed the limitations of the export system. As a result of the weakened demand for agricultural goods, employment in the countryside became scarce, driving peasants into cities.

The "massified city" derives from this situation, from the failure of the export economy. For Romero, the historical experience of this shift

---

[49] Hobsbawm writes, "The roaring 1920s were not a golden age on the farms of the USA" (90), but the observation could be extended beyond the United States to those regions, like Latin America, whose economic life depended on the farms.

consists of the following: "Suddenly it seemed that there were many more people" (319). Romero suggests that this migration amounted to a veritable "offensive of the countryside against the city" (321), a sort of return of the repressed. "The crisis of 1930," in Romero's pithy formulation, "visibly unified the Latin American destiny" (319), unified it, that is, in the sense of binding together antagonistic, incongruous elements. If the gap between city and countryside widened in the export era, even though this paradigm depended on agricultural production, the crisis of this model produced a situation in which city and countryside folded into one another, in which the inequalities of a peripheral nation could no longer be dismissed as a historical residue that would be overcome with development. Domestic industries emerged in the early twentieth century, spurred by either the wealth generated from exports or the slump in external demand. Moreover, after the 1929 crash, a motley mix of authoritarian, military, and popular regimes took power and actively pursued industrialization. But the factories would prove unable to absorb the newly arrived mass of migrants. Insofar as these masses were never fully integrated into the existing political and economic institutions, the shift from the bourgeois city to the massified city entails, according to Romero, the replacement of a "compact society with a divided one, in which two worlds were set against one another" (331). In the "bourgeois city," the emergent middle class aspires to the norms and standards of the oligarchy, but the coherence of this "compact society" is premised on the effective repression of the rural poor and corresponding conflicts over the meaning of the nation. In the "massified city," due to the internalization of the relation between the city and the countryside, these implicit conflicts become stark contrasts and explicit disagreements over norms. In the physical organization of this city, the "divided society" assumed the form of "the juxtaposition of isolated, anomic ghettos" (322). When the peripheral metropolis becomes massified, it thus actualizes in dramatic forms the tendency for poverty to produce Hegel's rabble. This may appear in the metropolis as a temporary crisis of poverty, unemployment, and anomie, but in the peripheral metropolis it becomes a more pervasive and stubborn crisis in the relations that make society into a coherent whole. Under these conditions, the rabble becomes, in Marx's words, a persistent reserve army of the unemployed, a "mass of human material always ready for exploitation by capital in the interests of capital's own changing valorization requirements" (*Capital: Volume 1* 784), a concept to which I will return in Chap. 5 via a discussion of Patrícia Galvão's *Parque industrial*. The writers and artists discussed in *Modernism in the Peripheral Metropolis* sensed that the crisis of the 1920s and 1930s would not be resolved despite the changes in political and economic institutions. The full implications of this impasse, however, would only become apparent in the second half of the twentieth century. Writing in the 1970s, the dependency theorist Ruy Mauro Marini identified in theoretical terms the intuition that the modernists had elaborated in formal terms. In *Dialectic of Dependency* (1973), Marini shows that the significance of Latin America's integration into the global capitalist economy lies not simply in the production of agricultural goods. What is crucial about this process, according to Marini, is that Latin American economies could only compensate for this unequal exchange by increasing exploitation. An international division of labor thus begins to take shape in which Latin America contributes to industrialization in the core of capitalism, to a regime of accumulation founded "on increasing the productive capacity of labor," even though Latin America's contribution was based precisely on greater exploitation (114).[50] Marini insists that this arrangement continues to shape the development of Latin American economies even beyond the export phase of the late nineteenth century and early twentieth century. As a consequence of this role in the international division of labor, "Latin American production does not depend for its realization on its domestic capacity for consumption" (132). Industrial nations, by contrast, develop in part through mass consumption, with the expanded reproduction of capital occurring on the basis of the worker's dual role as producer and consumer. But in the periphery the worker's personal consumption is rendered irrelevant since the regime of accumulation depends on increasing the exploitation of labor in production for the world market. As a result, "circulation separates from production" and "is carried out fundamentally

---

[50] Peripheral capitalism thus rests, for Marini, on super-exploitation. For Marini, following Marx, "super-exploitation" includes: 1. increasing the length of the working day; 2. increasing the intensity of labor; and 3. reducing the worker's consumption beyond its normal limits. All three have the effect that "the worker is denied the conditions necessary to replace his exhausted labor-power" since his or her work is "compensated below its value" (126–7). This aspect of Marini's argument has been controversial. I am not convinced that the specific concept of "super-exploitation" is necessary in Marini's argument. His account of the disarticulation of production and consumption only necessitates, it seems to me, relatively greater exploitation, but not super-exploitation in the specific sense described by Marx.

in the external market" (134). With production oriented toward the world market, peripheral capitalism will tend to "exploit as much as possible the worker's labor-power, without worrying about creating the conditions to replace the worker, so long as it can be replaced by means of the incorporation of new arms into the process of production" (134). Marini writes, "Latin American industrialization does not therefore create, like in classical economies, its own demand, but rather is born to attend to a preexisting demand, and it structures itself in accordance with market requirements coming from the advanced countries" (140).[51] Marini thus asserts that, in contrast to the integrated circuit of capital based on the productivity of labor, circulation in the periphery splits into two spheres: a "low" sphere corresponding to workers and based in domestic production; and a "high" sphere oriented toward non-workers and linked to "external production through import trade" (135). Within this structure, the former must be restricted, since its brutal exploitation is the source of profit, while the latter tends to expand as Latin American economies undergo industrialization. Latin American industrialization thus depends for its existence on a massive reserve army to both put downward pressure on wages and replace workers currently within the wage-relation. Indeed, as I will discuss in more detail in Chap. 5, the drive to increase exploitation in peripheral capitalism renders the working class and the reserve army effectively identical.

Over the course of the twentieth century, this reserve army-cum-rabble has increasingly become an urban phenomenon. As we have seen, it stems from what Fernando Henrique Cardoso and Enzo Faletto, when explaining the development of Lima in the early twentieth century, call "urbanization

---

[51] I provide the following quote to convey some of the details of Marini's powerful account of Latin American industrialization: "Dedicated to the production of commodities that do not enter, or enter very rarely, in the composition of popular consumption, industrial production in Latin America is independent of the wage conditions corresponding to workers; this is true in two senses: in the first place because, since it is not an essential element in the worker's personal consumption, the value of manufactured goods does not determine the value of labor power; thus it is not the devaluation of manufactured goods that will influence the rate of surplus value … In second place, because of the inverse relation that derives here from the evolution of the supply of commodities and the purchasing power of workers, that is, the fact that the former grows at the cost of the reduction of the latter, this does not create problems for the capitalist in the sphere of circulation, since, as we have noted, manufactured goods are not essential elements in the worker's personal consumption" (141–2). As a result, even when industrial production emerges and begins to orient itself toward internal demand, it focuses on luxury consumption goods.

without industrialization" (119). Mike Davis uses the same phrase in *Planet of Slums* (2006), his incisive account of urban poverty and Third-World megacities.[52] We should therefore see, I would argue, the interwar moment, the historical focus of *Modernism in the Peripheral Metropolis*, and our current planet of slums as aspects of a single historical process taking place over the course of the twentieth century, a process in which, as Davis describes it, the "global forces 'pushing' people from the countryside ... seem to sustain urbanization even when the 'pull' of the city is drastically weakened" (16–17).[53] In this way, the writers and artists examined here shed light not only on the global character of the interwar crisis of capitalism, but also on the historical development of issues of unevenness, dependency, indigenous migration, surplus populations, and normative instability: problems that have become increasingly acute in the over-urbanized Latin America of the present.[54] The crisis thus appears in their works not as a momentary disturbance but as the structuring principle of the peripheral form of social life. By elaborating the intuition of a collapsing social order, of an increasingly urbanized society lacking robust industrialization and without a fundamental reorganization of the relation between city and country, into an intelligible and sensible form, the writers and artists disclose the truth of a peripheral situation that somehow reproduces itself only by undermining its very conditions of reproduction.

---

[52] Davis also points to debt and structural adjustment programs as the forces driving the current proliferation of slums. When it comes to current circumstances of Third-World urbanization, what is perhaps most troubling in Davis's account is not only the disarticulation of urbanization and industrialization but the trend in which urbanization has been detached "from that supposed *sine qua non* of urbanization, rising agricultural productivity" (13).

[53] I think of *The Peripheral Metropolis* as complimenting Ericka Beckman's current work on Latin American literary representations of capitalist transitions in the countryside. Beckman's analysis, we could say, deals with this historical process from the perspective of the "forces pushing people from the countryside," while my project examines it from the vantage point of the "pull of the city." See Beckman, "Unfinished Transitions."

[54] I would even go so far as to suggest that the problems facing Latin American megacities are not specific to the Global South. Justin Read, along these lines, insists that we must discard the assumption that the Global South "lags behind" the more developed Global North. Instead, what we are seeing today is a process of "obverse colonialism," in which "If any 'time lag' now exists, it is only that nominally 'First World' cities are catching up nominally 'Third World' ones in the extent of their poverty" ("Obverse Colonization" 282). I return to this provocative idea in the conclusion.

"Dissonance Is the Truth About Harmony"[55]: Modernist Realism

III. La elegancia (1928), Tina Modotti

[55] Adorno, *Aesthetic Theory*, p. 110.

III. Los agachados (1934), Manuel Álvarez Bravo, © Archivo Horacio Coppola

In saying that the writers and artists in *Modernism in the Peripheral Metropolis* use modernist techniques to make coherent the incoherence of a form of sociality premised on disunity, I want to establish the realist character of modernism. Realism here is not a matter of local color or meticulous descriptions. Rather, this realism depends on the work's autonomy, on asserting a distance from immediate experience and a critical perspective on the duality of the peripheral situation. These works do not imitate a reality we already claim to know. Rather, by affirming their independence from the given opposition of cosmopolitan and national-popular orientations, these works can give shape to the way that crisis brings into focus the unity of a social order. This modernist realism grasps the totality of the peripheral situation not by adopting a position outside the crisis, not by merely registering the discordant experience of the moment, but precisely by tarrying with the contradictions animating the crisis. These works continue to compel conviction precisely because of this ability to pose questions about crises that have remained unresolved and, as a result, have acquired increasing urgency in the present.We can see this modernist realism at work in two photographs dealing with a specific peripheral metropolis, namely, Mexico City. First, Tina Modotti's *La elegancia* (Elegance, 1928). The force of *La elegancia* derives from the juxtaposition of an advertisement for elegant tuxedos and an exhausted worker— possibly unemployed, perhaps a recent migrant from the countryside— sitting on the sidewalk. The copy for the advertisement reads: "From head to food, we have everything a gentleman needs to dress elegantly." The disparity here is one of wealth, not a clash between colonial and bourgeois Mexico, between tradition and modernity. *La elegancia*, we could say, is a photograph of the sort of reserve army that the peripheral metropolis systematically produces, but its force does not derive from the image's indexical relation to a specific instance of urban poverty. Modotti's photograph presents a realistic, an entirely plausible scene that one might find on the streets of Mexico City, but it is not a document. It is, in fact, a photomontage. By deliberately constructing such a plausible scene, Modotti insists that the two images, the wealth and poverty, do not simply coincide but also belong together in some meaningful sense. The unity of *La elegancia*, its appearance of autonomy, thus turns on the way it posits a systematic relation between wealth and poverty. Both the elegant, tuxedo-clad man, and the (latent) worker, Modotti seems to say, are necessary to grasp Mexico City in this moment. But the very technique that unifies the photograph, the pasting of the two images, also explodes the appearance of autonomy. The need to paste, after all, betrays the existence of a cut. The moment of autonomy turns into dissonance when we see that the claim that the wealth and poverty belong together becomes the claim that they *should not* go together. *La elegancia* succeeds as a modernist account of the peripheral metropolis precisely in virtue of its ability to hold together autonomy and dissonance. Without autonomy, Modotti's photomontage would not appear separate from reality and, as a mere object, it could not compel conviction. Without dissonance, the artwork's separateness from reality would bear no critical relation to the reality from which it takes its materials. Through this dialectic of autonomy and dissonance, *La elegancia* makes sense of how the peripheral metropolis becomes what it is on the basis of disunity, how it reproduces itself by producing brutal forms of inequality, like a massive reserve army of the unemployed.

Manuel Álvarez Bravo's *Los agachados* (The Crouched Over/Submissive Ones, 1934) is less overtly political than *La elegancia*, but its form echoes Modotti's photograph and points to a similar critique of peripheral inequality.[56] Based on the setting, a small *comedor* or eatery, and the attire of the figures, the photograph clearly deals with urban workers; however, they do not appear as downtrodden as the worker in Modotti's photomontage. We might even infer, based on the shadow, that they are enjoying themselves to a meal after a day of work. But the photograph also

[56] Álvarez Bravo told a critic that *Los agachados* was one of his few "political" photographs (Mraz 89), but its political meaning is not presented directly.

intimates something sinister. Langston Hughes, a friend of Manuel Álvarez Bravo, for instance, hits on this when he observes: "Whereas the sun in a Bravo photo almost always has a sense of humor, one cannot be sure about the shadows" (141). The ambivalent shadow is, quite literally, at the center of *Los agachados*. As such, it does not illuminate the work, but its meaning, nonetheless, must be interpreted. Like *La elegancia*, the formal arrangement of Álvarez Bravo's photo highlights horizontal lines. In this case, the photo is divided into three rows, with the shadow mediating between the metal curtain and the workers' legs. Indeed, the photograph has been divided so starkly into these three rows that we might think that it is a montage, like Modotti's, but it is a straight photograph. The force of the photograph lies precisely in this striking formal composition, not in its indexical relation to a particular situation. The composition brings about the work's unity, but it is a peculiar unity, since the photograph achieves it through the negative space of the shadow. In this way, *Los agachados* calls to mind Paul Strand's *Wall Street* (1915), a photograph in which the massive windows of the J. P. Morgan and Co. building have, in Strand's own words, "the quality of a great maw into which people rush." In both photographs, the maw enacts a dialectic of autonomy and the dissonance that grasps the self-contradictory character of social reality. But if the tiny figures in Wall Street teeter along the edges of the windows of the J. P. Morgan and Co. building, narrowly avoiding the abyss of finance, the workers in *Los agachados* have already entered the maw. Álvarez Bravo's photograph, in other words, speaks to the peculiar form of poverty characteristic not of Manhattan but of the peripheral metropolis. *Los agachados* visualizes the crisis at the heart of the peripheral metropolis, namely, that it reproduces itself by consuming the workers because their very capacity for consumption has been rendered irrelevant. The workers in the photograph consume, seeking to sustain themselves, but in so doing, they are consumed by a city whose position in the international division of labor dictates that it systematically produces a reserve army and exploits its workers without any regard for their ability to reproduce themselves. As a result, the peripheral metropolis is ultimately indifferent to what is needed for its own reproduction. The dissonance of *Los agachados* thus does not merely register or reflect existing reality; it grasps the truth of a form of social life premised on crisis.

The realism of these works, therefore, is not simply a question of content. It depends on a formal organization that gives expression to that content. Modernists and critics of modernism sometimes disavow the importance of this formal mediation. In Roberto Schwarz's discussion of Oswald de Andrade's *pau-brasil* poetry, he draws attention to how the work consistently involves "the juxtaposition of elements characteristic of colonial Brazil with those of bourgeois Brazil" (*Misplaced* 110). This juxtaposition, Schwarz writes, is built into the "raw materials" themselves; it "could readily be observed in the day-to-day life of the country, long before it became an artistic effect" (110).[57] The duality, far from a mere artistic choice, follows from a socio-historical logic and thus describes a constitutive aspect of Brazilian society. But it would be a mistake to then conclude that Oswald's poetry merely indexes an immediate, non-artistic reality. When Schwarz accounts for the formal organization of this socio-historical material, he finds that the poetry "empt[ies] out of the antagonism between the colonial and (backward) bourgeois elements" (118). The apparent conflict between colonial and bourgeois Brazil is suspended and turned into "a picturesque contrast, where none of the terms is negative" (118). On this basis, Schwarz concludes that Oswald's poetry embodies a conservative modernization, an attempt to construct a modern Brazilian identity premised on quasi-feudal social relations, namely coffee plantations producing for the global market.[58] "*We could say,*" Schwarz writes, "*that Oswald's poetry was chasing the mirage of an innocent progress*" (Schwarz, *Misplaced* 121). We might also say that the disavowal of form in the name of an innocent reproduction of reality fails to grasp the truth of the peripheral situation.

I have selected these works by Tina Modotti and Manuel Álvarez Bravo above to underline that my account of realism, even in the case of photography, is not a matter of what Georg Lukács often calls a "photographic" imitation of reality. Lukács, of course, associates

[57] Or, to quote Nicholas Brown's gloss of Schwarz's argument, "here the raw materials are never quite random ... In semiperipheral cultural production this kind of juxtaposition is more or less immediately given geopolitical content, since the very texture of everyday life of the semiperiphery consists in the absolute contemporaneity of the residual and the emergent (the integration of Brazil into the world economy via the coffee industry, for example, both maintained quasi-feudal social relationships in the countryside and required a certain level of industrial development in the cities)" (*Utopian* 192–3).

[58] We see here a trademark of Schwarz's work, namely the insight that in the periphery non-capitalist social forms often play crucial roles in the reproduction of the international division of labor. As he explains it in the preface to *A Master on the Periphery of Capitalism*, he, along with others reading Marx's *Capital* in São Paulo, "reached the daring conclusion that the classic marks of Brazilian backwardness should be studied not as an archaic leftover but as an integral part of the way modern society reproduces itself, or in other words, as evidence of a perverse form of progress" (*Master* 3).

modernist techniques with such a photographic imitation of reality, but I would argue that his account of realism necessitates a modernist turn. In "Realism in the Balance," Lukács accepts that abstraction is constitutive of realist art and literature. But "everything depends" on the "direction" of this "movement" of abstraction ("Realism" 38). In abstracting from immediate experience, the realist aims to "penetrate the laws governing objective reality and to uncover the deeper, hidden, mediated, not immediately perceptible network of relationships that go to make up society" (38). The realist thus asserts her distance from immediacy, but she does so in order to produce "a new immediacy, one that is artistically mediated; in it, even though the surface of life is sufficiently transparent to allow the underlying essence to shine through (something which is not true of immediate experience in real life), it nevertheless manifests itself as immediacy, as life as it actually appears" (39). A realist work should thus appear familiar, but what makes this artistically mediated familiarity compelling is a critical distance, or abstraction, from immediacy. As Hegel writes in the *Phenomenology*, "What is familiar and well known as such is not really known for the very reason that it is *familiar and well known*" (20/¶ 31). Rather than leave immediacy behind or reify it, realism must make our familiar, but not known, world intelligible, which is not to say that it amounts to discursive or propositional knowledge. Along these same lines, Roberto Schwarz conceives form not as a structure belonging exclusively to a literary work; rather, form constitutes the "junction between novel and society," that is, the "mediating principle, which organizes the elements of fiction and of reality at a profound level, and is part of both" (*Two Girls* 22). Social relations are themselves "*something formed*," but this form does not appear immediately in experience; it must be "intuited and made objective by the novelist" (22). The realism of a work thus lies in "the mimetic value of the *composition*, as against the descriptive value of the parts" (17). To return to the examples above, *La elegancia* and *Los agachados* do not simply reproduce social reality in its immediacy; rather, the formal composition of the content raises questions about how we should understand salient aspects of the peripheral metropolis, namely, its brutal inequality and self-devouring character.

The question of the formal mediation of immediacy became critical for Lukács in an age of crisis. In modernist works, crisis often assumes the form of disintegration, the independence of parts from the whole. Indeed, we spontaneously experience a crisis in this way. But Lukács insists that this immediate experience inverts the truth of the social situation: "in periods when capitalism functions in a so-called normal manner, and its various processes appear autonomous, people living within capitalist society think and experience it as unitary, whereas in periods of crisis, when the autonomous elements are drawn together into unity, they experience it as disintegration" ("Realism" 32). It is precisely in a crisis that the "underlying unity" of capitalism, "the totality, all of whose parts are objectively interrelated, manifests itself most strikingly" (32). The essence of capitalism thus appears in a moment of crisis, but it does not appear as itself. In a crisis, the capitalist system becomes legible as a system, but this legibility depends on the formal mediation of familiar intuitions.

This question of crisis calls for modernist techniques, despite Lukács's opposition of realism to modernism. For Lukács, modernist techniques, like montage, only reproduce superficial aspects of a socio-historical situation, thus failing to "penetrate the laws governing objective reality."[59] Montage may be capable of striking effects, but once this technique "claims to give shape to reality," he believes "the final effect must be one of profound monotony" ("Realism" 43). "[T]he whole," based on the principles of montage, "will never be more than an unrelieved grey on grey," even if the "details may be dazzlingly colorful in their diversity" (43).[60] By describing montage as "grey on grey," Lukács evokes the following famous passage from Hegel's preface to the *Philosophy of Right*:

---

[59] It should be mentioned that the point for Lukács is not modernist techniques per se but mediation, that is, how these techniques relate to the work as a whole. In a later piece, "The Ideology of Modernism," Lukács makes this point more explicit through a comparison of Joyce and Mann. Stream-of-consciousness is present in both *Ulysses* and *Lotte in Weimar*, but whereas in Joyce "it is itself the formative principle governing the narrative pattern and the presentation of character," Mann uses it as one "technical device" in the service of a "compositional principle" that is fundamentally "epic" (*Realism* 18).

[60] Through this connection between montage and monotony (the "grey on grey"), Lukács alludes to an idea that would be more fully developed by the Italian theorist and historian of architecture Manfredo Tafuri. Montage, Tafuri argues, shares its logic with money as the universal equivalent. Tafuri proposes that when Georg Simmel writes, "All things float with equal specific gravity in the constantly moving stream of money. All things lie on the same level and differ from one another only in the size of the area which they cover," it appears "we are reading here a literary comment on a [Kurt] Schwitter *Merzbild*" (87–88). It is not incidental, Tafuri claims, "that the very word *Merz* is but a part of the word *Commerz*" (88). Just as money corresponds to the blasé attitude, which sees everything as grey and colorless, so montage resembles money in abstracting from the particular contexts (or use-value) of its materials. Tafuri and Lukács would disagree about the aesthetic value of montage, but this context clarifies the latter's comments on the monotony of montage as the basis of an aesthetic whole. According to Lukács, montage, like money, abstracts from content. Accordingly, it cannot grasp the dialectical mediation of part and whole that would be required to make explicit the unitary character of the crisis.

"When philosophy paints its grey in grey, a shape of life has grown old, and it cannot be rejuvenated, but only recognized, by the grey in grey of philosophy; the owl of Minerva begins its flight only with the onset of dusk" (23).[61] With the reference to this quote, Lukács seems to be saying that modernism and philosophy are united by a distance from historical reality. But whereas this historical distance makes conceptual understanding possible, it makes for bad artistic abstraction. The only connection of collage to history, for instance, comes from the superficial details of newspaper clippings. But I would argue that Lukács's rejection of modernist techniques betrays a similar distance from history. A realist work must, according to Lukács's account, retain the familiar while negating its immediacy. And if a crisis necessarily appears as disintegration, the realist work must somehow reconstruct that familiar experience so that its disunity becomes intelligible against the background of an underlying unity. The challenge for a modernist realism is to do justice to the fundamental uncertainty of the crisis, to grasp the unity of the crisis without purporting, like philosophy, to adopt a position outside the crisis from which one could gain knowledge of the outcome. Modernist realism's "awareness" of "crisis is disclosed by its poetic activity, i.e., by its capacity to shape spirit's objective reality anew or in an alternative way through intuition, imagination, and the power of images and language while still inhabiting the reality of crisis" (Nuzzo 428). The artistic expression of crisis thus demands the sort of dialectical relation of autonomy and dissonance that we have seen in the works of Martínez Estrada, Coppola, Oquedo de Amat, Modotti, and Álvarez Bravo.

Indeed, when dealing with the peripheral metropolis in the 1920s and 1930s, the need for realism to become modernist is even more urgent. In the context of the collapse of the export paradigm, the writers and artists

---

[61] The image of the owl of Minerva comes in the context of Hegel's claim that philosophy arrives "too late" to offer "*instructions* on how the world ought to be" (23). Critics of Hegel insist that this preface betrays his conservative intention to defend the status quo. But Hegel's point here has more in common with Marxian critique than any vindication of the Prussian state. When Hegel denies that it is philosophy's task to offer instructions, to determine how things ought to be, and instead affirms that philosophy "paints its grey in grey," he articulates the need for an *immanent* analysis of the historical present. If philosophy will have anything to say about the present, it must derive its critique from the recognition of history's rationality or internal dynamics, not from external standards. Additionally, Hegel writes that the owl of Minerva takes flight when "a shape of life has grown old, and it cannot be rejuvenated." Thus, "To paint gray on gray is," as Rebecca Comay nicely puts it, "to mark the exhaustion of the present" (143).

examined here sense that the rapid growth of cities in Latin America at the time was raising unexpected issues, but the specific form of urbanization remained a question. As I have argued in this chapter, the crisis does not represent a momentary phase after which things return to normal. It persisted throughout the twentieth century and fueled the development of what have come to be some of the most distressing expressions of our current "planet of slums." For this reason, modernist forms and techniques are particularly suited to the specificity of the peripheral situation. By tarrying with the uncertainty of the crisis and the contradictions it exposes while making it intelligible as a whole, these works of modernist realism allow us to grasp the various ways in which peripheral social formations "*stabilize a situation that, in other circumstances, would be a typical and unsustainable situation of crisis and anomie*" (Safatle, Cinismo 14), to grasp how this form of social life synthesizes incompatible normative commitments on the basis of brutal forms of inequality.

In the next chapter, "'Outline of Civilization': Maples Arce, O'Gorman, Modotti, and the Limits of the Mexican Revolution," I argue that the poet Manuel Maples Arce, the architect Juan O'Gorman, and the photographer Tina Modotti, despite regarding their works as contributions to the post-revolutionary process, ultimately insist on the autonomy of modernist form. In so doing, they make legible the failure of the revolution to solve the problems it set for itself. These artists are normally seen as espousing a technological, cosmopolitan vision, in contrast to the Mexican artists who formulated nationalist histories that synthesized pre-colonial, colonial and modern motifs. This tension between competing artistic visions resonated with the fabric of Mexico City at this time, namely its juxtaposition of indigenous ruins and the modernizing projects of the new revolutionary government. But I argue that the works of Maples Arce, O'Gorman, and Modotti are best understood as recasting this split between cosmopolitan and national-popular orientations in terms of the underlying forms of inequality in the city. Rather than subordinate their works to political goals in the avant-garde spirit of overcoming the antithesis of art and life, these artists acknowledge the continuing existence of this antithesis as evidence of the failure of the Mexican Revolution to overcome problems of inequality. Maples Arce, O'Gorman, and Modotti accomplish this by emphasizing, respectively, the collective solitude of poetry, the purpose of functionalist architecture at odds with its use as a tool for capital accumulation, and the technical potential represented by photography and its enduring distance from the masses.

The third chapter, "'Facet by Facet': José Carlos Mariátegui's Politics of the Modernist Essay," proposes that the modernist form of the essay was the necessary condition of possibility for Mariátegui's path-breaking Marxist interpretation of Peruvian society. Mariátegui is well-known as a theorist of indigeneity and the problem of the land, but I argue that these concerns must be understood in the context of the relation between Lima, the urban coastal region, and the rural, largely indigenous sierra, a tension that, for Mariátegui, is deeply connected to Peru's position in global capitalism at a moment of crisis. The essay, as a fragmentary genre, gave Mariátegui the form through which to make sense of these tensions by seeing Peru as a unity constituted precisely by the contradictory relation between city and countryside. Moreover, as a provisional genre, the essay allows Mariátegui to acknowledge this contradiction while positing its possible overcoming. He thus formulates a radical politics that aspire to universality without presupposing an underlying national identity, thereby challenging a tradition of writers who used the essay to articulate a spiritual, cultural identity and political thinkers who conflated anti-imperialism with the interests of the national bourgeoisie.

In the fourth chapter, "'The Century of Phrases': Roberto Arlt's Negative Dialectic of Belief and Distrust," I discuss the Argentine novelist Roberto Arlt's suggestion that cynicism is the fundamental expression of urban life. Critics often point to the uncanny, distressing proximity between conspiratorial politics in Arlt's *The Seven Madmen* and *The Flamethrowers* and contemporaneous events in Argentina. I argue that these novels must be understood as asserting a critical distance from the immediate political situation. I show how the misalignment of ideas and reality that characterizes cynicism becomes in Arlt's works a source of anguish for urban subjects and a form of political organization responding to an pervasive impasse of urban political power and rural economic power in Argentina. In so doing, Arlt grasps the fundamental anomie of Buenos Aires in the early twentieth century and in peripheral capitalism more broadly.

The fifth chapter, "'There's Only One Crisis. The Sexual Crisis': Modernist Dissociation and the Reserve Army in Patrícia Galvão's *Parque Industrial*," examines Galvão's proletarian novel in relation to Brazilian *modernismo* and the rapid growth of São Paulo. Critics often discuss the novel's depiction of working-class politics and Galvão's attempt to communicate with female proletarians in São Paulo, but I argue that what makes the novel compelling today is its use of formal techniques to grasp the contradictions of peripheral industrialization. Through anonymous characters and montage, Galvão articulates the connection in industrialization between brutal exploitation and non-exploitation, in other words, between those who receive a wage and those who depend on but do not receive a wage. *Parque industrial* suggests that industrialization in Brazil rests on a reserve army of disposable, latent workers who can be exploited without regard for their ability to reproduce themselves. Under these conditions, sexual liberation becomes a sexual crisis, incompatible sexual desires and an immense burden on social reproduction.

BIBLIOGRAPHY

Adorno, Theodor W. "On the Social Situation of Music." *Telos*, vol. 35, 1978, pp. 128–164.
———. *Aesthetic Theory*. Trans. Robert Hullot-Kentor, 1997.
Arantes, Paulo. *Sentimento da dialética na experiência intelectual brasileira: dialética e dualidade segundo Antonio Candido e Roberto Schwarz*. Paz e Terra, 1992.
———. *Zero à esquerda*. Conrad Editoria do Brasil, 2004.
Arlt, Roberto. *Los siete locos. Los lanzallamas*. Edited by Mario Goloboff, Colección Archivos, 2000.
Arteta, Álvaro Campuzano. "Carlos Oquendo de Amat o el socialismo en tono menor." *Revista de Crítica Literaria Latinoamericana*, vol. 33., no. 66, 2007, pp. 299–311.
Beckman, Ericka. "Unfinished Transitions: The Dialectics of Rural Modernization in Latin American Fiction." *Modernism/modernity*, vol. 23, no. 4, 2016, pp. 813–832.
Benanav, Aaron & Endnotes. "Misery and Debt: On the Logic and History of Surplus Populations and Surplus Capital." *Endnotes*, vol. 2, 2010.
Benhabib, Seyla. *Critique, Norm, and Utopia: A Study of the Foundations of Critical Theory*. Columbia University Press, 1986.
Bloch, Ernst. "Discussing Expressionism." *Aesthetics and Politics*, Verso, 1980, pp. 16–27.
Brown, Nicholas: *Autonomy: The Social Ontology of Art under Capitalism*. Duke University Press, 2019.
Candido, Antonio. "Literature and Underdevelopment." *The Latin American Cultural Studies Reader*, edited by Ana Del Sarto, Alicia Ríos & Abril Trigo, Duke University Press, 2004, pp. 35–57.
Cardoso, Fernando Henrique & Enzo Faletto. *Dependency and Development in Latin America*. Trans. Marjory Mattingly Urquidi, University of California Press, 1979.

Cavell, Stanley. *Must We Mean What We Say?* Cambridge University Press, 2002.
Clayton, Michelle. "Modes of Transport." *Poetics of Hispanism*, edited by Cathy L. Jrade & Christina Karageorgou-Bastea, Iberoamericana Vervuert, 2012, pp. 93–118.
Comay, Rebecca. *Mourning Sickness: Hegel and French Revolution*. Stanford University Press, 2010.
Coronado, Jorge. *The Andes Imagined: Indigenismo, Society, and Modernity*. University of Pittsburgh Press, 2009.
Cunningham, David. "The Concept of the Metropolis: Philosophy and Urban Form." *Radical Philosophy*, vol. 133, 2005, 13–25.
Davis, Mike. *Planet of Slums*. Verso, 2006.
Deckard, Sharae & Stephen Shapiro. "World-Culture and the Neoliberal World-System: An Introduction." *World Literature, Neoliberalism, and the Culture of Discontent*, edited by Sharae Deckard & Stephen Shapiro, Palgrave Macmillan, 2019, pp. 1–48.
Demaría, Laura. *Buenos Aires y las provincias: Relatos para desarmar*. Beatriz Viterbo Editora, 2014.
Frisby, David. *Cityscapes of Modernity: Critical Explorations*. Polity, 2001.
Gorelik, Adrián. *La grilla y el parque: Espacio público y cultura urbana en Buenos Aires, 1887–1936*. Universidad Nacional de Quilmes, 1998.
———. "Images for a Mythological Foundation: Notes on Horacio Coppola's Photographs of Buenos Aires." *Journal of Latin American Cultural Studies*, vol. 24, no. 2, 2015, pp. 109–121.
Greenberg, Clement. *Art and Culture: Critical Essays*. Beacon Press, 1961.
Halperín Donghi, Tulio. *The Contemporary History of Latin America*. Translated by John Charles Chasteen, Duke University Press, 1993.
Hegel, G. W. F. *Elements of the Philosophy of Right*. Trans. H. B. Nisbet, ed. Allen W. Wood, Cambridge University Press, 1991.
———. *The Phenomenology of Spirit*. Translated by Terry Pinkard, Cambridge University Press, 2018.
Hobsbawm, Eric. *The Age of Extremes: A History of the World, 1914–1991*. Vintage Books, 1996.
Hughes, Langston. "Pictures More Than Pictures: The Work of Manuel Bravo and Cartier-Bresson." *The Collected Works of Langston Hughes: Essays on Art, Race, Politics, and World Affairs*, edited by Christopher C. De Santis, vol. 9, University of Missouri Press, 2002, pp. 141–142.
Jacoby, Russell. "The Politics of the Crisis Theory: Towards the Critique of Automatic Marxism II." *Telos*, vol. 23, no. 3, 1975, pp. 3–52.
Jaeggi, Rahel. "Crisis, Contradiction, and the Task of a Critical Theory." *Feminism, Capitalism, and Critique: Essays in Honor of Nancy Fraser*, Palgrave Macmillan, 2017, pp. 209–224.

———. *Critique of Forms of Life*. Trans. Ciaran Cronin, Harvard University Press, 2018.
Larsen, Neil. *Modernism and Hegemony: A Materialist Critique of Aesthetic Agencies*. University of Minnesota Press, 1990.
———. *Determinations: Essays on Theory, Narrative and Nation in the Americas*. Verso, 2001.
———. "Literature, Immanent Critique, and the Problem of Standpoint." *Mediations*, vol. 24, no. 2, 2009, pp. 48–65.
———. "Race, Periphery, Reification: Speculations on 'Hybridity' in Light of Gilberto Freyre's *Casa-Grande & Senzala*." *Cultural Critique*, vol. 79, 2011, pp. 1–26.
Leland, Christopher T. *The Last Happy Men: The Generation of 1922, Fiction, and the Argentine Reality*. Syracuse University Press, 1986.
Lukács, Georg. *Realism in Our Time: Literature and the Class Struggle*. Trans. John & Necke Mander, Harper & Row, 1963.
———. "Realism in the Balance." *Aesthetics and Politics*, Verso, 1980, pp. 28–59.
Luxemburg, Rosa. *The Rosa Luxemburg Reader*. Eds. Peter Hudis & Kevin B. Anderson, Monthly Review Press, 2004.
Mao, Douglas & Rebecca L. Walkowitz. "The New Modernist Studies." *PMLA*, vol. 123, no. 3, 2008, pp. 737–748.
Mann, Geoff. *In the Long Run We Are All Dead: Keynesianism, Political Economy and Revolution*. Verso, 2017.
Mariátegui, José Carlos. *Invitación a la vida heroica. José Carlos Mariátegui. Textos esenciales*. Edited by Alberto Flores Galindo & Ricardo Portocarrero Grados, Fondo Editorial del Congreso del Perú, 2005.
Marini, Ruy Mauro. *América Latina, dependencia y globalización*. Ed. Carlos Eduardo Martins, CLASCO & Siglo del Hombre Editores, 2008.
Martínez Estrada, Ezequiel. *Radiografía de la pampa*. Edited by Leo Pollmann, Colección Archivos, 1996.
———. *La cabeza de Goliat. Microscopía de Buenos Aires*. Editorial Losada, 1994.
Marx, Karl. Marx, Karl. *Capital: A Critique of Political Economy, Volume I*. Translated by Ben Fowkes, Penguin, 1990.
———. *Grundrisse: Foundations of the Critique of Political Economy*. Translated by Martin Nicholaus, Penguin, 1993.
Masiello, Francine. *Lenguaje e ideología: Las escuelas argentinas de vanguardia*. Hachette, 1986.
Moretti, Franco. *Signs Take for Wonders: Essays in the Sociology of Literary Forms*. Trans. Susan Fischer, David Forgacs & David Miller, Verso, 1988.
Morse, Richard M. *From Community to Metropolis: A Biography of São Paulo, Brazil*. New York: Octagon Books, 1974.
Mraz, John. *Looking for Mexico: Modern Visual Culture and National Identity*. Duke University Press, 2009.

Mulder, Tavid. "Nonself Contemporaneity: José Carlos Mariátegui and the Question of Peripheral Modernism." *Comparative Literature Studies*, vol. 58, no. 2, 2021, pp. 371–396.
Nuzzo, Angelica. "Art in Times of Historical Crisis—A Hegelian Perspective." *Objektiver und absoluter Geist nach Hegel: Kunst, Religion und Philosophie innerhalb und außerhalb von Gesellschaft und Geschichte*, Brill, 2018.
Oquendo de Amat, Carlos. *5 metros de poemas*. Translated by Joshua Beckman & Alejandro de Acosta, Ugly Duckling Presse, 2010.
Pippin, Robert. *After the Beautiful: Hegel and the Philosophy of Pictorial Modernism*. The University of Chicago Press, 2014.
Postone, Moishe. *Time, Labor and Social Domination: A Reinterpretation of Marx's Critical Theory*. Cambridge University Press, 1996.
Pratt, Mary Louise. "Modernity and Periphery: Toward a Global and Relational Analysis." *Beyond Dichotomies: Histories, Identities, Cultures, and the Challenge of Globalization*, edited by Elisabeth Mudimbe-Boyi, State University of New York Press, 2002, pp. 21–47.
Prieto, Julio. *La escritura errante: Ilegibilidad y políticas del estilo en Latinoamérica*. Iberoamericana, 2016.
Rama, Ángel. "Las dos vanguardias latinoamericanas." *Maldodor*, no. 9, 1973, pp. 58–64.
Read, Justin A. "Obverse Colonization: São Paulo, Global Urbanization and the Poetics of the Latin American City." *Journal of Latin American Cultural Studies*, vol. 15, no. 3, 2006, pp. 281–300.
Romero, José Luis. *Latinoamérica: Las ciudades y las ideas*. Siglo Veintiuno, 2001.
Rosenberg, Fernando J. *The Avant-Garde and Geopolitics in Latin America*. University of Pittsburgh Press, 2006.
Ruda, Frank. *Hegel's Rabble: An Investigation into Hegel's Philosophy of Right*. Continuum, 2011.
Safatle, Vladimir. *Cinismo e falência da crítica*. Boitempo Editorial, 2008.
———. *Dar corpo ao impossível: O sentido da dialética a partir de Theodor Adorno*. Autêntica, 2019.
Sarlo, Beatriz. *Una modernidad periférica: Buenos Aires, 1920 y 1930*. Ediciones Nueva Visión, 1988.
———. *Jorge Luis Borges: A Writer on the Edge*. Edited by John King, Verso, 1993.
———. "The Modern City: Buenos Aires, The Peripheral Metropolis." *Through the Kaleidoscope: The Experience of Modernity in Latin America*, edited by Vivian Schelling, Verso, 2000, pp. 108–124.
Schwarz, Roberto. *Misplaced Ideas: Essays on Brazilian Culture*. Translated by John Gledson, Verso, 1992.
———. *A Master on the Periphery of Capitalism: Machado de Assis*. Translated by John Gledson, Duke University Press, 2001.
———. *Two Girls and Other Essays*. London: Verso, 2013.

Simmel, Georg. *The Sociology of Georg Simmel.* Trans. Kurt H. Wolff, The Free Press, 1950.
Siskind, Mariano. *Cosmopolitan Desires: Global Modernity and World Literature in Latin America.* Northwestern University Press, 2014.
Sohn-Rethel, Alfred. *Intellectual and Manual Labor: A Critique of Epistemology.* Macmillan, 1978.
Stasi, Paul. *Modernism, Imperialism, and the Historical Sense.* Cambridge University Press, 2012.
Suther, Jensen. "Black as the New Dissonance: Heidegger, Adorno, and Truth in the Work of Art." *Mediations*, vol. 31, no. 1, 2017, pp. 95–122.
Tafuri, Manfredo. *Architecture and Utopia: Design and Capitalist Development.* Translated by Barbara Luidia La Penta, The MIT Press, 1976.
Tejada, Roberto. *National Camera: Photography and Mexico's Image Environment.* University of Minnesota Press, 2009.
Tenorio-Trillo, *I Speak of the City: Mexico City at the Turn of the Twentieth Century.* University of Chicago Press, 2012.
Unruh, Vicky. *Latin American Vanguards: The Art of Contentious Encounters.* University of California Press, 1994.
Warwick Research Collective. *Combined and Uneven Development: Towards a New Theory of World-Literature.* Liverpool University Press, 2015.
Williamson, Edwin. *The Penguin History of Latin America.* Penguin Books, 1992.
Williams, Raymond. *The Country and the City.* Oxford University Press, 1975.
———. "Metropolitan Perceptions and the Emergence of Modernism." *Politics of Modernism: Against the New Conformists*, Verso, 2007, pp. 37–48.
Whitt, Matt S. "The Problem of Poverty and the Limits of Freedom in Hegel's Theory of the Ethical State." *Political Theory*, vol. 41, no. 2, 2013, pp. 257–284.
Yúdice, George. "Rethinking the Theory of the Avant-Garde from the Periphery." *Modernism and Its Margins: Reinscribing Cultural Modernity from Spain and Latin America*, edited by Anthony L. Geist & José B. Monleón, Routledge, 1999, pp. 52–80.

CHAPTER 2

"Outline of Civilization": Maples Arce, O'Gorman, Modotti, and the Limits of the Mexican Revolution

> *El procedimiento que sigue Manuel Maples Arce … es un procedimiento que requiere una constante gimnasia mental porque él no toma la imagen como la cámara fotográfica, en línea directa, sino que el objetivo llega al cristal receptor, podría decirse, mediante una combinación de espejos cóncavos y convexos: cuando los espejos han modificado la imagen, marcando poderosamente los rasgos característicos, él la traslada al lienzo, por sus temas no se puede ir en línea recta; debe desandarse la línea quebrada que él siguió sobre los cristales reflectores.*
>
> Early review of Manuel Maples Arce's *Andamios interiores: poemas radiográficas*

The 1933 "Pláticas sobre arquitectura" [*Talks on Architecture*] marked a decisive moment in Mexican architecture, staging an aggressive confrontation between modernist and traditional interpretations of the direction of this artistic medium and its nature as a social issue. Juan O'Gorman, one

---

This chapter is an expanded and revised version of my article, "The Torn Halves of Mexican Modernism: Maples Arce, O'Gorman and Modotti," which was originally published in *A Contracorriente*, 19.3 (2022): 260–290.

© The Author(s), under exclusive license to Springer Nature Switzerland AG 2023
T. Mulder, *Modernism in the Peripheral Metropolis*, New Comparisons in World Literature, https://doi.org/10.1007/978-3-031-34055-0_2

of the participants, would later become well-known for his organic designs and for the monumental mosaic of Mexican history on the Central Library at UNAM (The National Autonomous University of Mexico), but at the time he polemically endorsed the functionalism of Le Corbusier on the basis that "architecture will have to become international for the simple reason that man is becoming increasingly international" ("Conferencia" 74).[1] Committed to what had recently become known as the "International Style," O'Gorman opposed the need for a specifically Mexican style of architecture. Whereas the neo-colonial architect Carlos Obregón Santacilia, in his design for the Ministry of Health building, had used ornamental details to bring about a synthesis of indigenous motifs and classical European forms, thus conveying a continuous historical narrative about Mexican cultural identity,[2] O'Gorman built non-ornamental, geometrical houses and efficient, functional schools. This Mexican functionalist thereby called for a radical rupture with the colonial past and made a wager on the technological innovations of global modernity, like reinforced concrete.

The split between O'Gorman's functionalism and the neo-colonial style resonates with the account of Latin American modernism given by Ángel Rama in "Las dos vanguardias latinoamericanas" [The Two Avant-Gardes] (1973). As I discussed in the first chapter, Rama argues that modernist artists and works in Latin America can be distinguished in terms of whether they adopt a national-popular attitude or a cosmopolitan orientation. Whereas national-popular modernists attempt to calibrate universal or European literary forms to national situations, cosmopolitan artists seek an "abrupt rupture with the past" (62). If the former aspires to communicate with "a social community" by drawing on

---

[1] O'Gorman's comments echo Manuel Maples Arce's imperative a decade earlier in the *estridentista* manifesto "Actual No. 1" (1921) to "become cosmopolitan" [*Cosmopoliticémonos*] (45). To my knowledge, O'Gorman and the *estridentistas* never directly collaborated, most likely because O'Gorman became active as an architect in the late twenties and early thirties, a few years after the *estridentistas* moved to Xalapa and then disbanded.

[2] Not surprisingly, José Vasconcelos, the Minister of the post-revolution Secretariat of Public Education, supported neo-colonial architecture because of its affinities with his concept of the "cosmic race," a synthesis of all existing races that was destined to inaugurate a new spiritual age of civilization. Moreover, Elizabeth Olsen argues that neo-colonial architecture, by conveying a sense of continuity, gained broad appeal to the extent that it "would prove a reassuring message to those conservatives who feared the Revolution and the full imposition of the Constitution, as well as to those progressives who believed that the key to Mexico's future was a recovery of its past" (7).

what presumably unities that community—for example, indigenous cultures, the language of popular sectors—the latter "intensified their link with the structure of the European avant-gardes" (62).[3] Rama's account grasps the terms of the debate in the "Pláticas sobre arquitectura," but it could also be extended to Mexican modernism more broadly. For instance, the split between national-popular and cosmopolitan orientations can be seen in the differences between a Mexican muralist like Diego Rivera, with his epic narratives of Mexican culture stretching from pre-conquest times to the revolutionary present, and the *estridentistas*, with their technological, cosmopolitan utopias. If the muralists embodied the attempt to communicate with a non-elite, national-popular audience—and, indeed, public murals were perhaps uniquely suited to addressing the illiterate masses and peasants in Mexico—the *estridentistas* rejected the past and nationalist commitments by engaging in a dialogue with Futurism and Dadaism.

O'Gorman's polemical intervention indeed evokes this conflict between national-popular and cosmopolitan tendencies, but it stems from a more fundamental issue. Ultimately, according to O'Gorman, the choice is not between Mexican or International style, but rather between, on the one hand, "technical architecture," which "serves the majority" and "man," and, on the other hand, "academic architecture," which "serves the minority" and "money" ("Conferencia" 75). O'Gorman rejects neo-colonial architecture not because it embodies a particularist, Latin American cultural identity; rather, he highlights the fact that the neo-colonial style, with its expensive Baroque ornamentation, could only be enjoyed by those who could afford it. Functionalist architecture, by contrast, represented the attempt to mobilize the medium to address the gap between rich and poor. In this way, O'Gorman suspends the familiar opposition between Latin American content and putatively universal, European forms, in favor of focusing on how modernist works can make normative claims in relation to inequalities based on the social power of money.

---

[3] "un sector del vanguardismo, más allá del rechazo de la tradición realista en su aspecto formal, aspira a recoger de ella su vocación de adentramiento en una comunidad social, con lo cual se religa a las ideologías regionalistas; otro sector, para mantener su formulación vanguardista, que implica abrupta con el pasado y remisión a una inexistente realidad que les espera en el futuro, intensifica su vinculación con la estructura del vanguardismo europeo, esto lo forzará a crear un posible ámbito común para las creaciones artísticas de uno y otro lado del Atlántico, lo que obligadamente pasa por la postulación de un universalismo."

By highlighting this form of inequality, O'Gorman identifies the issue that underlies the familiar opposition of national-popular and cosmopolitan orientations in Latin American societies. To return once again to Roberto Schwarz's crucial insight, peripheral social formations are characterized by "forms of inequality so brutal that they lack the minimal reciprocity ... without which modern society can only appear artificial and 'imported'" (*Misplaced* 15). That is, because of their dependent position in global capitalism, peripheral social formations lack the formal coherence that ostensibly characterizes "modern," metropolitan nations. Indeed, critics often claim that the Mexican "nation" did not pre-exist the revolution because, prior to that moment, it was only in the most "artificial" sense that, for instance, an indigenous peasant in Oaxaca and a bourgeois intellectual in Mexico City could be said to experience themselves as belonging to the same national community. Moreover, despite the claims of the post-revolution state, these brutal forms of inequality would persist throughout the twentieth century, becoming, if not more brutal, at least starker. Given such conditions, the modernists examined in this chapter would call into question Ángel Rama's presupposition of the possibility for artists to directly communicate with the masses. This chapter will show, instead, how modernism makes legible the way in which the peripheral nation systematically disarticulates the synthetic impulse characteristic of modern, metropolitan nations. The truth of the peripheral situation, as we will see, unfolded palpably in Mexico City as modernization projects lost the emancipatory character associated with the revolution. Ultimately, the modernization of the city amounted to no more than an "outline of civilization," to use the stunning phrase of the *estridentista* Arqueles Vela.

In this chapter, I focus on the relation between modernist form and inequality in the works of the poet Manuel Maples Arce, the architect Juan O'Gorman, and the photographer Tina Modotti. These artists are normally seen as espousing a technological, cosmopolitan vision, in contrast to the Mexican artists who formulated nationalist histories that synthesized pre-colonial, colonial, and modern motifs. But, for Maples Arce, O'Gorman, and Modotti, this modernist vision did not entail the abandonment of problems specific to the Mexican context. Indeed, this modernist orientation was integral to their avowed goal of contributing to the post-revolution project. In this way, Maples Arce, O'Gorman, and Modotti may appear as avant-garde artists who sought to overcome the antithesis of art and life by subordinating their works to a political purpose. I will hold, however, that what makes these works most compelling is the way they make legible the limits of the Mexican Revolution, its failure to solve the problems it set for itself. These works accomplish such a critique not by subordinating their works to an external purpose but by insisting on the work's formal autonomy. In contrast to the avant-garde project, formal autonomy here involves the acknowledgment of the alienation of art from life, not its overcoming, and thereby the persistent problem of inequality at the heart of Mexico City and peripheral society more broadly. As I will argue, Maples Arce, O'Gorman, and Modotti formulate such a critique of the limits of the Mexican Revolution by emphasizing, respectively, the collective solitude of poetry, the purpose of functionalist architecture at odds with its use as a tool for capitalist accumulation, and the technical potential represented by photography and its enduring distance from the masses.

"AXEBLOWS OF SILENCE" IN MAPLES ARCE'S *URBE*

In Roberto Bolaño's *The Savage Detectives* (1998), Amadeo Salvatierra tells Cesárea Tinajero that the Mexican avant-garde group *estridentismo* represented the attempt "to get us where we really want to go ... To modernity ... to goddamned modernity" (460/433). The crucial question is what this "goddamned modernity" would look like.[4] For the *estridentistas*, it would undoubtedly exhibit the speed and dynamism of the Futurist imaginary. Marinetti famously wrote in the manifesto of the Futurist movement that "a roaring automobile ... is more beautiful than the Victory of Samothrace" ("Founding and Manifesto" 51). *Estridentismo* enthusiastically echoed the message, calling for rapid modernization as Mexico rebuilt after a decade-long revolution. Manuel Maples Arce, the founder of the movement, repeats Marinetti's words in his own manifesto, "Actual No. 1" (1921), and offers a complementary formulation: "with half a glass of gasoline, we literally gulped down Avenida Juárez, 80 horse

---

[4] As Bolaño's novel also dramatizes, twentieth-century critics in Mexico were largely in agreement that *estridentismo*, in its obsession with technology, committed itself to an uncritical vision of modernity and that the avant-garde movement ignored Mexican identity in favor of industrial culture. The critic Carlos Monsiváis clearly articulated this sentiment when he wrote, "At bottom, it was Edison, not Marinetti and Marx, who presided over this adolescent enthusiasm for the benefits of civilization" (173). In choosing Edison over Marx, the *estridentistas* apparently forfeited critique precisely when it was most necessary—that is, in peripheral conditions where the material conditions of modernity were largely absent.

power" ("Actual No. 1" 44).[5] Across various media, including poetry, murals, and woodcuts, the *estridentistas* expressed their passion for the technologies of the modern metropolis, largely ignoring indigenous cultures and the colonial past.[6] *Estridentismo* would thus apparently exemplify the cosmopolitan orientation that posits a rupture with popular traditions in order to strengthen its ties with the international avant-gardes. Indeed, Maples Arce explicitly calls in "Actual No. 1" for Mexican intellectuals and artists to "become cosmopolitan" [*Cosmopoliticémonos*] (45). And yet, as an avant-garde project aiming to fuse art and life,[7] *estridentismo* could not disavow the immediate context that it wanted to modernize: namely, Mexico City. Elissa Rashkin explains that the *estridentistas* called for, on the one hand, "a public art, rooted in the daily life of the metropolis with its factories and workers, cars and trolleys, cinemas, jazz bands and flappers, shop windows and electric signs, carnivals and demonstrations, telegraph wires, concrete and steel," and, on the other hand, "a linguistically complex, cosmopolitan intellectualism in dialogue with an international avant-garde, but unlikely to engage a mass audience" (Rashkin 22). It would thus be more accurate to say, in contrast to the view that the movement favors modernity at the expense of national issues, that the *estridentistas*, in sustaining an orientation toward popular, urban life, and the experimental techniques of the avant-gardes, attempt to suspend the

[5] "*En medio vaso de gasoline, nos hemos tragado literalmente la avenida Juárez, 80 caballos.*" In "Actual No. 1" Maples Arce also insists that *estridentismo* departs from futurism insofar as it privileges the present moment over the future: "Nada de retrospección. Nada de futurismo. Todo el mundo, allí, quieto, iluminado maravillosamente en el vértice estupendo del minuto presente; atalayado en el prodigio de su emoción inconfundible y única y sensorialmente electrolizado en el 'yo' superatista, vertical sobre el instante meridiano, siempre el mismo y renovado siempre. Hagamos actualismo" (46).

[6] It would be wrong to claim that modern technologies, the obsession of the *estridentistas*, had no place in Mexico City at the time. In the twenties, "radiotelegraphy was introduced in the communications system, as well as the first direct commercial flights in transportation, the use of the telephone and cinema became generalized, and the automobile displaced the horse-drawn carriages and mule-driven trams, bringing the first traffic jams to Mexico City" (Aguilar Camín and Meyer 77).

[7] It is easy to misinterpret this idea. Marjorie Perloff provides a helpful clarification: "'Literature is a part of life!' meant in practice ... (1) form should not call attention to itself; (2) the 'high' artwork should incorporate and come to terms with elements from 'low' culture—the newspaper headline, the popular song, the advertising poster; and (3) the making of art could become a collective enterprise, designed for what was perceived to be a newly collective audience" (37–38). All of these definitions could be said to describe the project of *estridentismo*.

tension between national-popular and cosmopolitan priorities, acknowledging first and foremost the alienation of art from social life. In the heady atmosphere of post-revolution Mexico, they imagined they could overcome this alienation through artistically mediated technological advances that would extend the revolution into the cultural domain. And yet, I will argue that Manuel Maples Arce's *Urbe: Super-poema bolchevique en 5 cantos* [City: Bolshevik Super-Poem in 5 Cantos] (1925), perhaps the movement's most important work, asserts its independence from external ends—for example, the use of the work by a revolutionary audience—thereby thematizing the failure of the Mexican revolution, namely, its disarticulation of modernization and social needs.

Critics have argued that Maples Arce's *Urbe* marks a shift in the political valence of *estridentismo*. Tatiana Flores, for instance, holds that "*Urbe* represents Maples Arce's attempt to unite Estridentismo to socialist politics" since "he leaves behind his utopist vision of the city, describing the urban environment as a contested space, rife with social problems" (184). *Urbe*, indeed, articulates a commitment to the politics of class struggle, but, as my discussion will show, the poem ultimately exhibits a more tragic conception of working-class politics. Rashkin thus identifies a disjuncture in *Urbe* between, on the one hand, the way "the activism of workers and campesinos was a source of profound inspiration" and, on the other hand, "the continued violence and instability," which "created feelings of insecurity and distress" (116). Rashkin's comments echo Maples Arce's own recollections about the composition of the poem. In his memoirs, he writes that after walking home during the May 1st workers' marches in 1923, he sat down to write "a canto beating with hope and desperation" (*Soberana* 148).[8] The ambivalence of this remark would seem to confirm the suspicion held by many critics that *estridentismo*'s radical politics were tepid or insincere. According to this account, the movement's elitist, cosmopolitan aspect ends up overshadowing its commitment to popular culture. It ultimately prefers a pure, imaginary modernity over the messiness of mass politics. But *Urbe*'s most compelling claim, I will show, concerns not its immediate attitude toward national-popular culture but a narrative of the Mexican Revolution in which such an attitude becomes irrelevant, in which the attempt to overcome art's alienation turns into an assertion of autonomy.

---

[8] "un canto en que latía la esperanza y la desesperación."

Maples Arce presents *Urbe* as a revolutionary work, evoking the Bolshevik Revolution in the title and carrying a dedication "To the workers of Mexico." To carry out the promise contained in these paratexts, the work effects a shift from the private individual to revolutionary collectivity. According to Evodio Escalante's persuasive account of *Urbe*, the poem requires a "*libidinal sacrifice*," in which "modernity can only be achieved by getting rid of the figure of the beloved" (51).[9] Modernity appears as a collective achievement that demands the disavowal of personal, bourgeois values. Canto I thus praises the revolution and the modern, industrial city, but when it addresses a female figure, a more pessimistic tone surfaces. At this point, the world seems to withdraw from the poetic speaker in a movement that intimates the eventual failure of the revolution. The second canto again alternates between the politicized masses and the absent beloved, turning to the port as both an industrial space and a metaphor for leaving. Canto III abounds in violent metaphors and images that suggest the decomposition of the revolution. This pessimistic tone resounds in the fourth canto as Maples Arce evokes the aftermath of the Great War and "winds of tragedies" from Soviet Russia. The beloved at this point has been reduced to mute, fragmented memories. Once this figure has been eliminated and the privatized individual subsumed into collectivity, modernity has indeed been achieved, but it is not the modernity promised in the beginning of the poem. Rather, the poem indicates that revolutionary modernization has destroyed its own emancipatory potential. *Urbe* ends with an arresting image: "the sky, frayed / is the new / flag / that flutters / over the city" (23).[10]

To attend more closely to *Urbe*'s treatment of the Mexican Revolution and its claims about art's relation to society, I will focus on the relation between noise and silence in the poem. The modern city, Maples Arce writes in Canto I, is "all tense / with wires and effort, / all noisy / with motors and wings" (5).[11] These lines evoke "The Art of Noise," Luigi Russolo's Futurist manifesto, in which he wrote, "In the nineteenth century, with the invention of machines, Noise was born" (133). For Russolo

---

[9] *Urbe*, Escalante continues, accordingly has four moments: the constitution of the modern poet through the experience of catastrophe; the modern poem as the coordination of multiple spatial and temporal planes; libidinal sacrifice; return of the sacrificed, "the weight of the dead continues to loom over the economy of the poem in the form of a resistance, a burden that sabotages the euphoric ideology of the text" (54–55).

[10] "y el cielo, deshilachado, / es la nueva / bandera / que flamea / sobre la ciudad."

[11] "toda tensa / de cables y de esfuerzos, / sonora toda / de motores y de alas"

and Maples Arce, silence prevails in nature, but the city has a "musical" character that derives from its "mechanical rhythms" (Maples Arce, *Urbe* 11). Noise in *Urbe* also reflects the entrance of the masses onto the historical stage. Indeed, the masses constitute in Maples Arce's poem a musical form that displaces bourgeois compositions. "The unhinged masses / splash musically in the streets" (9),[12] and this collective noise stands in stark contrast to the images of silence that appear whenever Maples Arce turns to the beloved, the private concern of the poet. Noise, in other words, becomes a figure for, on the one hand, a dialogue between the poet and the masses in which art seeks to overcome its alienation by becoming part of the workers' struggle, and, on the other hand, a form of social life in which the technologies of the industrial city are developed in accordance with the needs of the masses.

Urbe aspires to effect "a raucous / conversion to the Left" (19),[13] to construct a "poor syndicalist city / scaffolded / in cheers and shouts" (15, translation modified),[14] but the relation between silence and noise undergoes a fundamental shift in the final canto. The streets, which were initially teeming with musical crowds and mechanical rhythms, remain "noisy," but we now find that they are "deserted" (23). Whereas the noise previously expressed the unity of humanity and technology, of production and consumption, this unity has now been torn asunder, leaving machines apparently operating in the absence of workers. In the image of "Noisy, deserted / streets," the development of humanity's productive capacities seems to take on a life of its own. In the reconfiguration of the final canto, silence also undergoes a shift, indicating not the ineffectual existence of the bourgeois individual but the destructive fate of the modernization project: "Iron architectures fall / under the axeblows of silence" (21).[15] This silence symbolizes a force that smashes modern architecture's revolutionary promise to construct a technological space attentive to social needs. The Mexican Revolution itself, *Urbe* implies, contradicted its emancipatory potential not because it abandoned modernization. After all, the streets still resound with the noise of machines. Rather, modernization here assumes a destructive, alienated form in which the development

---

[12] "La multitud desencajada / chapotea musicalmente en las calles"
[13] "Y la vida, es una tumultuosa conversion hacia la izquierda"
[14] "pobre ciudad sindicalista / andamiada / de hurras y de gritos"
[15] "Bajo los hachazos del silencio / las arquitecturas de hierro se devastan"

of the productive forces no longer obeys the qualitative logic of social norms determining the unity of production and consumption.

By the end of the poem, the problem of the alienation of art from society has turned into the alienation of human subjects from capitalist modernization. Rather than a celebration of the industrial metropolis as the expression of revolutionary workers, the city ends up more closely resembling what Arqueles Vela called "the outline of civilization." The poet in *Urbe* may have overcome his alienation from the masses, but to the extent that production and consumption remain divorced and mediated by capital instead of social needs, the poet and the masses alike become alienated from modernization. Arqueles Vela captured this paradox well when he wrote that in Maples Arce's poetry "excessive individuality finds its social resonance. The poet's anguish sings not its solitude alone, like the romantic or the surrealist, but the *solitude refined in the crowds*" (qtd. in Escalante 45, my emphasis). The poetic voice in *Urbe* is thus neither a *flâneur*, a detached observer who takes satisfaction in his aesthetic rendering of the crowd, nor a member of an organic community. Within the space of the poem, the opposition of poet and crowd is suspended, and yet solitude remains. *Urbe* promises a revolutionary politics that would overcome its alienation by adjusting to the demands of a mass audience, but it delivers a far more modest politics: "not the overcoming of our isolation, but the sharing of that isolation" (Cavell 229). By sharing, not overcoming, isolation and alienation, *Urbe* acknowledges its own silence and solitude: in other words, its autonomy from external ends and the ongoing antithesis of art and life. The poem abruptly shifts from noise, as a figure of communication, to mechanical noise in the absence of human subjects, and finally ends with a shuddering silence. This silence is not the same as the one at the beginning of the poem. At the outset, silence attaches to the private individual as something to be overcome, but by the end it stands for the alienation of the masses from the post-revolutionary world they have produced. In the context of this peripheral metropolis, modernization does not overcome the alienation of the elite from the masses, of art from life; rather, it exacerbates this alienation through its own indifference to human needs as such. The assertion of autonomy in *Urbe*, therefore, both acknowledges the persistence of inequality in modernization, as it turns into "the outline of civilization" and leads to the institutionalization of the Mexican Revolution, and projects the possibility of a social form that remains to be constructed.

Interlude: Mexico City and the Revolution

The *estridentista* Arqueles Vela wrote in his column for *El Universal Ilustrado* that "The mechanism of modern cities tends to synthesize everything. To compress everything. We will not be anything more than the *outline of civilization*" (qtd. in Schneider 85, my emphasis).[16] Via this mechanization, the city, the putatively highest representation of civilization, becomes an outline, an empty form devoid of content. As a mere "outline of civilization," the city assumes an increasingly abstract form alienated from human needs. In the Mexico of the 1920s, Vela's assertion may appear out of place, a comment on urbanization elsewhere, not a reflection on the then-traditional character of Mexico City. But, rather than dismiss the assertion as an index of the avant-garde cosmopolitanism of an *estridentista* poet, it would be more accurate to see it in terms of the intuition that urbanization in Mexico City was not living up to its own claims, that it was assuming unexpected and disquieting forms. During the twenty years following the revolution, the development of Mexico City would vindicate Vela's and Maples Arce's critique of modernization insofar as it would make it increasingly apparent that modernization would not produce a coherent form of social organization.

The events of the revolution contributed to Mexico City becoming a metropolis, but they also put that modernity at odds with itself. The population of the city grew rapidly from 541,516 in 1900 to 729,153 in 1910, and then to nearly one million in 1921 (Davis 26).[17] But this population growth, a defining feature of any metropolis, was not exactly a function of the industrial foundations of the city; rather, it was largely due to the migration of rural populations to the city in order to escape fighting in the countryside in the 1910s. And since the territorial size of the city remained unchanged in this decade, population density shot upward, creating severe housing problems.[18] The portion of workers in agricultural production dropped and the urban population increased, but these developments were not straightforward effects of modernization. "Mexico was still" living and dying, Aguilar Camín and Lorenzo write, "according to the

---

[16] "El mecanismo de las urbes modernas tiende a sintetizarlo todo. A comprimirlo. Nosotros no seremos más que el esquema de la civilización."
[17] The numbers vary depending on how the city is defined. Olsen says that the population increased from 471,066 in 1910 to 615,367 in 1921 (4).
[18] "[D]ensity increased from 486.01 inhabitants per square kilometer in 1910 to 610.97 in 1921, principally in the shantytowns in the eastern and norther sections of the city" (Olsen 4).

patterns of a predominantly rural society" (73). These dynamics specify the character of Mexico City as a peripheral metropolis. Mexico City was a rapidly expanding, increasingly technological social space, but these transformations were largely the result of what had been happening in the countryside.

Indeed, the Mexican Revolution was principally a rural phenomenon. Rather than radiate out from the city, the revolution, as the historian Alan Knight writes, "originated in the provinces, established itself in the countryside, and after years of a costly war was finally able to conquer an alien and sullen capital" (2).[19] For instance, a pivotal, but by no means definitive, moment came in 1914, when the peasant forces of Emiliano Zapata and Pancho Villa, coming from Morelos and Chihuaha respectively, took control of Mexico City. Zapata and Villa would not stay in the capital, and would be replaced (or murdered) by other figures in the revolution, but when the fighting stopped and the dust settled, "political support in Mexico City proper" became "absolutely critical" to the project of constructing a post-revolution government (Davis 22).[20] This meant, as Diane Davis has shown in great detail, prioritizing the reconstruction of the city to address the scarcity of housing and transportation problems. Housing was a major problem because, as I mentioned above, the population of Mexico City rose significantly between 1910 and 1920 without any corresponding expansion of the city limits or an increase in construction projects. This situation also put pressure on transportation services, and the *tranviarios* (trolley workers) were some of the most militant workers in the city, a fact that was not lost on Maples Arce. His poems and manifestos are littered with references to trams, perhaps as an allusion to the revolutionary *tranviarios*. In effect, by prioritizing those issues common to inhabitants of the capital in order to shore up political support, "national political dynamics were now subordinated to local ones," namely the urban development of Mexico City (Davis 25). If these political develop-

---

[19] Insofar as this language suggests an invasion of alien territory, it represents the flipside of the language of what has been called internal colonialism. This concept was meant to demonstrate how relationships between regions within Mexico closely resembled the relationship of an empire and its colonies. Accordingly, the reversal of this relationship in the Mexican Revolution takes the form of an invasion, even though the city and country exist within the same nation.

[20] Indeed, although Carranza and Obregón were suspicious of the political sentiments of Mexico City's inhabitants, they relied on this urban base of support in their struggle against Villa and Zapata, the more radical, peasant-oriented segments of the revolution.

ments reflected an inequality with respect to the countryside and the needs of the peasantry, this inequality would also find its way into the city. The landlords who fled the countryside during the revolution settled into the newly established *colonias* west of the *centro histórico,* bought large plots of land, and effectively became urban landlords. Accordingly, the "cityscape" throughout the twenties came to display "the steady concentration of power in the hands of a ruling clique" (Olsen 30). That is, as the revolution passed into post-revolution, the city developed at the expense of the countryside, but it also internalized the antagonism of rural and urban that had fueled the revolution.[21]

Just as Mexico City remained the center, albeit an internally divided one, of the political and economic structures of post-revolution Mexico, the capital also became the locus of different interpretations of the revolution and of the modern nation. As I mentioned above, the Mexican nation cannot be said to truly pre-exist the revolution. Instead, it is principally a byproduct of revolutionary struggles and subsequent attempts to construct an ideology based on indigenous, colonial, and revolutionary motifs. The capital played a crucial role in this invention of nationhood. As Horacio Legrás writes, "Mexico City was asked to represent Mexico to the eyes of Mexico itself" (27). Although the revolution forcefully exhibited what Legrás calls the "extension" of Mexico, namely, its immense variety of cultures and regions, meaning that it had to abandon "the centuries-old prejudice that Mexico City was all there was to Mexico" (31), the conviction remained that to speak of Mexico City was to speak of the nation. What the revolution meant for the nation, however, was far from self-evident. The revolution simultaneously challenged oligarchical control of the country and pursued modernization. These commitments overlapped, but they were not always identical. "Mexico City's built environment indicates," according to Elizabeth Olsen, that "it was impossible to conduct both [projects] at once" (xv).

---

[21] The prevailing opinion has been that the inhabitants of Mexico City were opposed to the revolution and felt particular disdain for what they saw as the "barbaric horde" of peasants following Zapata and Villa. This is not entirely accurate, as Horacio Legrás has recently argued: "The portrait of a capital oblivious to the revolt and dismally beholden to its European linings is as colored by myth as the story retold so many times of Obregón's defacement of the city. Mexico City did not preserve its identity through the tumultuous years of revolutionary upheaval. It was both challenged and changed. It underwent an educational process out of which it emerged, by and large, a different city. As usual, purification was by fire" (32).

In terms of the city and architecture, the debate over the meaning of the revolution amounted to a question of continuity and restoration or modernization, with the philosopher and Secretary of Education José Vasconcelos and neo-colonial architects on one side and functionalists on the other. According to the neo-colonialists, the *Porfiriato*—with its oligarchical modernization, imitation of French styles, and Haussmann-inspired urbanization[22]—represented a departure from Mexican culture and national history. The revolution established the possibility of restoring an authentic Mexican culture by appropriating the colonial architecture of the *centro histórico*.[23] That is, the neo-colonial style—with its intricate ornamentation—took its inspiration from the past and was thus premised on conceiving "the revolution in opposition to the dangers of capitalist modernization" (Legrás 78). Moreover, this architectural style attenuated some of the uncertainty of the post-revolution period to the extent that it "was able to project order upon a society newly recovering from the destruction of civil war" (Olsen 6). José Vasconcelos, in his philosophical and political work, insisted on neo-colonial architecture, along with the muralist movement, as an intrinsic element of the spiritual and aesthetic education of the nation. Vasconcelos "was consciously trying to restore the golden age of New Spain, a time when he felt that the moral and cultural values of Mexica had been at their highest point" (Méndez-Vigata 66). The fundamental ingredient of this golden age, for Vasconcelos, was the racial composition of colonial Mexico. The Mexican people, he argued constituted the "cosmic race," a synthesis of all existing races that was destined to inaugurate a spiritual stage of civilization. Neo-colonial architecture, with its intricate combinations of indigenous motifs and Renaissance forms, embodied Vasconcelos's "syncretic notion of the people it was meant to serve" (Carranza 55). At the end of his essay *La raza cósmica* (1925), Vasconcelos explains how the SEP building (Secretaría de Educación Pública) articulated the link between his philosophical account of history and race and neo-colonial architecture:

---

[22] Paseo de la Reforma, for instance, was modeled on Haussmann's transformation of the Champs-Élysées.
[23] "It was well before the revolution, in the formative decades of the Porfiriato, that the colonial downtown of Mexico City appeared to the Mexican elite as an inheritance that they could neither refuse nor engage … How could this past be reconciled with the pulsating modernity that was also a defining trait of the emergent social order?" (Legrás 77).

On the panels at the four corners of the first patio, I had them carve particular civilizations that have most to contribute to the formation of Latin America. Immediately below these four allegories, four stone statues should have been raised, representing the four great contemporary races: The white, the red, the black, and the yellow, to indicate that America is home to all and needs all of them. Finally, in the center, a monument should have been raised that in some way would symbolize the law of the three states: The material, the intellectual and the aesthetic. All this was to indicate that through the exercise of the triple law, we in America shall arrive, before any other part of the world, at the creation of a new race fashioned out of the treasures of all the previous ones: The final race, the cosmic race. (39–40)[24]

Indeed, in Vasconcelos's grand project, this neo-colonial architecture would make Mexico City into what he called "Universópolis," the metropolis of the Latin American continent. It was precisely because it evoked historical continuity, in opposition to modernity, that neo-colonial architecture could fulfill this function for Vasconcelos and others.

Functionalism, conversely, entailed a radical rupture with the colonial past. Whereas neo-colonial architecture evoked a national past, functionalism made its wager on technological innovations—like reinforced concrete—and global modernity. Moreover, the prohibitive cost of neo-colonial ornamentation was ill-equipped to address social needs in a peripheral nation struggling to recover from a decade of civil war. In the early thirties, Narciso Bassols became the new head of the Secretary of Education, and his tenure entailed a decisive shift toward secular, socialist education and functionalism in architecture. Beyond the issue of cost, Bassols saw neo-colonial architecture as incompatible with these political goals.[25] The insistence on modernization and functionalism, however, struck many as inauthentic since its abstract, geometric, international forms appeared indifferent to Mexican culture. When confronted with indigenous ruins or the colonial architecture of the *centro histórico*, functionalism would have seemingly responded that "little of this past should be preserved and that it was the duty of the revolution to break with

---

[24] Vasconcelos admits here that in the finished building the Renaissance forms outweighed the indigenous elements. This was most likely because the neo-colonial style was highly decorative and thus prohibitively expensive for a nation recovering from war. For a detailed discussion of the SEP building and how it expressed Vasconcelos's philosophy, see Carranza, Chapter 2.

[25] Bassols concluded that the "colonial cloister was not a suitable structure to house the socialist classroom" (Olsen 85).

tradition in favor of new concepts and especially new materials" (Legrás 77–78).[26] For functionalists like Juan O'Gorman, the colonial past and cultural identity mattered little when compared to the current needs of the masses. And yet, as I will discuss in the next section, the development of functionalist architecture coincided with a shift away from public funding and toward the investment of private capital. Although it seemed to be the most rational solution to the nation's needs for housing and education, functionalism turned into a tool for capital accumulation because of its ability to increase productivity. To the extent that modernization followed the logic of capital, Mexico City would become an "outline of civilization," a social space alienated not only from its colonial and indigenous past but also from the needs of its inhabitants.

O'Gorman's Functionalism: Does (Aesthetic) Form Follow (Capitalist) Function?

The architect Juan O'Gorman is perhaps best known for designing the central library in the *Ciudad Universitaria* of The National Autonomous University of Mexico (UNAM). Following in the footsteps of the muralist movement, the library is a public monument that uses architecture to construct a narrative of Mexican cultural history. The façade of each side of the building consists of an intricate mosaic of symbols relating to three stages in the nation's history: pre-conquest, colonial, and modern. The mural is remarkable, but it is also perplexing when one considers that O'Gorman began his career as a devout functionalist who opposed all ornamentation. Against the neo-colonial architecture of someone like Carlos Obregón Santacilia, whose Centro Escolar Benito Juárez (1924–1925) included decorative spires and a colonial tile roof, O'Gorman, as we have already seen, endorsed the ideas of Le Corbusier.[27] For O'Gorman, functionalism represented a fundamental break from "academic architecture," because it served the needs of the "majority," rather

---

[26] According to Legrás, this impasse between functionalism and neo-colonialism would only be overcome in the work of Mario Pani, the first Mexican architect who built a housing complex in the style of Le Corbusier and oversaw the architecture of Ciudad Universitaria, which combines the International Style and indigenous motifs.

[27] He claimed to have read the Swiss architect's *Vers une architecture* (1923) multiple times during his formative years in the twenties. In Nicolás Cabral's *Catálogo de formas*, a contemporary novel about O'Gorman, Le Corbusier's *Vers une architecture* has biblical connotations, being referred to as "the Book."

than the needs of a wealthy "minority." However, for O'Gorman, this did not entail the subordination of architecture to an external end. It is only in the autonomy of the medium that architecture can serve the "majority." For this reason, as I will explain in more detail below, O'Gorman ultimately abandoned functionalism once it became the preferred architectural style for the accumulation of capital.

O'Gorman's early commitment to functionalist architecture is perhaps most evident in the dual studios he designed for Diego Rivera and Frida Kahlo. With their zig-zag roofs and exterior concrete staircases, the studios closely resemble the designs included in Le Corbusier's *Vers une architecture*. Adhering strictly to the principle "form follows function," O'Gorman did not hide functional elements—like electrical wires—behind walls, and he left water tanks exposed on the roof. The design and construction of the house was guided by a simple principle that O'Gorman reiterated time and again in those years: "maximum efficiency for minimum effort/cost." Indeed, the cost of the studios for Rivera and Kahlo was equivalent to that of workers' housing (Fraser 44). Because of this combination of modern design and efficiency, Rivera recommend O'Gorman to Narcisso Bassols, the newly appointed Secretary of Public Education in 1932.[28] Acting on the state's commitment in the 1917 Constitution to universal, rational, non-clerical education, and on his own socialist politics, Bassols sought an architect to design buildings for the nearly 30,000 children without schools in Mexico City (Rodríguez Prampolini 29–30).[29] O'Gorman took on the project and achieved the remarkable feat of building twenty-four primary schools for a million pesos. At every step, the designs were informed by his dictum "maximum efficiency for minimum effort/cost." O'Gorman eschewed all ornamental, superfluous elements and built austere, geometrical, and functional forms that could be reproduced, with slight modifications, in multiple locations.

[28] Bassols is a fascinating figure. He attempted to move the Ministry of Education in a decidedly socialist direction. Bassols's tenure, however, was short-lived. On Bassols and his relationship to architecture, see Olsen 84–86. As Nicolás Cabral recounts the meeting in his novel *Catálogo de formas*, Bassols asked O'Gorman how he would build a school, to which he replied, "Desterrando el arte, atendiendo estrictamente la función, impidiendo los sobornos. Hagamos algunas entonces, le dije, preséntese mañana en mi oficina" (36).

[29] José Vasconcelos, Bassols's predecessor, emphasized the importance of education, but he preferred the prohibitively expensive neo-colonial style. As a result, few schools were built during his tenure.

As the studios and schools demonstrate, O'Gorman turned to functionalism for social and political reasons. Because of its "maximum efficiency," functionalism promised to modernize Mexico and fulfill the revolution's commitment to addressing social needs for housing and education. It constituted, in other words, an attempt to extend the revolution into architecture. It is in this commitment to revolution that O'Gorman departs from the principles of his teacher, Le Corbusier. At the end of the first section of *Vers une architecture*, Le Corbusier states emphatically, "It is a question of building which is at the root of the social unrest of to-day: architecture or revolution" (8).[30] For Le Corbusier, the question of architecture and revolution revolves around the issue of housing, specifically the increasing gap between modern technologies (steel and concrete) and the inadequacy of traditional housing. "The machinery of Society," Le Corbusier writes, is "profoundly *out of gear*" (8). In effect, Le Corbusier suggests that technology has advanced beyond its social conditions, and he conceives functionalism as the means of overcoming this imbalance and restoring harmony. The situation in post-revolution Mexico seems to be precisely the opposite. As Luis Carranza writes with regard to O'Gorman, "the Revolution had already taken place. The country now needed architecture" (135). That is, post-revolution Mexico appeared to O'Gorman to have brought about a transformation in social relations, but technical conditions remained relatively unchanged. If Le Corbusier saw the need to bring housing in line with modern technologies, O'Gorman strove to advance the technical forces to meet the social conditions of post-revolutionary Mexico.

By seemingly subordinating architecture to external ends, to the needs of urban populations, O'Gorman's functionalism appears to eschew aesthetic autonomy. Moreover, even though he was profoundly influenced by Le Corbusier, O'Gorman never shared his insistence on the aesthetic beauty of modern engineering and pure geometrical forms. In the 1933 "Pláticas sobre arquitectura," he railed against "academic architecture" for distorting architecture's function by making "spiritual needs ... intervene in the composition of architecture" (69). Spiritual needs, for O'Gorman,

---

[30] Fredric Jameson argues this formula is not, as critics often assume, a straightforwardly reactionary statement. Le Corbusier, of course, was not "committed to 'revolution' ... because he saw the construction and the constitution of new space as the most revolutionary act, one that could 'replace' the narrowly political revolution of the mere seizure of power" (50–51).

amount to little more than advertising, vanity, or aestheticism. Functionalist architecture, by contrast, addresses the objective needs of the majority and thus has little concern with ornamentation. "The form of the building," he writes, "would be the simple result of technical application" (74).[31] In this way, the influence of Adolph Loos stands alongside Le Corbusier, since O'Gorman regards ornamentation as a "criminal" waste of materials and labor, a grave violation of his principle "maximum efficiency, minimum effort/cost."

Given his orthodox functionalism, it is striking that O'Gorman abruptly abandoned these ideas in the second half of the 1930s. The first glimpses of O'Gorman's hesitations appear in his essay "Arquitectura capitalista y arquitectura socialista" (1936). Under the conditions of capitalism, O'Gorman argues, "maximum efficiency for minimum effort/cost" ceases to be a way to efficiently satisfy social needs and becomes, instead, "maximum efficiency for maximum profit."[32] Although O'Gorman promoted this formula as an attempt to use scarce resources in post-revolution Mexico to address issues of housing and public education, the increased productivity implied by "maximum efficiency for minimum effort/cost" also constitutes the lever by which capital increases surplus-value. The compatibility of functionalism and capitalism ultimately demonstrated to O'Gorman that "there could be no 'socialist' architecture, given the structural relations that determine the nature and meaning of any particular work: only when all private property and the means of production were in the hands of the people could there be an architecture under socialism"

---

[31] On this basis, O'Gorman also responds to complaints that functionalist architecture is a foreign form: not "Mexican," but Swiss, German, or international. O'Gorman writes that just as "The size of the door of a worker's house will be the same as the door of the philosopher's house" (69), certain needs are universal and will be mystified if they are made to have a specifically national character. The point of functionalist architecture, for O'Gorman, is not to construct abstract forms in the style of European architecture, but to address human needs in the most efficient manner possible. And in this sense functionalism may be more "Mexican" than neo-colonial architecture: in terms not of identity but of local needs. Moreover, O'Gorman argues, sounding very much like Maples Arce, that "architecture will have to become international for the simple reason that man is becoming increasingly international" (74).

[32] O'Gorman saw this play out first hand when the Tolteca Cement Company embraced functionalist ideas and aggressively advertised for their application.

(Carranza 160).[33] In short, a cultural revolution—in architecture, among other artistic forms—cannot replace social revolution. O'Gorman premised his project on the idea that functionalist architecture could constitute a unity of production and consumption, constructing buildings to satisfy the social needs of the masses, but he failed to register the extent to which this form of social reproduction could be subordinated to the quantitative logic of capital accumulation. Functionalism represented an architectural advance in humanity's productive capacities, but, as Theodor Adorno remarked, modern architects only produced "a small portion of their work," since "the same society which developed human productive energies to unimaginable proportions has chained them to conditions of production imposed upon them" ("Functionalism" 14). In this way, O'Gorman functionalism highlights the limits of the modernization achieved by the Mexican Revolution. In the absence of a genuine socialist revolution, the attempt to expand Mexico's productive capacities and satisfy social needs could not be extricated from the imperatives of capitalism.

All of this appears to suggest that O'Gorman would be deeply hostile to any claims about the autonomy of architecture. Technical architecture, it seems, is determined by an external end—namely, the needs of those who would live in the building—not by any formal standards. In his critique of academic architecture, O'Gorman acknowledges and seeks to overcome the alienation of architectural design from the masses and their needs, but his frustration over the transformation of functionalism into a capitalist style indicates that he also opposed the idea of subordinating design to the preferences of dwellers. Indeed, after O'Gorman finished the studios for Rivera and Kahlo, he was surprised to learn that Rivera found his house aesthetically pleasing: "he had designed the house to be useful and functional, not beautiful" (Fraser 42). Rivera's preference was irrelevant because for O'Gorman preference is only contingently related to what mattered, namely, the inherently purposeful character of the medium. O'Gorman's functionalism entails not simply an economic calculation concerning efficiency and scarce resources but also a normative claim about what architecture should be in a modern society. It is not a claim

---

[33] For a more detailed discussion of this article, see Carranza 158–167. Most accounts of O'Gorman's "dissatisfaction" with functionalism jump rather quickly from the early thirties to his reflections on organic architecture in the fifties. This approach bypasses the question of architecture's relationship to capitalism and gives the impression that he initially abandoned functionalism because it was insufficiently "Mexican" or because it was not attuned to the natural environment. I would argue that O'Gorman's trajectory is better understood as a continuous commitment to the medium of architecture.

that instrumentalizes architecture for an external purpose, which is precisely what academic architecture and capitalism do by orienting production towards market preferences and "spiritual necessities." The normativity of O'Gorman's claim about architecture's purpose—that purpose is its medium—is inseparable from the assertion of functionalism's independence from immediate responses, be it aesthetic pleasure, use, or the self-satisfaction of owning a modern home. In effect, O'Gorman turns the economic principle "maximum efficiency, minimum effort/cost" into a formal principle for autonomous architecture, pointing both toward and beyond the dwellers of the buildings. Along these lines, Adorno wrote, "architecture is in fact both autonomous and purpose-oriented," meaning "it cannot simply negate men as they are. And yet it must do precisely that if it is to remain autonomous" (14). Functionalist architecture, for O'Gorman as for Adorno, is "worthy of human beings [if it] thinks better of men than they actually are. It views them in the way they could be according to the status of their own productive energies as embodied in technology" (14). As purposeful, the medium of functionalist architecture cannot be divorced from the needs of the dweller. But, as *inherently purposeful*, it demands to be taken on its own terms, not subordinated to an external end, namely, the preferences of a market. The insistence on the autonomy of architecture projects the possibility of a social form freed from the valorization of capital, the realization of modernity's possibility—the expansion of productive capacities to eliminate absolute scarcity—not on the basis of the existing forms of inequality in capitalism but on a rupture with its prevailing logic in order to satisfy existing needs.

THE FORM OF SOCIAL PRODUCTION, OR MODOTTI'S MODERNIST PHOTOGRAPHY

Like O'Gorman, the Italian-American Tina Modotti insists on the autonomy of photography at the same time that she seemingly disavows art. In one of her few essays, she expresses her discomfort when the label "artistic" is attached to her work. "Photography," she writes, "because of the single fact that it can only be produced in the present and based on what objectively exists in front of the camera, is clearly the most satisfactory medium for registering objective life in all its manifestations" (qtd. in Tejada 87). The medium "has documentary value," and, as a result, it "deserves *a place in social production*, something to which all of us should contribute" (87). For Rubén Gallo, these comments indicate an unambiguous position on the debate over the camera as a machine or an artistic tool. In this way, according to Gallo, Modotti distances herself from Edward Weston, with whom she lived and collaborated in Mexico during the mid-1920s. As a formalist, Weston ignores Mexico's modern architecture and industrializing cityscape, preferring instead the beautiful forms of traditional subject-matter, but Modotti "uses a modern medium to document modern technologies" (Gallo 35). Rather than use the camera for aesthetic purposes, Modotti strips this machine of its aura and "partakes of the automatism that characterizes the modern era" (37). To say that photography has a place in social production would thus mean, in Gallo's account, to insist on the medium's indexical character over its artistic pretensions. But I would argue that if the camera is reduced to a machine embedded in an industrial process of production, then decisions about formal composition become subordinate to the preferences of an anonymous market. As we will see below, Modotti would emphatically deny such a conception of the relation between photography and social production.

IV. Tina Modotti, Workers' Parade (1926), Digital image copyright, The Museum of Modern Art. Licensed by SCALA/Art Resource, New York

V. Tina Modotti, *Mella's Typewriter / La técnica* (1928). Digital image copyright, The Museum of Modern Art. Licensed by SCALA/Art Resource, New York

Modotti's "Workers' Parade," for instance, illustrates the limits of this sort of interpretation. As a photograph of protesting peasants, it certainly has documentary value. Its meaning, it could be said, depends on the audience's response, on the peasants who recognize themselves in the struggle or on the urban reading public who would learn about the protest through this image and the newspaper in which it appeared.[34] In this case, the photograph matters as an index of a specific protest, as a document that can inform and motivate others to political action. Our interest in the photograph, accordingly, would "drop through"[35] to its subject-matter, ignoring interpretive questions about Modotti's formal decisions in taking this photograph. But what is most distinctive about the photograph is the

---

[34] "Workers' Parade" was published in *El Machete*, the newspaper for the Mexican Communist Party.
[35] On "dropping through" and its opposite, revelatory photographs, see McIver Lopes 36–47.

pattern of *sombreros*. By foregrounding this formal arrangement, Modotti expresses a meaning that cannot be reduced to subject matter or its social, documentary character. John Mraz thus argues that Modotti "filled Westonian form with social content" (85), utilizing formal composition like Weston, but replacing his peppers, toilets, and nautilus shells with objects invested with social meaning—for example, sombreros, a sickle, and the *mazorca*.[36] While Mraz rightly reinstates the importance of the formal dimension to Modotti's photographs against the tendency to reduce them to documents, he assumes that the social and political character of her works derives from their subject-matter or content. I argue, instead, that the commitment to autonomous form in these photographs has a crucial political valence. For instance, the workers represented in "Workers' Parade" would seem to have no use for this photograph. With their backs turned toward the camera, the photograph could not serve as a portrait for individual peasants. Instead, "Workers' Parade" seems to insist on the fiction that they are not being viewed.[37] They are absorbed in their political struggle, independently of the fact of their representation. The content of the photograph, in other words, does not fuse with, or fill in, the form; rather, form and content are at odds with one another. To see the beauty of the formal arrangement of *sombreros* necessarily separates one from the immediate political struggle of the peasants. The politics of form here consist in highlighting the social division between those who can make protest into a formal composition and those who are absorbed in the protest to overcome their poverty. The disarticulation within "Workers' Parade," in other words, points to continuing forms of inequality and the alienation of art from immediate social purposes and preferences.[38]

---

[36] See also Sarah Lowe's argument about Modotti's use of still-life, namely, her ambition, in Lowe's words, "to transform the tangible into the intangible, to transmute matter into ideology" (205).

[37] I am alluding here to Michael Fried's notion of "absorption." The peasants, in other words, are emphatically anti-theatrical.

[38] In this interpretation of "Workers' Parade," I owe a debt to Walter Benn Michaels's reading of the photographs of Walker Evans in *Let Us Now Praise Famous Men*. These photographs of poor tenant farmers, according to Michaels, stage a social difference relating to the ability to see beauty in poverty. The condescending idea that "they can't see the beauty in these pictures … is just the flip side of" the idea that "only the rich see the beauty of poverty" (126). Michaels adds that "it would be a mistake to conclude from this that the beauty of these pictures therefore compromises their political meaning. On the contrary, it's what *gives* them their political meaning. It is only if you can see the photographs as art that you can see the 'superiority' of the person who made them and of the people who admire them to the people who are in them. It's only as works of art—their beauty invisible to their subjects—that they can inscribe on themselves the inequality that is the condition of their production" (126-7).

Modotti's claims about photography are most powerfully articulated in "Mella's Typewriter" (1928). This typewriter belonged to the Cuban Communist Julio Antonio Mella, Modotti's lover at the time. With its peculiar angle and cropping, its attention to the details of a machine, the image calls to mind the precisionist photographs of Alfred Stieglitz and Charles Sheeler. Like the Futurists, the precisionists celebrated the new technological age and, adhering to the principle "form follows function," found beauty in the pure, geometrical forms of modern engineering.[39] Moreover, the photograph contains a textual fragment that explicitly articulates the motivations of precisionist art, namely a quote from Leon Trotsky's *Literature and Revolution* (1924): "Technique will become a more powerful inspiration for artistic work" (205). In the original passage, Trotsky insists that socialism must draw on, not turn away from, the unprecedented development of productive forces in capitalism.[40] If art is to contribute to the goals of socialism, it must also find its inspiration in technology.

Trotsky begins the section from which Modotti takes this quote by speculating on the "monumental tasks" that the Bolsheviks will carry out: "the planning of city gardens, of model houses, of railroads" (202). Beyond feats of engineering, these projects would entail that the "wall between art and industry will come down" (203). In tearing down this barrier, Trotsky does not mean to suggest that art will be subsumed under technique in a socialist society. The "artistic imagination," he writes, "will be directed toward working out the ideal form of a thing," not toward the ornamental "embellishment of the thing as an aesthetic premium to itself" (203). The artist, in other words, imagines the thing as it should be; he or she does not simply decorate it, giving the illusion that the thing is already more than itself. Trotsky then adds that another wall will fall, that between art and nature: "the contradiction itself between technique and nature will be solved in a higher synthesis" (205).[41] It is not that in a socialist society art will return to a pre-modern imitation of nature. Rather, Trotsky insists

---

[39] Weston references "form follows function" in his notebooks when he decides to explore the aesthetic possibilities of photographing a toilet. Taken in 1925, Weston's "Excusado" was, at least in part, the result of his collaboration with Modotti in Mexico and likely his contact with the Mexican avant-gardes.

[40] It would have come as no surprise to Trotsky that precisionist art was primarily an American phenomenon. "The passion for mechanical improvements, as in America, will accompany the first stage of every new socialist society" (Trotsky 205).

[41] Modotti also used the quote as an epigraph for the text that accompanied her solo exhibition in Mexico City. When the text was later published, she deleted the quote for political reasons. She was a member of the Mexican Communist Party at the time, and she tended to support Stalin against Trotsky.

here on the development of humanity's productive capacities, the ways humanity has transformed nature to satisfy its needs and reproduce itself. Therefore, when Trotsky writes at the end of the passage that the "contradiction between technique and nature will be solved on a higher synthesis," he envisions a relation between humanity and nature dictated not by the domination of the other but by their mutual enrichment and collaboration. Art has a role to play in the synthesis of nature and technique precisely because it suspends its subordination to external purposes, as in ornamentation, and makes normative claims about what the object should be.

For it to "work out the ideal form of a thing," the artwork must oppose the existing world. Trotsky's statement about art may seem to contradict Modotti's own remark about art and photography "deserving a place in social production." With regard to "Mella's Typewriter" specifically, Mella himself wrote in a letter to Modotti that her photograph has "socialized" the typewriter "with [her] art" (qtd. in Noble 97). If socialized production seems incompatible with the autonomy of art, this is largely because capital has determined what counts as "social." We would do well to remember Theodor Adorno's enigmatic claim that artworks are "products of social labor" (*Aesthetic Theory* 225). In capitalism, the social character of labor lies in its commodity-producing character, but Adorno, as the preeminent theorist of aesthetic autonomy, has in mind a different sense of sociality. As Josh Robinson explains, the "concept of social labor thus contains a tension between two different kinds of sociality," the capitalist meaning, on the one hand, of "the organization of society on the basis of production of commodities for sale to anonymous others," and, on the other hand, "the cooperation inherent in ... 'genuinely human activity'" (168). When Adorno insists that artworks are the products of social labor, he rejects the idea that artistic activity is a private activity and makes explicit the artwork's implicit claim that "Exchangeability is not the only possible basis for the sociality of labor" (Robinson 170). And when Modotti insists that photography "deserves a place in social production," she suggests that artworks call for a social existence that cannot be achieved on the basis of existing commodity relations, that is, by reducing the photograph to an anonymous beholder's interest in its subject-matter.

In "Mella's Typewriter," Modotti makes these claims about art, technology, and capitalism through formal decisions. Perhaps the most striking thing about the photograph is the framing. Rather than present the typewriter directly, as if one were sitting in front of it and ready to write,[42] Modotti chooses an unfamiliar angle. Moreover, she crops the object so that only a corner remains within the frame. Through these formal decisions, Modotti decontextualizes the typewriter, removing it from the role it would play for a secretary in an office, for instance.[43] The photograph is a document in the sense that Modotti has not manipulated the image, but interest in "Mella's Typewriter" cannot be reduced to the interest in seeing Mella's typewriter. The framing ensures that the photograph is more than an index because it reveals the typewriter in a way that we would not experience it as a useful machine.[44] In this way, the object in the photograph is less than itself. The framing also leaves out a significant portion of the machine and Trotsky's quote; all that remains of the passage is: "inspiration"; "artistic"; "in a synthesis"; and "between the."[45] Although the quote is only partially communicated, this partiality is crucial to the photograph's meaning. By presenting neither the entire machine nor a complete message, Modotti asserts a meaning that suspends the photograph's indexical character and points toward the "higher synthesis" that does not yet exist.[46] Art itself cannot overcome the contradiction between technique and nature, which is also the contradiction between the cooperation inherent in genuine human activity and the accumulation of capital, but it can assert this possibility by decontextualizing its objects and working out their "ideal form." "Mell's Typewriter" *deserves* a place in social production neither because it merely reproduces the machine nor strives to meet

---

[42] Weston, one imagines, would have photographed the typewriter in this way. He does not, for instance, present is peppers and nautilus shells from unfamiliar angles. And yet, we might say that Modotti and Weston achieve the same effect through different means: defamiliarization.

[43] In the "Frame" section of *The Photographer's Eye*, John Szarkowski writes: "To quote out of context is the essence of the photographer's craft. His central problem is a simple one: what shall he include, what shall he reject? The line of decision between in and out is the picture's edge. While the draughtsman starts with the middle of the sheet, the photographer starts with the frame ... The edge of the photograph dissects familiar forms, and shows their unfamiliar fragment ... The photographer edits the meanings and patterns of the world through an imaginary frame. This frame is the beginning of his picture's geometry. It is to the photograph as the cushion is to the billiard table" (70).

[44] Dominic McIver Lopes calls this the "first art" of photography. See McIver Lopes, pp. 36–47.

[45] These translations from the Spanish do not exactly correspond to the English translation of Trotsky's Russian.

[46] As Roberto Tejada writes, the "synthesis is deferred into the future" (92).

the existing demands of an anonymous beholder but rather because it expresses the social meaning the typewriter could have if the asocial form of capitalist sociality were abolished.

"Mella's Typewriter" thus indicates that it would be inaccurate to say that Modotti either strives to adapt photographic modernism to Mexican reality in order to subordinate the meaning of her works to the responses of a given national-popular audience, or that she seeks a tighter link with the European avant-gardes through the rupture with the past. Modotti was undoubtedly committed to photographic modernism but not for national-popular or cosmopolitan reasons. A "good photograph," she writes, "is that which accepts the limitations inherent in photographic technique, and which takes advantage of all the possibilities and characteristics offered by the medium" (qtd. in Tejada 87). In light of this comment, Modotti's rejection of "artistic" photography can be clearly recognized not as a categorical denial of the possibility of artistic photography but as the modernist critique of pictorial photographers who, in the attempt to imitate painting, ignored the specific qualities of the medium.[47] It is only by working through these limitations, which are also conditions of possibility, that the modernist photographer can both produce "good photographs" and imagine the sort of sociality that capitalism denies by systematically disarticulating production and consumption and generating the brutal forms of inequality characteristic of the peripheral situation. The value of photography, in other words, lies not in partaking in the "automatism that characterizes the modern age," as Gallo would have it, but in what Paul Strand refers to as the "immense possibilities in the creative control of one form of the machine, the camera" (146). These are the immense stakes of modernist photography in Strand's "Photography and the New God" (1922). In using this machine for artistic ends, the photographer, Strand argues, responds to the demand that the machine "must be humanized lest it in turn dehumanize us" (151). "Mella's Typewriter" suggests that Modotti would have agreed not only with Strand's argument about the objectivity of the photographic medium but also with his claim about its ability to insinuate the possibility of

---

[47] At the time "artistic" photography was effectively synonymous with "pictorial" photography, a style that imitated painterly effects by manipulating the negative, through soft-focus and natural landscapes.

humanizing social production.[48] The Mexican Revolution failed to achieve this goal. The development of humanity's productive capacities remained tied to the accumulation of capital, and machines, as the material expression of the logic of capital, threatened to dehumanize society. It is for this reason that the revolution could not live up to either of its apparently incompatible aims: develop the nation or vindicate indigenous claims. To the extent that the accumulation of capital determined post-revolution modernization, it could not even accomplish one of the aims at the expense of the other. Over the course of the twentieth century, it would become increasingly obvious that both aims were sacrificed, culminating in the highly unstable megalopolis that we know as Mexico City today. O'Gorman, Maples Are, and Modotti, working in the early stages of this historical process of dehumanizing production, acknowledge the forms of inequality in peripheral capitalism through their commitment to autonomy, through their recognition and appropriation of art's ongoing alienation from social life. At the same time, this assertion of autonomy holds onto the possibility of a "higher synthesis," of a coherent form of sociality that comes into view negatively against the dissonant foreground of the present.

Bibliography

Adorno, Theodor W. "On the Social Situation of Music," *Telos*, vol. 35, 1978, pp. 128–164.

———. "Functionalism Today." *Rethinking Architecture: A Reader in Cultural Theory*, edited by Neil Leach, Routledge, 1997a, 4–18.

———. *Aesthetic Theory*, translated by Robert Hullot-Kentor, University of Minnesota Press, 1997b.

Brown, Nicholas. *Autonomy: The Social Ontology of Art under Capitalism*. Duke University Press, 2019.

Cabral, Nicolás. *Catálogo de formas*. Editorial Periférica, 2014.

---

[48] This is, in effect, about the question of intention in photography. Critics tend to assume that the camera, because it mechanically reproduces what is in front of it, undermines the photographer's intentions. These critics, however, work with an inflated, misguided sense of intention. One might respond that the camera poses no problems for intention, that it is simply a tool like a paintbrush, but this also seems inadequate because we often have to ask different interpretive questions of a photograph than of a painting. I would argue, however, that photography raises interesting questions about intention, and particularly in the context of Mexican modernism, it becomes a question of the work of art's ability to negate a social horizon in which productive forces seem to outstrip human control.

Carranza, Luis E. *Architecture as Revolution: Episodes in the History of Modern Mexico*. University of Texas Press, 2010.
Cavell, Stanley. *Must We Mean What We Say?* Cambridge University Press, 1976.
Echeverría, Bolívar. *Crítica de la modernidad capitalista*. Vicepresidencia del Estado Plurinacional de Bolivia, 2011.
———. "'Use-Value': Ontology and Semiotics." *Radical Philosophy*, vol. 188, 2014, pp. 24–38.
Escalante, Evodio. *Elevación y caída del estridentismo*. Conaculta, 2002.
Fraser, Valerie. *Building the New World: Studies in the Modern Architecture of Latin America 1930–1960*. Verso, 2000.
Flores, Tatiana. *Mexico's Revolutionary Avant-Gardes: From Estridentismo to ¡30-30!*. Yale University Press, 2013.
Gallo, Rubén. *Mexican Modernity: The Avant-Garde and the Technological Revolution*. MIT Press, 2005.
Jameson, Fredric. "Architecture and the Critique of Ideology." *The Ideologies of Theory: Essays, 1971–1986*, vol. 2, University of Minnesota Press, 1988, pp. 35–60.
Klich, Lynda. *The Noisemakers: Estridentismo, Vanguardism, and Social Action in Postrevolutionary Mexico*. University of California Press, 2018.
Le Corbusier. *Towards a New Architecture*. Dover Publications, 1986.
Legrás, Horacio. *Culture and Revolution: Violence, Memory, and the Making of Modern Mexico*. University of Texas Press, 2017.
Lowe, Sarah. "The Immutable Still-Lifes of Tina Modotti: Fixing Form." *History of Photography*, vol. 18, no. 3, 1994, pp. 205–210.
Maples Arce, Manuel. *Soberana juventud*. Plenitud, 1967.
———. "Andamios interiores: Poemas radiográficos." *El estridentismo: Antología*, edited by Luis Mario Schneider, UNAM, 1983, pp. 11–26.
———. "Actual No. 1." *El estridentismo: México, 1921–1927*. Edited by Luis Mario Schneider, UNAM, 1985, pp. 41–48.
———. *City: Bolshevik Super-Poem in 5 Cantos*. Translated by Brandon Holmquest, Ugly Duckling Presse, 2010.
Marinetti, F. T. "The Founding and Manifesto of Futurism." *Futurism: An Anthology*, edited by Lawrence Rainey, Christine Poggi & Laura Wittman, Yale University Press, 2009a, pp. 49–53.
———. "Le Futurisme." *Futurism: An Anthology*, edited by Lawrence Rainey, Christine Poggi & Laura Wittman, Yale University Press, 2009b, pp. 98–104.
McIver Lopes, Dominic. *Four Arts of Photography: An Essay in Philosophy*. Wiley, 2016.
Michaels, Walter Benn. *The Beauty of a Social Problem: Photography, Autonomy, Economy*. The University of Chicago Press, 2015.

Monsiváis, Carlos. "Los estridentistas y los agoristas." *Los vanguardismos en América Latina*, edited by Oscar Collazos, Casa de las Américas, 1970, pp. 169–173.
Mraz, John. *Looking for Mexico: Modern Visual Culture and National Identity*. Duke University Press, 2009.
Mulder, Tavid. "The Torn Halves of Mexican Modernism: Maples Arce, O'Gorman and Modotti." *A Contracorriente*, vol. 19, no. 3, 2022, pp. 260–290.
Noble, Andrea. *Tina Modotti: Image, Texture, Photography*. University of New Mexico Press, 2001.
O'Gorman, Juan. "Conferencia en la Sociedad de Arquitectos Mexicanos." *Juan O'Gorman: Arquitecto y pintor*, edited by Ida Rodríguez Prampolini, Universidad Nacional Autónoma de México, 1982a, pp. 69–77.
——. "¿Qué significa socialmente la arquitectura modern en México?" *Juan O'Gorman: Arquitecto y pintor*, edited by Ida Rodríguez Prampolini, Universidad Nacional Autónoma de México, 1982b, pp. 87–90.
Oles, James. "The Modern Photography and Cementos Tolteca: An Utopian Alliance." *Mexicana: Fotografía modern en México, 1923–1940*, Generalitat Valenciana, 1998, pp. 273–275.
Olsen, Patrice Elizabeth. *Artifacts of Revolution: Architecture, Society, and Politics in Mexico City, 1920–1940*. Rowman & Littlefield Publishers, 2008.
O'Rourke, Kathryn E. *Modern Architecture in Mexico City: History, Representation, and the Shaping of a Capital*. University of Pittsburgh Press, 2016.
Rama, Ángel. "Las dos vanguardias latinoamericanas." *Maldoror*, vol. 9, 1973, pp. 58–64.
Rashkin, Elissa J. *The Stridentist Movement in Mexico: The Avant-Garde and Cultural Change in the 1920s*. Lexington Books, 2009.
Robinson, Josh. *Adorno's Poetics of Form*, State University of New York Press, 2018.
Rodríguez Prampolini, Ida. *Juan O'Gorman: Arquitecto y pintor*. Universidad Nacional Autónoma de México, 1982.
Russolo, Luigi. "The Art of Noises: A Futurist Manifesto." *Futurism: An Anthology*, edited by Lawrence Rainey, Christine Poggi & Laura Wittman, Yale University Press, 2009, pp. 133–139.
Schneider, Luis Mario. *El estridentismo, o una literatura de la estrategia*. Ediciones de Bellas Artes, 1970.
Schwarz, Roberto. *Misplaced Ideas: Essays on Brazilian Culture*. Translated by John Gledson, Verso, 1992.
Szarkowski, John. *The Photographer's Eye*. The Museum of Modern Art, New York, 1966.
Tejada, Roberto. *National Camera: Photography and Mexico's Image Environment*. University of Minnesota Press, 2009.

CHAPTER 3

"Facet by Facet": José Carlos Mariátegui's Politics of the Modernist Essay

El caos civil, producido por la famélica concurencia urbana de cancerosa celeridad, se ha constituido, gracias al vórtice capitalino, en un ideal: el país entero anhela deslumbrado arrojarse en él, atizar con su presencia el holocausto del espíritu.

Sebastián Salazar Bondy, *Lima la horrible*

In June 1929, the first Latin American conference for the Communist International was held in Buenos Aires. José Carlos Mariátegui, who was unable to attend for health reasons,[1] sent Julio Portocarrero and Hugo Pesce to represent the Peruvian delegation. Portocarrero and Pesce offered Victorio Cordovilla, the director of the conference, a copy of Mariátegui's *Siete ensayos de interpretación de la realidad peruana* (Seven Interpretive Essays of Peruvian Reality, 1927). As the historian Alberto Flores Galindo

---

[1] Due to complications from a childhood injury, one of Mariátegui's legs was amputated in 1924, meaning that at the time of the conference he was confined to a wheelchair. Before his death in 1930, Mariátegui seriously considered moving to Buenos Aires for better medical treatment and because he was finding it difficult to continue his political activities in Peru. On Mariátegui's connections with Argentine intellectuals, especially Samuel Glusberg, see Horacio Tarcus, *Mariátegui en la Argentina*.

© The Author(s), under exclusive license to Springer Nature Switzerland AG 2023
T. Mulder, *Modernism in the Peripheral Metropolis*, New Comparisons in World Literature,
https://doi.org/10.1007/978-3-031-34055-0_3

recounts, Cordovilla "found it unbearable" (*Agonía* 27). According to Cordovilla, the essay, as a form of writing, had no place in Communist politics. Its claims are "provisional," its analysis involves "guesswork," and it conveys a tone of "uncertainty," but "Reality was sharply defined, such that one thing or another must be done; the correct line did not admit discussion, and 'essays' were left for intellectuals" (27–28). What was needed, Cordovilla claimed, were pamphlets like the one Ricardo Martínez de la Torre published on the Peruvian workers' movement in 1919.

Contrary to Cordovilla's preferences, Mariátegui's *Siete ensayos* has come to be regarded as perhaps the seminal work of Latin American Marxism. And yet, it would seem that this reputation has been established in spite of the fact that the work is a collection of essays. Critics have largely ignored the question of Mariátegui's form of writing or dismissed the essay as the unfortunately limited articulation of what could have been a more comprehensive analysis of Peruvian society. Álvaro Campuzano Arteta challenges this neglect in a beautiful passage where he compares Mariátegui's writings to the cubist mosaics of the Argentine Emilio Pettoruiti:

> When encountering the irregular and changing whole of Mariátegui's writings, which expresses, as in Pettoruti's mosaics, the historical undulations of the beginning of the past century, careful attention to the whole and every detail obeys the attempt to recognize in its flickering lights, in its revolutionary sparks, the formation of constellations in movement that spark the imagination of another modernity. (*Modernidad imaginada* 301)

But even Arteta at times describes Mariátegui's work as "interrupted and unfinished" (22), echoing the common view that the essay is not a form in its own right but a temporary articulation that would be superseded at a later point. This dismissive attitude toward the form of the essay points to a broader division in Mariátegui scholarship. For most of the twentieth century, Mariátegui was presented as primarily a social and political thinker. However, a quick look at his complete works in the Biblioteca Amauta edition reveals that close to half of his oeuvre deals with art, literature, philosophy, and culture. In recent years, various critics have rightly recovered Mariátegui's insights as a cultural thinker.[2] But few have closely analyzed the form of Mariátegui's writings,[3] much less insisted that the essay makes possible his distinctive interpretation of Peruvian reality. This is precisely the line of thought that I will pursue in this chapter. In the *Siete ensayos*, Mariátegui insists: "my aesthetic conception is intimately linked (se unimisma) in my consciousness with my moral, political and religious conceptions, and, without ceasing to be strictly aesthetic, it cannot operate independently or differently" (204).[4] I hope to do justice to this claim by asking what relation the essay holds to Mariátegui's thought.[5] I argue that he turns to the essay neither for contingent, circumstantial reasons nor as an inessential placeholder for a prospective, complete analysis, but because the form of the essay offers a compelling framework for making sense of the shape of peripheral societies. The essay discloses what he calls the inorganic character of Peruvian social reality, namely, the way that it assumes its identity precisely through the split between coast and sierra, or city and countryside. As in the essay, so for Peru, the parts do not compose a coherent whole, but they also cannot be conceived independently of the whole. As a social category, the inorganic thus designates the crisis of a form of life, the way it breaks down in light of its normative self-conception as a unified collectivity and fails to reproduce itself. The inorganic, in failing to be organic, grasps the dependent, not self-sufficient,

[2] Vicky Unruh's "Mariátegui's Aesthetic Thought: A Critical Reading of the Avant-Gardes" was a path-breaking work for appreciating the extent to which Mariátegui engaged with European and Latin American avant-gardes. Estuardo Nuñez's *La experiencia europea de José Carlos Mariátegui* is an invaluable source for biographical information on Mariátegui's connections with European artists and avant-garde movements, not to mention post-WWI radical politics. Mariátegui also wrote on Latin American artists and writers and cultivated a circle of artists in Lima by hosting reunions at his house on Calle Washington. For a variety of recent perspectives on connections between Mariátegui and art, see the *Mariátegui y los estudios latinoamericanos*, edited by Mabel Moraña and Guido Podestá.

[3] Michelle Clayton's "Mariátegui y la escena contemporánea," not to mention her personal feedback, inspired me to attend to the formal dimension of Mariátegui's works.

[4] "Pero esto no quiere decir que considere el fenómeno literario o artístico desde puntos de vista extraestéticos, sino que mi concepción estética se unimisma, en la intimidad de mi conciencia, con mis concepciones morales, políticas y religiosas, y que, sin dejar de ser concepción estrictamente estética, no puede operar independiente o diversamente."

[5] Put differently, the essay allows Mariátegui to explore what Flores Galindo calls the "agony" he experienced between "avant-garde art and *indigenismo*, between the West and the Andean world, between the vindication of heterodoxy and the exaltation of discipline, between the national and the international, between Mexico (the native side of Latin America) and Buenos Aires (the port towards Europe)" (*Agonía* 11–12).

character of the periphery, that is, how the circulation of capital, in such a situation and in contrast with the core of the world-system, cannot sustain itself. I begin by examining Mariátegui's comments on his own form of writing and by putting his work in the context of the essay in Europe and Latin America. I then show how this form allows us to trace the movement of his thoughts on the relation between the city and the countryside (or the coast and sierra) in Peru, especially in the "Regionalism and Centralism" essay of the *Siete ensayos*. I then conclude by drawing out the politics of the essay by connecting this formal arrangement to the disagreement between Mariátegui and Víctor Raúl Haya de la Torre, a polemic over the need for a socialist united front of workers and indigenous peasants versus the populist anti-imperialism of Haya de la Torre's Alianza Popular Revolucionaria Americana. Throughout the chapter, I argue that Mariátegui utilizes the essay not in order to represent a fragmentary external reality but to express a crisis in the peripheral form of social life, the contradiction between who these subjects are and who they take themselves to be, since the very commitment to a modern nation negates itself in this context and requires brutal forms of inequality. In carrying out such a self-negation, the essay indeed evokes uncertainty, but this uncertainty does not simply appear as a lack relative to a pamphlet, which seeks to inform the reader of a problem and provide readymade solutions. Rather, the essay makes its inherent uncertainty into a normative demand to transform the practices and self-conceptions that lead to these forms of inequality.

THE ESSAY AND INORGANIC FORM

Given that JoséCarlos Mariátegui's *Siete ensayos deinterpretación de la realidad peruana* (1927) has been lauded as one of the most significant analyses of Latin America society, Mariátegui's tentative words in the "Author's Note" may strike the reader as incongruous. Mariátegui explains that, like his first published book, *La escena contemporánea* (1923), these essays do not form "an organic book" (13). Indeed, each essay is perhaps only "the outline, the plan, of an autonomous" work (13). The *Siete ensayos*, in other words, is incomplete, and Mariátegui highlights this unfinished status when he references an eighth essay he intended to include but now realizes should be reserved for another book. Mariátegui even goes so far as to insist that none of his works "is finished; they never will be as long as I live and think and have something to add to what I have written, lived, and thought" (13). This quote compels us to redescribe Mariátegui's previous statements about the composition of the book. Not simply commenting on the contingent conditions that prevented him from completing the work, Mariátegui also asserts his commitment to a particular mode of thinking and writing. Along these lines, he identifies with Nietzsche, who "loved not the author under a contract for the intentional, deliberate production of a book, but rather the one whose thoughts formed a book spontaneously and without premeditation" (13).[6] Accordingly, Mariátegui does not conceive the essay as a mere constraint that would be overcome with the completion of his analysis; rather, this form and the content of his interpretation are adequate to one another. My goal in this section is to delineate the form of the essay by reviewing its history and the specific ways Mariátegui thinks about this inherently self-reflexive form of writing. We will then be able to see clearly what makes the essay a compelling formal medium for working through the contradictions of Peruvian reality.

The essay has a rich history in Latin America, especially in the early twentieth century. Martin Stabb has argued that the proliferation of essays in this historical moment should be viewed as a rejection of the positivist and materialist legacy of the nineteenth century.[7] It appeared to these essayists that the exclusive focus on utilitarian values and technical progress left no room for what Latin America urgently needed, namely, an exploration of the region's spiritual and cultural identity. José Enrique Rodó's *Ariel* (1900), the most influential essay of the period, made such an argument through allusions to Shakespeare's *The Tempest*. According to Rodó, Latin America must uphold the noble, spiritual values of Ariel in opposition to the base materialism of Caliban, whom the Uruguayan writer associates with the United States, the new industrial and imperial

---

[6] This is a reference to the epigraph Mariátegui chose for the *Siete ensayos*. It comes from "The Wanderer and His Shadow," a section of *Human, All Too Human*. The quote, which Mariátegui includes in German, reads as follows: "Ich will keinen Autor mehr lesen, dem man anmerkt, er wollte ein Buch machen; sondern nur jene, deren Gedanken unversehens ein Buch werden."
[7] See Stab, *In Quest of Identity*, Chapter 5.

giant in the region.[8] For Rodó and others of this generation, the essay, because of its distance from scientistic approaches, seems uniquely suited to this task of articulating a specifically Latin American identity, of addressing a need that cannot be satisfied by material goods. We should not, however, take Mariátegui to be a straight-forward representative of this generation of essay writers. As we will see, Mariátegui shares a critique of positivism, but the form of the essay leads him to think about identity in very different terms.[9]

Mariátegui's use of, and reflections on, the essay draw on three crucial aspects of its form and history. First, the essay dialectically mediates the aesthetic and the cognitive, the sensible and the intelligible, preserving and cancelling their mutual antagonism. This is the focus of one of the great essays on the essay, Georg Lukács's "On the Nature and Form of the Essay."[10] This text, which opens Lukács's *Soul and Form* (1908), begins not dissimilarly to Mariátegui's *Siete ensayos*. Lukács asks himself "whether one is entitled to publish such works—whether such works can give rise to a new unity, a book" ("Essay" 16). But this leads to a different question: what kind of unity? Does the essay possess the sort of unity belonging to science: logical necessity and conceptual clarity? Or is its unity that of art,

---

[8] It is often noted that Rodó, writing *Ariel* in the wake of the Spanish American War, recognized that the United States, not Spain, would be the main threat to Latin American independence in the new century. In defeating the Spanish, the United States also thwarted the Cuban independence movement. Although Cuba nominally became an independent state after the war, the Platt Amendment emptied its independence of any real content. In this context, it bears mentioning that the Cuban Roberto Fernández Retamar reversed Rodó's judgment and made Caliban the symbol of a revolutionary, anti-imperialist Latin America culture.

[9] I share Claire De Obalida's judgment that the "shortcomings" of most studies of the essay in Latin America have to do "with the fact that they are more concerned with the ways in which the content of essays reflect the history of ideas and the cultural identity of their countries than with the form itself" (61). My focus in this chapter is limited to Mariátegui, so I cannot say much about the Latin American essay in general, but I do aim to give the form of the essay the attention it deserves.

[10] In one sense, Lukács's essay is not an essay at all. Rather, it is written as a letter to his friend Leo Popper. In a discussion of this essay, Peter Uwe Hohendahl suggests that it is because the "essay form articulates this loss [of representative speech] as the absence of a clearly defined public that the critic wants to address" (221), that it is appropriate for Lukács to write this essay as a letter to a personal friend. Lukács also claims that "the greatest essayist who ever lived or wrote" is Plato, an author of dialogues ("Essay" 29). The dialogue format could be another way of dealing with the "absence of a clearly defined public," insofar as it incorporates the audience within the essay.

which, in Lukács's enigmatic formulation, "offers us souls and destinies" (18)? Along the lines of this last quote, Lukács recasts the issue of the essay, from science vs. art into form vs. life. These two poles stand in apparent opposition. From the perspective of form, life lacks order. From the vantage point of life, form appears as devoid of content.[11] The essay—being neither science nor art, or being both science and art[12]—"succeeds simultaneously in providing form with life (without which it remains an empty shell, pure abstraction) and life with form (without which it remains inarticulate, inchoate immediacy)" (De Obalida 105). This idea becomes more concrete when Lukács discusses the fundamental irony of the essay: that the critic is "always speaking about the ultimate problems of life, but in a tone which implies that he is only discussing pictures and books, only the inessential and pretty ornaments of real life" ("Essay" 25). In the essay, the inessential, contingent details of life become the occasion for reflecting on questions of universal significance. But this does not mean that the object of the essay becomes a mere example of a universal, as would be the case in scientific writing. Rather, the essay enables us to see form—that is, the universal—unfolding from within life—that is, the particular object.

Along these same lines, Mariátegui conceives of the essay neither as a pre-existing form to be applied to an object nor as mere vehicle for an analysis of Peruvian social reality that he has already elaborated. Rather, the form and content of the essay reciprocally determine one another in the process of articulation. The essay thus expresses Mariátegui's conviction, cited above, that his "aesthetic conception is intimately linked (se unimisma) in [his] consciousness with [his] moral, political and religious conceptions, and without ceasing to be strictly aesthetic, it cannot operate independently or differently" (*Siete ensayos* 204).[13] When Mariátegui refers to the "aesthetic" in this quote, he does not mean to evoke the idea that art gives form to an inchoate social reality. Rather, the "aesthetic" here is a matter of formal intelligibility. As we see in what follows, the essay makes

---

[11] This is a version of the Kantian distinction between concept and intuition, so we should keep in mind Kant's stipulation that "concepts without intuitions are empty, intuitions without concepts are blind."

[12] Adorno notes in his "The Essay as Form" that Lukács ultimately makes the essay into an art form, rather than insist on its dialectical mediation of art and science ("Essay" 5).

[13] "Pero esto no quiere decir que considere el fenómeno literario o artístico desde puntos de vista extraestéticos, sino que mi concepción estética se unimisma, en la intimidad de mi conciencia, con mis concepciones morales, políticas y religiosas, y que, sin dejar de ser concepción estrictamente estética, no puede operar independiente o diversamente."

sense of the social organization of Peruvian reality, allowing individuals to recognize the structure of the life they inhabit. Through a focus on formal arrangement, Mariátegui overcomes schematic analysis and discloses his interpretation of Peruvian reality as a concrete issue of life.

Second, the essay has historically been a vehicle for skeptical criticism. For Montaigne, the father of the modern essay, this mode of writing was uniquely suited to skeptical philosophy because it enabled him to entertain contradictory and incommensurable ideas. Writing in the epistemological crisis of the Renaissance, with modern rationality beginning to displace traditional authority, Montaigne repeatedly asks himself in the *Essais*, what do I know? And, like a good skeptic, he concludes: nothing with certainty. The dilemma, as Montaigne articulates it, is that "Man cannot avoid the fact that his senses are both the sovereign regents of his knowledge, and yet, in all circumstances, uncertain and fallible"; thus "we are forced to conclude ... that there is no such thing as knowledge" (669). In such a situation, Montaigne suggests that we ought to respond with "doubt and suspense of judgment" (561), what Pyrrhonian skepticism calls *epoché*. The essay, as an open-ended genre for "weighing" an object, allows Montaigne to examine his object from multiple angles, thus undermining the dogmatic truth of traditional authority. And yet, the proto-modernist technique of "weighing" an object also opposes the new ideal of scientific discourse. Whereas science aims at a pure "view-from-nowhere," for which subjectivity is simply a source of error, the essay embodies the idea that a conclusion is binding only if it can make the reader respond to the object in the relevant way.

Mariátegui does not share Montaigne's epistemological skepticism, but he does consistently oppose the putative certainty of positivist philosophies. Rejecting the evolutionist assumptions of Second International Marxism, Mariátegui always emphasizes subjectivity, creativity, and the need for faith.[14] Moreover, as I will show in more detail in the final section of this chapter, the necessity of uncertainty informs Mariátegui's politics.

---

[14] This led Mariátegui to write enthusiastically about George Sorel. This is a divisive issue in Mariátegui scholarship. The first generation of critics tended to dismiss these references to Sorel, while later critics took them as a sign of Mariátegui's heterodox tendencies. For an excellent discussion of Mariátegui's reception of Sorel, and the reception of Mariátegui's reception of Sorel, see De Castro, *Bread and Beauty*, Chapter 3.

Third, the form of the essay is characterized by a peculiar anti-systematic system.[15] This constitutive tension is developed and worked through in Theodor Adorno's "The Essay as Form" (1958). Indeed, Adorno's own philosophy shares with the essay a dialectical relation between system and its opposite. As Terry Pinkard aptly puts it, "Adorno is some sort of holist, so he believes that one cannot understand social life ... without understanding how the distinct elements function in the whole. Yet he also seems to think that any attempt to be systematic in philosophy necessarily ends up falsifying what it studies since it necessarily must try to cram too many individualities into a premade system" ("Negative Dialectics" 459). Adorno thus needs some way of conceiving the whole as distinct from system, and the essay is precisely the form that makes such a concept possible. In "The Essay as Form," this project revolves around the rejection of Cartesian method. In his *Discourse on Method*, Descartes famously sets down four rules: first, clear and distinct perceptions and "indubitable certainty"; second, "the division of the object into 'as many parts as possible, and as might be necessary for its adequate solution'"; third, moving step by step from the simplest to the most complex; fourth, to develop "exhaustive enumerations" and thereby include everything (Adorno, "Essay" 14–15). By contrast, the essay: learns from error and rejects the ideal of certainty; emphasizes mediation over immediacy or the self-sufficiency of parts; "starts from the most complex"; and, replaces the seamless continuity of enumeration with discontinuity. The point of Adorno's distinction between Cartesian method and the essay, however, does not amount to a shift from hierarchical organization to disorder. Rather than disavow the category of totality; the essay "has to cause the totality to be illuminated in a partial feature" (16). The essay does not embody disorder but a different kind of order. A system imposes unity on its elements, subsuming particular objects under universal concepts, whereas the essay coordinates particulars into a "force field." "It is not," Adorno writes, that the essay is "unlogical; it obeys logical criteria insofar as the totality of its propositions must fit together coherently" (22). But it "does not develop its ideas in accordance with discursive logic. It neither makes deductions from a principle nor draws conclusions from coherent individual observations. It coordinates elements instead of subordinating them" (22). Neither inductive nor deductive, the essay makes particular elements meaningful and

---

[15] Adorno's way of putting this is that "the essay proceeds, so to speak, methodically unmethodically" ("Essay" 13).

intelligible only through its immanent form, not by some principle or system whose validity is established prior to and independently of those elements.[16]

In these ways, the essay resonates with modernist dissonance. The artwork initially appears as an organic whole where the parts can only be understood through the whole and the whole only understood through the parts. It thus separates itself from reality, but, at the same time, by exhibiting the historical deformation of its socio-historical materials, the artwork also discloses the work's social determination. Through the acknowledgment of the gap between its autonomy and its deformed material, the modernist work expresses what *should not be*, the self-contradiction in our failure to live up to who we take ourselves to be. In a different way, the essay initially appears in the guise of occasional thoughts—scattered reflections on friendship, cannibals, cruelty, etc.[17]—not as organic wholeness. But, in the experience of reading these essays, one discovers that these incongruous elements somehow belong together, that they compose a whole that is more than the sum of its parts and thereby mean something, even if this meaning is not a proposition from which all else can be deduced. The dissonance of the essay, we might say, lies in discovering the unity of what appears to fall apart, the necessary interdependence of seemingly contingent elements. Accordingly, the essay embodies a form for working through and reflecting on the experience of crisis.

Critics agree that the crisis of the early 1920s was crucial to Mariátegui's political formation, but I would also argue that it is a key for understanding the development of his form of writing. In the 1910s, the period Mariátegui would later call his "stone age," his writings would more accurately be called *crónicas* or impressionistic sketches.[18] The mature Mariateguian essay, by contrast, is a product of his reflections on, first, the crisis, which he witnessed while living in Europe in the early twenties, and, second, the need to articulate a Marxist interpretation of Peruvian society when he returned to Lima in 1923. I will elaborate on the first moment here, leaving the second for the next section.

---

[16] Along these lines, Josh Robinson usefully clarifies that "Adorno's essay is focused less on the essay-form as abstraction than on the form which can be identified within an individual essay" (128).

[17] To list just a few of the topics covered in Montaigne's *Essais*.

[18] For an excellent analysis of Mariátegui's often overlooked early writings, see Álvaro Campuzano Arteta, *La modernidad imaginada: Arte y literatura en el pensamiento de José Carlos Mariátegui (1911–1930)*.

Mariátegui's time in Europe was, to use Álvaro Campuzano Arteta's apt phrase, a "friendly form of exile" imposed on him by President Augusto Leguía (*Modernidad* 44). In 1919, Leguía became the president of Peru through a peculiar route. He won the election, but, believing that the oligarchy would not honor the results, he then staged a coup d'état. To secure his tenuous grasp on power, Leguía sought to rid the nation of some of its strongest critics and thus encouraged, with stick and carrot, Mariátegui and others to leave Peru. Mariátegui left for Europe in 1920 and spent the next three years living in Italy, France, and Germany, writing articles for newspapers back in Lima and immersing himself in radical politics and avant-garde art. Upon returning to Peru in 1923, Mariátegui set himself the task of reconstructing the present conjuncture for a national audience. He began giving a series of lectures at the recently established Popular University on what he called the "History of the Global Crisis." He then developed these lectures into a variety of articles published in the local newspapers *Variedades* and *Mundial*. Finally, Mariátegui collected these articles under the title of *La escena contemporánea* (The Contemporary Scene), which was published in 1925. The book, like the lectures, deals with the fundamental issues of the interwar period: the emergence of fascism, the crisis of democracy, the challenges facing socialism, antisemitism, and what he calls the "message of the Orient."

The book also contains a brief, yet remarkable, note in which Mariátegui reflects on his form of writing. As in the "Author's Note" for the *Siete ensayos*, Mariátegui's note in *La escena contemporánea* presents the essay not only as a provisional, incomplete attempt to study its object but also as the form that is adequate to the content of his analysis. It is worth quoting a long passage:

> Gathered together and coordinated in a volume, under the title "The Contemporary Scene," these hasty and fragmentary impressions do not claim to form an explanation for our epoch. But they contain the primary elements of a sketch of this epoch and its tempestuous problems, an interpretive essay or rehearsal of what I may dare to attempt in a more organic book. I do not think that it is possible to apprehend in a theory the entire panorama of the contemporary world. It is not possible, above all, to fix its movement in a theory. We have to explore it and know it episode by episode, facet by facet. Our judgment and our imagination will always feel lagging with respect to the totality of the phenomenon. As a result, the best method to explain and translate our time might be a method that is a little bit journalistic and a little bit cinematographic … I know very well that my

view of the epoch is neither very objective nor very unastigmatic. I am not an indifferent spectator of the human drama. I am, on the contrary, a man with an affiliation and a faith. This book only has the value of being a faithful document of the spirit and sensibility of my generation. I thus dedicate it to the new men and the new youth of Indo-Iberia America (*La escena* 11)[19]

This note is a veritable catalog of tropes associated with the essay. We have, working backwards: the rejection of the scientific view-from-nowhere and the acknowledgment of the author's own fallible subjectivity; the affinity with artistic forms of presentation, namely cinematic montage, but also implicitly analytic cubism and perspectivism; an insistence on the gap between the form of presentation and what is presented; the refusal of a pre-existing system from which one could deduce particular objects; an indication that these texts are merely preparation for the elaboration of a more complete work. While Mariátegui indeed states that he may at some point "dare" to develop these "hasty" thoughts into a "more organic book," suggesting that this form of writing could be dispensed with, the note's more compelling claim is that this form is necessary because it is not possible "to apprehend in a theory the entire panorama of the contemporary world. It is not possible, above all, to fix its movement in a theory." Accordingly, an analysis contemporaneous with this "tempestuous" historical situation could never be definitive.[20] The essay, in contrast to a putatively complete account, appears as the adequate form for the

---

[19] "Agrupadas y coordinadas en un volumen, bajo el título de 'La Escena Contempránea,' no pretenden estas impresiones, demasiado rápidas o demasiado fragmentarias, componer una explicación de nuestra época. Pero contienen los elementos primarios de un bosquejo o un ensayo de interpretación de esta época y sus tormentosos problemas que acaso me atreva a intentar en un libro más organico. Pienso que no es posible aprehender en una teoría el entero panorama del mundo contemporáneo. Que no es posible, sobre todo, fijar en una teoría su movimiento. Tenemos que explorarlo y conocerlo, episodio por episodio, faceta por faceta. Nuestro juicio y nuestra imaginación se sentirán siempre en retardo respecto de la totalidad del fenómeno. Por consiguiente, el mejor método para explicar y traducir nuestro tiempo es, tal vez, un método un poco periodístico y un poco cinematográfico ... Sé muy bien que mi vision de la época no es bastante objetiva ni bastante anastigmática. No soy un espectador indiferente del drama humano. Soy, por el contrario, un hombre con una filiación y una fe. Este libro no tiene más que el de ser un documento leal del espíritu y la sensibilidad de mi generación. Lo dedico, por esto, a los hombre nuevos, a los hombres jóvenes de la América indo-íbera"

[20] I discuss Mariátegui's thoughts on the relationship between contemporaneity and avant-garde art in "Nonself Contemporaneity: José Carlos Mariátegui and the Question of Peripheral Modernism."

presentation of the moment precisely because it acknowledges the totality and its failure to grasp it exhaustively.

In order to make sense of this apparent paradox, we need to make explicit Mariátegui's modernist critique of representation.[21] The assertion that "Our judgment and imagination will always feel lagging with respect to the totality of the phenomenon" initially appears to be the familiar materialist principle that ideas merely reflect a pre-existing reality. But we could also read this comment with the emphasis on "totality," in which case it closely resembles a claim often made by Fredric Jameson, namely, that the totality—that is, capitalism—cannot be represented as such. To take an example that resonates with Mariátegui's own language, Jameson writes:

> No one has ever seen that totality, nor is capitalism ever visible as such, but only in its symptoms. This means that every attempt to construct a model of capitalism—for this is now what representation means in this context—will be a mixture of success and failure: some features will be foregrounded, others neglected or even misrepresented. Every representation is *partial*, and I would also stress the fact that every possible representation is a *combination of diverse and heterogeneous modes of construction or expression*, wholly different types of articulation that cannot but, incommensurable with each other, remain a *mixture of approaches that signals the multiple perspectives from which one must approach such a totality and none of which exhaust it* (*Representing* 6–7, my emphasis)[22]

If no single representation will disclose the totality, then, to use Mariátegui's language, we must approach it "facet by facet," assembling a mosaic that will never possess the continuity of a panorama. And yet, I argue that Mariátegui goes further in that he challenges the underlying assumption of representation. The representation, in this picture, mediates a subject and an independent object. But, as Mariátegui indicates by disavowing any

---

[21] Although I cannot develop the argument here, I would argue that modernism is anti-representational but not for the reasons we usually believe. It is not simply that modernists realized that language does not represent the world or that the realist desire to represent the world was a conservative impulse. Rather, the anti-representationalism of modernism should be seen as a way of working through the contradictory self-understanding that mediates our practical activities in the world.

[22] Jameson also insists in this passage that "*This very incommensurability is the reason for being of the dialectic itself,* which exists to coordinate incompatible modes of thought without reducing them to ... one-dimensionality" (*Representing* 7).

position as a contemplative spectator, we are not dealing here with an independent object but with a historical process or a form of social life in which we all participate. Our fundamental mode of being in the world is not as epistemological subjects representing objects but as historical and social agents who act in light of normative self-conceptions. The essay offers a form for making explicit and working through these underlying commitments. "[T]he tension between the presentation and the matter presented" (Adorno, "Essay" 22), which is the moment of dissonance in the essay, thus discloses our failure to be who we take ourselves to be. It discloses, in other words, the crisis of a form of life that has become uninhabitable to the extent that our activities no longer make sense within the horizon of normative expectations, to the extent that our practices negate themselves by leading to incompatible commitments.

If Mariátegui renounces a contemplative position, articulating, instead, the contradictory character of his participation in an ongoing crisis, the intended reader likewise cannot be seen as merely observing the situation from an external perspective. We ought to remember this when we note the incongruity of the dedication to "the new men and the new youth of Indo-Iberia America" and the fact that *La escena contemporánea* does not deal with contemporary Latin America. Mariátegui wants his Peruvian and Latin American audience to learn about world-historical developments during and after WWI. But Mariátegui's project goes beyond informing his national community about events in other parts of the world. Rather, he underlines time and again the inseparability of the fate of the working class and indigenous masses in Peru with the situation in Europe. In 1929 he would reaffirm this commitment, writing: "In the struggle against foreign imperialism we are fulfilling our duties of solidarity with the revolutionary masses of Europe" (Mariátegui, *Anthology* 272). In his lectures at the Popular University and publications in *Variadades* and *Mundial*, he sought to address radical intellectuals and the working class in Lima and thereby compose an internationally oriented "we" grounded in the struggle within Peru. Mariátegui also actively worked to establish connections with indigenous organizations, but given the conditions of illiteracy and the weakness of the existing means of communication between coast and sierra, these efforts were unfortunately limited. But, crucially, he conceives of the essay as an attempt to articulate the urgent nature of the crisis as something that the European and Peruvian masses already inhabit and whose outcome depends on their political activities.

Mariátegui's preferred term for the crisis of the contemporary scene—and, as we will see, for the character of Latin America—is the "inorganic." But, once again, the social stakes of this term only fully emerge when we also take into account its formal and aesthetic character. In the author's notes for both *La escena contemporánea* and the *Siete ensayos*, Mariátegui states that these books are not organic. The idea of an "organic" work calls to mind Peter Bürger's account of the historical avant-garde and its self-critique of art. Bürger, drawing on Walter Benjamin's theory of allegory, identifies an opposition between the organic work of art, which implies a self-contained structure based on the "necessary congruence between the meaning of the individual parts and the meaning of the whole," and the constitutive incompletion of the avant-garde work, in which "the parts lack necessity" and are "'emancipated' ... from a superordinate whole" (80). The harmony of classical art thus passes into the various forms of modernist fragmentation in the early twentieth century. And yet, the avant-garde work does not simply disintegrate. As Bürger clarifies in his analysis, the meaning of avant-garde art cannot be reduced to its disparate parts. This would destroy meaning as such. Instead, the avant-garde work continues to express a "total meaning" but its "unity has integrated the contradiction within itself. It is no longer the harmony of the individual parts that constitutes the whole; it is the contradictory relationship of heterogeneous elements" (82). The inorganic character of the avant-garde work, in other words, is not synonymous with fragmentation; rather, it embodies unity-in-difference through its emphasis on contradictory relations.

We can see Mariátegui working through this conception of the inorganic in his review of Blaise Cendrars's *L'Or* (1925). Mariátegui, I would argue, recognizes in Cendrars's novel something of his own essayistic mode of composition, making this apparently occasional piece into one of Mariátegui's most significant reflections on the formal dimension of his writing. What strikes Mariátegui about Cendrars's work are its "cinematographic scenes" (*El artista* 114), a term, as we have already seen, he uses to describe his own method.[23] In his review of *L'Or*, he includes a long passage in which Cendrars employs paratactic construction to convey the disjointed experience of New York City:

---

[23] The cinematic, montage character of Cendrars's novel was not lost on Sergei Eisenstein, who wanted to make a film adaptation of *L'Or*.

The port of New York. All the shipwrecked ones from the Old World disembark there. The shipwrecked one, the disgraced, the discontent, the free men, commodities. Those who have had setbacks; those who have risked it all on a single card; those who have been tormented by a romantic passion. The first German socialists, the first Russian mystics ... Since the French Revolution, since the Declaration of Independence, in full growth, in full development, New York has never seen its docks so continuously invaded. The immigrants disembark day and night and in each boat, in every human shipment, there is at least one representative of strong race of adventurers. (Qtd. in Mariátegui, *El artista* 111–112)[24]

As Mariátegui explains, "in a single page of rapid, brief, precise and abrupt prose," Cendrars gives us "an integral phrase in the formation of the United States" (111). Moreover, since the story of Suter and the gold rush in *L'Or* traverses the globe, we could even say that Cendrars gives us an integral phrase in the formation of the capitalist world-system. Cendrars's aspiration, in other words, is the same as Mariátegui's in *La escena contemporánea*, and both writers construct their accounts "facet by facet," through the coordination of parts. The whole in *L'Or* and *La escena* is neither a pre-existing system, from which one could deduce the elements, nor an aggregate, a mere sum of individuals indifferent to the form of the whole. The whole here is organic, albeit a broken organism. In an organic structure, the whole exists for the sake of the parts, and the parts exist for the sake of the whole. By contrast, the whole disintegrates in the avant-garde work, the parts becoming "emancipated" from the whole, in Bürger's words. But Mariátegui claims that in *L'Or* "no scene is excessive" [ningún cuadro sobra] (114).[25] The parts are no longer merely the role they play in the whole, but neither are they independent. They remain bound to a whole that has lost its binding character. This is why Mariátegui insists on the "*in*organic." This negative determination suggests that the whole fails to be what it should be, a self-reproducing

---

[24] Mariátegui was drawn to similar passages in Dos Passos's *Manhattan Transfer*. Mariátegui briefly stopped in New York during the long trip in boat from Lima to Europe, and the emphasis on these passages in Dos Passos and Cendrars suggests that he was fascinated by the chaotic, montage-like juxtaposition of people in the metropolis. Uprooted from tradition and organic communities and placed in the "empty space" of the city, these people marked the historical possibility of internationalism, which Mariátegui signals by quoting the moment in *Manhattan Transfer* in which deported immigrants sing "L'Internationale." See Mariátegui, *Signos* 152–159.

[25] "ningún cuadro sobra."

organism. The dissonance of *L'Or* and the Mariáteguian essay thus derives from the peculiar manner in which the parts do and do not belong together. The inorganic, in other words, offers as a way of conceptualizing crisis, of making explicit the form of a social reality whose unity is disclosed precisely in the way it breaks down, in the way its contradictory relationships unfold.

Shifting from the crisis of the interwar moment to the forms of inequality in the periphery, Mariátegui frequently uses the "inorganic" to describe Latin American societies.[26] I would like to close this section by highlighting one particular moment when these threads come together: Mariátegui's review of Pedro Henríquez Ureña's *Seis ensayos en busca de nuestra expresión* (Six Essays in Search of Our Expression, 1928). Mariátegui begins the review by situating Henríquez Ureña's work in opposition to "the superamericanist demagogy" and "messianism" that had taken hold of many Latin American intellectuals (52). I will say more about the political dimension of this polemic in the final section of this chapter, but what bears emphasizing now is the conception of Latin America shared by Henríquez Ureña and Mariátegui. The demagogues appeal to some putatively pre-existing cultural identity that would organically give rise to a national form of representation. But this organic conception of national identity breaks down in the context of the periphery's brutal forms of inequality.[27] Henríquez Ureña thus insists on the need to "search" for "our expression."[28] The task faced by Latin American literature, in his

---

[26] Along similar lines, Paulo Arantes discusses Antonio Candido's use of the essay form. The "variation in angles of approach" (*Sentimento* 10), Arantes writes, must be understood in terms of the essay's object, namely, the social experience of peripheral duality that we discussed in Chap. 1.

[27] As Neil Larsen argues in "The 'Hybrid' Fallacy, or, Culture and the Question of Historical Necessity," "Peru appears to invert this dialectic" of a cultural content giving rise to its national form, "for here history has produced the abstract, rational form of the nation as a result of the nineteenth-century wars of independence without, as yet, having produced the content—'*peruanidad*'—that should have acted as its organic substratum" (*Determinations* 89). Larsen argues that Mariátegui clearly recognizes the problem but cannot see the solution. He thus turns to the novels of Machado de Assis in light of Roberto Schwarz's path-breaking interpretations. I am in complete agreement with Larsen when it comes to the main thrust of his argument. I would simply add that an attention to form in Mariátegui—namely, the essay—allows us to see beyond this impasse within Mariátegui's own work.

[28] Mariátegui follows the same line of thought in "El proceso de la literatura," his interpretation of Peruvian literature, which was included as the last essay of the *Siete*.

analysis, deals with the "inorganic" (53) character of peripheral societies, namely, that its unity is not given but something to be achieved. In the absence of a pre-existing and unified cultural content, Henríquez Ureña's writings are *essays* in search of an expression, provisional articulations of what Latin Americans take themselves to be. This is not a question of representing an independent reality, namely, a national-cultural identity. Rather, it is a project that must be sustained by these subjects as they actively strive to be what they take themselves to be, even as these commitments undermine themselves. Mariátegui, citing Henríquez Ureña, thus insists that "only effort and discipline" (53) could bring about the organic unity they have failed to achieve. The essay, through the dissonance of its presentation and the matter presented, makes explicit this contradictory self-relation and discloses the inorganic character of this form of social life, since these subjects could actualize their normative commitments only by taking responsibility for the brutal forms of inequality that these subjects sustain in their practical activities.

Piecing Together the City and the Country

To review, I have argued that the form of the essay offers José Carlos Mariátegui a compelling way to make sense of Peruvian social reality. More than simply the draft of an analysis that he would complete at a later date, the essay plays a necessary role in his thinking insofar as it makes possible and intelligible his interpretation of the inorganic character of peripheral societies, of a whole that fails to adequately reproduce itself because its parts both do and do not belong together. In this way, Mariátegui insists that the provisional character of the essay does not only index an external limit—for example, the material constraints that prevented him from fully developing his thoughts—rather, through a reflexive relation to these material conditions, the essay makes explicit the internal contradictions of Peruvian society and conveys the normative force to transform the practices and self-understanding that have led to this inorganic form of life. Having reconstructed these formal dynamics, we can now more adequately grasp the content of Mariátegui's interpretation. In this section, I will discuss Mariátegui's reflections on the city/country divide in Peru—that is, the split between the coast and sierra—in light of the essayistic form of the inorganic. I will pay particular attention to his analysis in "Regionalism and Centralism," the sixth of the *Siete ensayos*, for it demonstrates persuasively how this central opposition in Latin American societies can be recast in terms of a unified, albeit contradictory, historical process.

Mariátegui's early writings often exhibit a romantic, anti-urban attitude that, as we will see, he would later denounce in the "Regionalism and Centralism" essay. For instance, on July 28, 1918, the day of Peruvian Independence, a young José Carlos Mariátegui left behind the national celebrations, the "fiestas patrias," in Lima. In the text, "¡28 de Julio!," he evokes the joyous atmosphere in Lima—"the illuminated city, jubilant and wrapped in flags, ... a verse of the National Anthem on the lips, ... a cup of champagne in the right hand" (*Invitación* 106–107)—but, as Mariátegui shows through juxtaposition, this national pride does not extend outside the capital. In fact, this is precisely what draws Mariátegui to the sierra. Mariátegui does not lament the lack of "fiestas patrias" in the sierra; rather, he yearns for what is absent in the city. He writes, "We are here as travelers, as pilgrims and wanderers, because for a long time our soul has been in need of solitude, our eyes in need of multiple panoramas and our heart eager to feel a little more bohemian, more nomadic and vagrant than normal" (107). Mariátegui thus articulates the disparity of city and country in the romantic framework of urban alienation. He feels compelled to escape the artificial, foreign culture of Lima and to experience renewal in the midst of nature. And yet, Mariátegui finds that he is irrevocably divorced from organic, rural life. Even from "the cold and steep heights" of the Andes, he cannot "talk to the city about what [he] finds interesting but only about what interests [the city]" (*Invitación* 107). He also discovers his own inability to communicate outside the boundaries of Lima when he attempts to talk to locals in search of a non-urban perspective on Peru. This is "the city's revenge": "We believe we have left her behind. And in reality we remain in her the same as before" (107).

The "city's revenge" hints at an insight that will become more explicit during Mariátegui's travels throughout Europe in the early twenties, namely, the interdependence of urban and rural. After spending three years in Rome, Paris, and Berlin, Mariátegui writes in "La urbe y el campo" (The City and the Country, 1924) that "[w]hile the city educates man in collectivism, the countryside excites his individualism" (*Invitación* 246). This observation evidently emerged out of the events Mariátegui witnessed in Europe in the early twenties: the failure of the Turin communists, the emergence of fascist rural fantasies in Italy and Germany, the civil war in Russia. This urban orientation also indicates Mariátegui's turn toward Marxism, which traditionally has privileged the role of the urban working class in revolutionary struggles. In this theoretical framework, the city, insofar as it brings the masses together and cultivates social consciousness, creates the necessary conditions for socialism, whereas "the countryside loves tradition too much" and sets individual ownership of property as its ultimate goal (245). Mariátegui's principal advance in "La urbe y el campo," however, does not reside in the shift from countryside to city but in the dialectical reversal of these terms. For instance, when Mariátegui discusses Italian fascism, he notes the paradox that its imagery derives from the countryside, in opposition to the corrupt, "red" cities, and its base of support was ultimately rural, but, he writes, "fascism was born in Milan, in an industrial and opulent city" (*Invitación* 246). The anti-urban sentiment also surfaces when Mariátegui mentions Spengler, for whom "the last phase of a culture is urban and cosmopolitan" (247). Spengler expresses in apocalyptic terms the popular impression that "the city will be reabsorbed by the innumerable, anonymous countryside" (248). Mariátegui does not accept this impression of the supposed decadence of the city, but he is drawn to it because it exhibits the dialectical inversion that characterizes the relation between rural and urban in the current crisis. The countryside appropriates the innumerable anonymity that would seem to be proper to the city, and the city, no longer an expanding monster, becomes a passive entity. This reversal articulates Mariátegui's point that the crucial distinction is not between city and country but within each term: "To speak of revolutionary city and reactionary province would, however, entail accepting a classification that is too simple to be exact. In the city and the country, society divides into two class" (246). Mariátegui ultimately insists on the mutual mediation of the urban and the rural, seeing their interdependence and incommensurability as results of the contradictory internal dynamic of capitalism.

When Mariátegui returns to Peru in 1923, he would continue to see the urban/rural divide not as an external opposition but as a contradictory relationship of two internally divided terms. Politically, he addressed workers and radical intellectuals in Lima, but he also worked to build alliances with indigenous organizations in the sierra. The "Regionalism and Centralism" essay represents the culmination of Mariátegui's reflections on the crisis of urbanization in Lima in the context of the relationship between, on the one hand, the relationship between coast and sierra in Peru and, on the other hand, the international division of labor.[29] Despite the recent, dramatic changes in the Peruvian capital, Mariátegui insists that this growth is prone to crisis because it is not self-reproducing—that is, it depends on external mechanisms and disavows that dependence at the same time. "The hegemony of Lima," he writes, "[c]orresponds to an epoch, a period of national historical development. It rests on reasons that are liable to grow old and expire" (190).[30] With a century of hindsight, this judgment on peripheral urbanization appears self-evident, but at the time it contradicts the perception of Lima's *belle époque*. "The new neighborhoods, the asphalt avenues, car rides at seventy or eighty miles," Mariátegui writes, "easily persuade the *limeño*—beneath his epidermic and cheerful skepticism, the *limeño* is much less incredulous than he appears—that Lima is quickly following the path of Buenos Aires and Río de Janeiro" (*Siete ensayos* 190).[31] But the rapid modernization of Lima, according to Mariátegui, is proving to be literally and figuratively superficial. The surface of the city had extended, especially to the south, but "[t]he growth of the surface of Lima exceeds the growth of the population. The two processes, the two terms do not coincide. The process of urbanization is advancing on its own" (191).[32] And if it is advancing on its own, without an adequate social basis, this urbanization is bound to break down.

This latent crisis reveals the specificity of Lima and its position within the social structure of Peru.[33] Whereas most modern cities have been

---

[29] Many of these comments already appeared in the newspaper *Mundial* two years earlier with the title "El porvenir de Lima" (The Future of Lima).

[30] "La hegemonía limeña reposa a mi juicio en un terreno menos sólido del que, por mera inercia mental, se supone. Corresponde a una época, a un período del desarrollo histórico nacional. Se apoya en razones susceptibles de envejecimiento y caducidad."

[31] "Los barrios nuevos, las avenidas de asfalto, recorridas en automóvil, recorridas en automóvil, a sesenta u ochenta kilómetros, persuaden fácilmente a un limeño—bajo su epidérmico y risueño escepticismo, el limeño es mucho menos incrédulo de lo que parece—, de que Lima sigue a prisa el camino de Buenos Aires o Río de Janeiro."

[32] "la superficie de Lima supera exorbitantemente al crecimiento de la población. Los dos procesos, los dos términos no coinciden. El proceso de urbanización avanza por su propia cuenta."

[33] In this account, Lima appears bigger than its population. In subsequent decades, this situation will be reversed: there never seems to be enough space for the population as it is constantly moving from the countryside to the city. The main point, however, is that Mariátegui identifies that this disjuncture of the size of the city and its population will mark the city throughout the twentieth century.

fueled by industry or trade, Lima is primarily a political or administrative unit.[34] Lima may be the capital of the nation, but Callao is the major port. Referencing the work of his friend César Falcon, Mariátegui highlights the specificity of this situation by contrasting it with Buenos Aires:[35] "the reasons for the stupendous growth of Buenos Aires are fundamentally economic and geographical. Buenos Aires is the port and market of Argentine agriculture and livestock. All the great commercial routes in Argentina flow into it" (*Siete ensayos* 192).[36] In the age of the export paradigm, Buenos Aires plays a crucial role in the international division of labor. Peru occupies a similar position in the global economy, but Lima does not quite perform the same function, making its growth even more precarious. Because of the inorganic character of this city, its parts failing to perform their role in the reproduction of the whole, Mariátegui casts doubt on the idea of a rapidly modernizing Lima, on the image of the city's future: Lima "is the capital today, but will it be the capital tomorrow?" (198).[37] By calling into question the fate of Lima, Mariátegui points toward what I have been calling the peripheral metropolis, a crisis-ridden urban space whose identity and disunity must be understood in terms of the global capitalist economy and the urban-rural divide within Peru.

Mariátegui's interpretation of Lima also implies a judgment about Peru, and, in order to draw out these implications, we need to examine the interconnection of city and nation in the context of early-twentieth-century Peru. As I alluded to above, Lima underwent an intense period of modernization during the *oncenio* (1919–1930), the eleven-year presidency of Augusto Leguía. Though nowhere near as large as Mexico City or Buenos Aires in the 1920s, the city's population more than doubled in the first decades of the twentieth century, from 140,884 inhabitants in 1908 to around 280,000 in 1931 (Elmore 38). The growth and

[34] "The development of a city is not a question of political and administrative privileges. It is, rather, a question of economic privileges" ["el desarrollo de una urbe no es una cuestión de privilegios políticos y administrativos. Es, más bien, una cuestión de privilegios económicos"] (*Siete ensayos* 191).

[35] "Regionalism and Centralism" makes references to London, Berlin, New York, and Vienna, but Mariátegui leans most heavily on the comparison with Buenos Aires, recognizing that a structural distinction exists between the peripheral metropolis in Latin America and the metropole in Europe and the United States.

[36] "las razones del estupendo crecimiento de Buenos Aires son, fundamentalmente, razones económicas y geográficas. Buenos Aires es el puerto y el mercado de la agricultura y la ganadería argentinas. Todas las grandes vías de comercio argentino desembocan ahí."

[37] "Es la capital hoy, pero ¿será también la capital mañana?"

transformation of Lima at the time were partially due to Leguía's quasi-reformist government, which sought, in rhetoric at least, to break with the nation's oligarchical class—the *civilistas*—and initiate a modern future for Peru. Although successful to a limited degree in combatting the *gamonales*—Peru's quasi-feudal landowning class—Leguía's government primarily carried out a shift in economic power from one set of landowners and export capitalists on the northern coast to a different group of landowners and capitalists on the southern coast of Lima.[38] The city itself expanded toward the south, eventually incorporating Miraflores and Barranco.[39] In large part, Leguía's urbanization projects were fueled by a massive increase in US investments after the opening of the Panama Canal, from 10% of total investment in 1900 to 74% in 1924 (Klarén 243). Broad avenues were never built in Lima and the city was never subjected to a totalizing urban project like other post-Haussmann cities, but Leguía's modernization had a major impact on the capital. "By the 1930s, Lima had definitely acquired a new physiognomy" (Aguirre and Walker 101).[40] But, as Mariátegui anticipated, the new belied an old and persistent problem.

The eventual failure of this modernization project repeated, now in the context of US imperialism, previously frustrated experiments in urbanization. Peter Elmore has argued that these failures were epitomized in the demolition of the walls surrounding the colonial center of Lima in 1870 (35–36). These walls, which were initially erected to stop pirates from raiding the heart of Spain's colonial administration in South America, were removed in order to make room for modernization projects and the expansion of Lima beyond its colonial limits. This urbanization effort, however, would prove to be short-lived. When the War of the Pacific ended in 1883, Chile occupied Lima and left the Peruvian capital in ruins. As Peru's defeat

---

[38] See Kristal 177–80. For a useful overview of the contradictions of the Leguía government as it relates to Mariátegui, see Moore 29–43.

[39] Barranco, a resort town in this period, provides the setting for Martín Adán's avant-garde novel *La casa de cartón* (1928).

[40] Guillermo Rodríguez Mariátegui, one of Leguía's urban engineers, articulated Leguía's role in these changes in more elevated language: "Leguía! And like the Napoleonic eagle that flew from bell tower to bell tower, from Cannes to Paris, Leguía's tenacious spirit, inherited from his Basque forefathers, irradiated torrents of progress from the capital to the hamlet that thrust Peru forward, and whose momentum we still leisurely enjoy" (131). I am not sure if José Carlos Mariátegui was related to Guillermo Rodríguez Mariátegui. José Carlos was distantly related to Leguía, so I suspect that Guillermo Rodríguez could have come from that side of the family.

brought urbanization projects to an abrupt halt, the uncertain fate of the city fueled the growing awareness of the fragility of the nation—as a political agent, as a cultural identity, and as a socio-economic formation within global capitalism. *Indigenismo* emerged as the most significant intellectual response to this moment of crisis. Manuel González Prada (1848–1883), the father of *indigenismo* in the late nineteenth century, attributed Peru's defeat in the War of the Pacific to the fact that the indigenous masses, who formed the majority of the Peruvian army, had been systematically excluded from the nation and thus felt no commitment to the war effort. The war thus disclosed to González Prada the gap between what the national authorities—the "trinity" of governors, priests, and judges—took themselves to be and the forms of inequality that their institutions sustained. In this way, *indigenismo* primarily expressed the profound social and ideological distance separating coast and sierra.

But, as Ángel Rama has argued, *indigenismo* was largely an urban phenomenon. Despite its investment in the figure of the *indio*, *indigenismo* emerged in response to the incomplete modernization of Peru's urban center and social hierarchies. The artists and theorists of *indigenismo* were middle-class mestizos, not indigenous, and for Rama the call to vindicate indigenous culture served as a vehicle for the expression of the middle-class's frustration with a stagnant urban culture in Lima, with institutions dominated by an entrenched, traditional oligarchy.[41] In this way,

---

[41] See Rama, *Narrative Transculturation* Chapter 3. Rama goes so far as to argue that Mariátegui's Marxism was an expression of his position as a middle-class mestizo. Mariátegui's insistence on realist literature and economic factors, Rama argues, has nothing to do with the vindication of indigenous peasants; rather, they constituted a bourgeois, modernizing project seeking to displace the oligarchy. See Rama 103–6. At a very high level of abstraction, Rama is right to point to the way socialism in the twentieth century, when it assumed a decidedly materialist, positivist, determinist character, often worked to facilitate the transition from feudalism to capitalism, not as a challenge to capitalism. But there are a number of problems with this account, especially as it relates to Mariátegui. Coronado astutely criticizes Rama's attempt to retrospectively judge Mariátegui's modernism by the peculiar form of modernization that took root in subsequent decades (30–1). I would also argue that Rama's class terms do not adequately elucidate social structures in Peru. While it makes sense to speak of a rising middle class in opposition to an aristocratic oligarchy in nineteenth-century Europe, the distinction between oligarchy and bourgeoisie tends to collapse in twentieth-century Latin America. Postcolonial studies in general illustrate some of the ways in which critics, and Marxists in particular, have overemphasized the political role of the middle class or bourgeoisie, leading these critics to exaggerate the differences between "East" and "West."

indigenismo and its critique of the oligarchy do not simply index the dominance of Lima over the rest of the country; they also express the failures or impasses of urban modernity in Peru. Put differently, *indigenismo* emerges out of the transition from what, as we discussed earlier, José Luis Romero calls "bourgeois cities" to "massified cities." Whereas the former, as the centers of merchant capital, flourished with the growth of Latin America's export economies, enabling these cities to be remade in accordance with the desire of the oligarchy and the bourgeoisie for luxury and private spaces, the latter were characterized above all by the presence of more people, migrants who sought work in the city but soon found they were superfluous in a global depression and in a city whose meager economic growth made employment scarce.[42] Rather than indicating the unquestioned supremacy of the coast over the sierra, *indigenismo* registers an urban crisis that is itself the reflection of a deeper crisis in the global economy and the periphery's reliance on commercial activities within industrial capitalism.

The modernization of Lima was partial at best, and it certainly did not translate into the comprehensive development of the nation. Insofar as its growth was based largely on foreign investment and not sustained by its own economic foundations, the modernization of Lima appeared promising but proved to be unstable. It could hardly sustain itself, much less the rest of the country. "Lima is Peru," the writer Abraham Valdelomar famously claimed. But during these divisive times, this sentiment could be variously interpreted as the idea that Lima was the heart of Peru's Hispanic culture or as the idea, in the words of Peter Elmore, "that the city not only lived with its back to Peru, but at its expense" (62). Lima was simultaneously praised as a "colonial Arcadia," a myth at which Sebastián Salazar Bondy took aim in his *Lima la horrible* (1964), and derided for its lack of connection to the rest of the nation.

And yet, it would be a mistake to think that urban intellectuals lived in complete ignorance of the sierra and its conflicts. Even though the *indigenistas* were typically urban subjects whose aesthetic proposals and political demands were shaped by the impasses of urban modernity in Lima, they closely followed news about peasant rebellions, which were increasing in frequency, and often established connections with indigenous organizations. Alberto Flores Galindo claims that around fifty revolts occurred

---

[42] See Romero, Chapters 6 and 7.

in the southern Andes between 1919 and 1923 (*In Search* 167). These rebellions, expressing indigenous opposition to *gamonalismo*, a quasi-feudal form of landed property, made conditions in the sierra an urgent issue for intellectuals and workers on the coast.

In this spirit, Mariátegui offers a dialectical critique of *gamonalismo* in "Regionalism and Centralism," seeing in this institution the enigma of Peru's inorganic social reality. Like feudal landed property, *gamonalismo* rejected wage-labor in favor of "local power: privatization of politics, fragmentation of authority, and control over a town or province" (Flores Galindo, *In Search* 153). In the context of the late nineteenth century, as Peru was progressively integrated into global capitalism through its export economy, *gamonalismo* appeared increasingly anachronistic, as a feudal remnant that hindered the nation's progress. As Flores Galindo explains, "gamonal was a Peruvianism coined in the nineteenth century that likened landowners to parasitic plants" (153). But Mariátegui will insist, against the view that *gamonalismo* is a parasite that does not fit in a modern nation, on the necessary role it plays in the brutal process of the political unification of Peru and its incorporation into the international division of labor. Despite its appearance as a specifically regional power structure, Mariátegui holds that "*gamonalismo*, within the unified, central republic, is the capital's ally and agent in the regions and provinces" (179).[43] The continued existence of *gamonalismo*, as Flores Galindo would later explain in Mariátegui's footsteps, is due to the paradox of a modern nation whose liberal institutions were based on the exclusion of the masses: "The state needed gamonales to control the indigenous masses excluded from voting and other liberal democratic rituals and whose customs and language greatly differentiated them from urban residents" (154). *Gamonalismo* thus betrays the inorganic character of Peru, since, insofar as it is a modern nation, this quasi-feudal form of landed property does not belong, but as a peripheral nation whose participation in global capitalism is based on expanding exploitation, it does belong.

Having established that the modernization of Lima rests on shaky foundations and that *gamonalismo* is a necessary premise of current economic arrangements in Peru, Mariátegui recasts the traditional narrative of nineteenth-century Latin America, namely, as a conflict between

---

[43] "El gamonalismo, dentro de la república central y unitaria, es el aliado y el agente de la capital en las regiones y en las provincies."

regionalism and centralism.[44] Mariátegui provocatively insists that it is a false problem, one that cannot be solved on its own terms. At the very least, it is "an obsolete, anachronistic polemic" (*Siete* 173).[45] But, even more importantly, when the conflict is "displaced from the exclusively political plane to a social and economic plane" (173),[46] regionalism appears not as a defense of local, popular traditions, but as a justification of the interests of the *gamonales*. At the same time, centralism depends on the *gamonales* in order to erect its centralized structures and liberal policy of export for a world market. Mariátegui's dialectical approach allows him to state that "one of the vices of our political organization is, without doubt, its centralism" (173)[47] and, at the same time, that "decentralization ... would increase the power of *gamonalismo* against a solution inspired by the interests of the indigenous masses" (178).[48] In other words, Mariátegui rejects what Antonio Gramsci in "Some Aspects of the Southern Question" (1926) calls the "magical formula" of mere decentralization, of breaking up political and economic power without addressing the overarching socio-economic structure of the nation.[49] The conflict between centralism

---

[44] Mariátegui's thoughts on the city and the countryside closely parallel those of Antonio Gramsci. Mariátegui and Gramsci met during the famous Livorno Conference in which Gramsci and others broke from the Socialist Party and established the Communist Party of Italy. It is tempting to imagine that they were in closer contact than what the historical record indicates, but it is more important to appreciate how their thoughts developed out of overlapping contexts. On Gramsci and Mariátegui, see Terán and Flores Galindo, *La agonía de Mariátegui*. For a more recent comparison that looks at Gramsci and Mariátegui from a decolonial perspective, see Mignolo. See Harootunian (Chapter 3) for a very competent and comprehensive comparison of Gramsci and Mariátegui.

[45] "La polémica entre federalistas y centralistas, es una polémica superada y anacrónica como la controversia entre conservadores y liberales."

[46] "se desplaza del plano exclusivamente político a un plano social y económico."

[47] "Una de los vicios de nuestra organización política es, ciertamente, su centralismo."

[48] "la descentralización ... aumentaría el poder del gamonalismo contra una solución inspirada en el interés de las masas indígenas."

[49] As Gramsci explains at the beginning of the text, critics had claimed that Gramsci and his journal *L'Ordine Nuovo* advocated a "magical formula": to "divide up the great landed estates among the rural proletariat" (*Pre-Prison* 313). Gramsci does not deny his support for land reform, but he insists that this formula is not sufficient onto itself. In part, the redistribution of land often fails to accomplish its stated goals because of the poor quality of the land and the lack of access to technology. Accordingly, Gramsci insists that the Turin Communists "wanted this distribution to take place within the context of a general revolutionary action on the part of the two allied classes, under the leadership of the industrial proletariat" (315). The possibility and necessity of this alliance derives from the interconnection of north and south, in contrast to the prevailing idea that "the South is the ball and chain that is holding back the social development of Italy" (316).

and regionalism, according to Mariátegui, ultimately boils down to a disagreement between a quasi-feudal aristocracy and a nascent national bourgeoisie, even though this disagreement conceals their mutual dependence. Recasting the opposition to thereby point beyond it, Mariátegui writes, "Peru must opt for the *gamonal* or for the Indian. This is its dilemma. There is no third way" (189).[50] *Gamonalismo*, rather than being an archaic remnant of the countryside, mediates regionalism and centralism. It can thus be overcome neither through centralism, which depends on the *gamonal* for its existence, nor through decentralization, which would only weaken any structures of opposition to *gamonalismo*, but only through a political organization of rural and urban forces on the basis of the needs of the working and indigenous masses.

Just as the form of the inorganic makes possible the thought that *gamonalismo* both does and does not belong in the whole of modern Peru, it also informs Mariátegui's interpretation of the limits of Lima's capacity for expanded reproduction. It, in other words, allows him to distinguish his critique from the "anti-Limaism," which "has not, in this respect or others, gone beyond dramatic complaint" (*Siete* 190).[51] Challenging both the urban optimism buoyed in the *belle époque* and the anti-urban prejudice among his regionalist contemporaries, Mariátegui bases his critique on an analysis of the social structure of Lima in terms of the relation between periphery and metropolis. Industry constitutes the engine of industrialization, but the historical foundation of Lima derives from its role as an administrative unit in the colonial system. As we saw in the introduction, this peripheral position in the international division of labor, producing raw materials for consumption and industrial production in the core of global capitalism, will constrain attempts to develop industry in Latin America. Industry, Mariátegui notes, has the peculiar feature that it "does not follow consumption; it precedes and overflows it. It is not enough for it to satisfy needs; sometimes it must create them, discover them" (195).[52] This is, indeed, what happens in the metropolis. As workers are absorbed into wage-labor, they not only produce commodities; they also become a

---

[50] "El Perú tiene que optar por el gamonal o por el indio. Este es su dilema. No existe un tercer camino."

[51] "El anticentralismo de los regionalistas se ha traducido muchas veces en antilimeñismo. Pero no ha salido, a este respecto como a otros, de la protesta declamatoria."

[52] "Y, como muchos economistas observan, la industria en nuestros tiempos no sigue al consumo; lo precede y lo desborda. No le basta satisfacer la necesidad; le precisa, a veces, crearla, descubrirla."

source of demand, thereby contributing to expanded reproduction. Capitalism entails the systematic disarticulation of production and consumption, but the metropolis "is fundamentally a market and a factory" (195), the space that historically has mediated these two moments of social reproduction. But Mariátegui intuits that capitalism will not unfold in this way in the peripheral metropolis. It is not simply that industry has not yet developed in Lima. The most important economic activities in Peru, as a peripheral nation, involve the agricultural production of raw materials for the world market, leading to an economic arrangement in which Lima, as an administrative unit, does not play a major role.[53] Moreover, insofar as the Peruvian economy attends to a pre-existing and external demand coming from the core of capitalism, it does not give rise to an industrial process of creating and then satisfying new needs. To the extent that production in Peru does not depend for its realization on an internal capacity for consumption, peripheral urbanization will have an inorganic character. Its parts do not work together in concert to reproduce the whole, but they remain bound to one another insofar as the whole is determined by its position in the international division of labor. The peripheral metropolis thus becomes what it is in virtue of, not in spite of, its inherent tendency toward crisis.

THE EIGHTH ESSAY, OR THE POLITICS OF THE INORGANIC

In light of the inorganic character of Peruvian society, Mariátegui denies the validity of the regionalism/centralism polemic without positing some notion of a unified cultural identity. In the same way that the essay denotes a provisional arrangement, the inorganic implies a lack of cohesion, an identity that needs to be achieved. The parts of the inorganic essay do not compose a harmonious whole; the Peruvian nation cannot persuasively claim to embody a unified cultural identity because of the history of antagonism between coast and sierra. And yet, the parts are somehow bound together in the essay, and Mariátegui likewise does not insist on independence of regions. The essay thus raises the question of organization, an

[53] Mariátegui's reasons for doubting the possibility of industrial development in Lima can at times seemingly lapse into geographical determinism. For instance, he writes that the "physical geography of Peru proves to be anti-centralist. The other cause of industrial gravitation in a city is the proximity of a site of production to certain raw materials" (*Siete* 196). We should note that geographical determinism is partially warranted in this case to the extent that the peripheral economy revolves around raw materials.

urgent issue in peripheral social formations and the topic of the eighth essay that Mariátegui never completed. But, in a certain sense, Mariátegui already answered the question of organization. The eight essay is just the form of the essay, the inorganic form that subsists in all his writings and structures his interpretations. Ofelia Schutte suggests something similar when she writes, "The 'shape' given to the *Seven Essays* is not dissimilar to the one he would have preferred giving to his political organizing: a loose confederation of ideas—or, in politics, a coalition of groups brought together from within the society rather than by means of an external, teleologically directive force (e.g., the Party central command)" (33). Mariátegui, indeed, opposed excessively centralized organization, whether it took the form of dictates from the Comintern or the demagogic populism of Víctor Raúl Haya de la Torre's APRA (Alianza Popular Revolucionaria Americana). In this final section, I will reconstruct Mariátegui's attempt to articulate thoughts on organization "between APRA and the International," to borrow Flores Galindo's phrase. I argue, once again, that the question of organization should be understood in relation to the essay. More than an arbitrary collection of ideas, the essay constitutes a specific way of holding together elements that do not fully cohere. In this way, it discloses the contradictory relation between who these subjects are and who they take themselves to be and thus embodies the demand to sustain or live up to one's normative commitments, which may mean transforming our self-conception or renouncing incompatible practices. Likewise, by casting Peruvian reality in terms of the inorganic, Mariátegui insists on the need to acknowledge the divide between coast and sierra, along with the colonial and indigenous histories it entails, in order to overcome the practices and self-interpretations that have led to forms of inequality and negate the commitment to freedom.

Before addressing the disagreements with Haya de la Torre over political organization, we should review Mariátegui's contribution to the "intellectual meridian debate" because it clarifies how the Peruvian essayist conceives the contours of the problem of organization. This debate ignited in 1927 when Guillermo de Torre, the Spanish avant-garde poet, published an article entitled "Madrid, Intellectual Meridian of Spanish America" in *La Gaceta Literaria*. Minimizing any regional or cultural differences, Guillermo de Torre emphasizes the continuity between Spain and Latin America, and on this basis, he proposes that Madrid could serve as the center of this cultural formation. To most of his Latin America contemporaries, this proposal reflected little more than a pathetic attempt to reassert Spain's imperial legacy. Juan De Castro, for instance, observes that De Torre's article expresses "the implicit nostalgia for the colonial literary and cultural system" within "much of Spanish intelligentsia" (*Spaces* 34). The contributors to the Argentine magazine *Martín Fierro*, despite being close to Guillermo de Torre in terms of avant-garde poetry, playfully ridiculed the idea that Madrid could be their cultural north star and insisted on the need for the autonomy of Latin American culture. Mariátegui, in his article "La batalla de *Martín Fierro*" (The Battle of *Martín Fierro*, 1927), echoes this critique and points to the deep irony of claiming Madrid as the intellectual meridian when the proto-fascist Primo de Rivera had just limited cultural freedom in Spain. Mariátegui admits that Madrid continues to be the center of Spanish-language publishing. It is, in other words, the literary market for Latin America and Spain. But this commercial role should not be confused with the leadership of an intellectual meridian. More fundamentally, Mariátegui challenges the assumption of a cultural continuity or identity that would justify any intellectual meridian for Latin America or the Spanish-speaking world more broadly. In language that should now be familiar, Mariátegui claims that "[o]ur peoples still lack the consistency necessary to agree on a single headquarters. Spanish America is still an *inorganic* thing. But the ideal of the new generation is precisely to give it unity" (*Temas* 117, my emphasis).[54] In this way, Mariátegui not only dissents from the proposal to make Madrid into an intellectual meridian; he also questions the anti-imperialist call in *Martín Fierro* for a meridian rooted in Latin American culture. Mariátegui suggests that Buenos Aires indeed *could* become the center of an intellectual-cultural formation, but unless the brutal forms of inequality and pervasive illiteracy in peripheral nations have been overcome, its intellectual leadership would reproduce the alienation of literary elite and masses. Buenos Aires may play the role of intellectual meridian, but only through and at the end of the struggle to give unity to Spanish America by overcoming material and cultural inequalities. As we will see, Mariátegui expresses suspicion at anti-imperialist politics when they fail to acknowledge the inorganic character of Latin America societies.

In more traditional political terms, Mariátegui sees the need for a united front, where, again, that unity is understood as something to be achieved,

---

[54] "Nuestros pueblos carecen aún de la vinculación necesaria para coincidir en una sola sede. Hispanoamérica es todavía una cosa inorgánica. Pero el ideal de la nueva generación es, precisamente, el de darle unidad."

not a given. As Oscar Terán suggests,[55] the deepest affinity between Gramsci and Mariátegui derives from their shared commitment to the idea of the united front during a moment in which this organizational strategy was frequently abandoned by their contemporaries.[56] Gramsci, for instance, concludes that the question of the rural/urban divide in Italy raises the issue of "hegemony," the need for the proletariat to obtain "the consent of the broad peasant masses" (*Pre-Prison* 316). This need to obtain consent implies that the division between urban masses and rural peasantry remains, that it must be acknowledged, not ignored through the facile presumption of identical interests. City and countryside remain, to an extent, distinct perspectives, but their internal divisions and mutual dependency in the nation enable a hegemonic project of the united front. Seen in this light, the political implications of Mariátegui's proposal in "Regionalism and Centralism" become more explicit. When Mariátegui says that they must opt between *gamonalismo* and the Indian, he insists on the tension within the sierra, seeing this as the basis of a political alliance between urban workers in Lima and indigenous peasants. *Gamonalismo*, as we saw in Mariátegui's analysis, was not simply a historical residue restricted to non-urban areas. Rather, it constituted the lynchpin of a nation apparently divided into coast and sierra, the coercive point of mediation for a peripheral social formation whose forms of inequality follow from its position in the international division of labor. A united front of proletarians and indigenous peasants would remain an inorganic thing, but without such a fragile alliance, any attempt to overcome the inequality within Peru and to challenge imperialism would be one-sided.

The insistence on internal divisions and on the mass-based united front plays a crucial role in perhaps the defining political moment of 1920s Peru: the split between Mariátegui and Víctor Raúl Haya de la Torre.[57] As

---

[55] "This adhesion to the united front—anachronistic for the program of the Comintern—had however a company as illustrious and marginal as would become the figure of Gramsci within the same 'third period'" (Terán 106). The "third period" refers to a Stalinist period in the history of the Comintern during which Social Democrats were considered "social fascists." On Mariátegui and the united front, see also Flores Galindo, *La agonía*.

[56] Despite the assumption that Gramsci outlined different political strategies for the West and the East—the war of position and the war of maneuver—Peter Thomas has shown that the united front was Gramsci's "fundamental orientation" (212), an internationalist perspective made possible by the unity of the capitalist state-form. See Thomas 197–241.

[57] In my opinion, the best discussions of Mariátegui's disagreement with Haya de la Torre are still the ones contained in Alberto Flores Galindo's *La agonía de Mariátegui*, Chapter 4, and Oscar Terán's *Discutir Mariátegui*, Chapter 5.

one of the leaders of the University Reform movement in Peru, Haya de la Torre was partially responsible for opening university education to Lima's working-class population. But Haya de la Torre's continuing activism in the twenties made his relationship with the Leguía government increasingly strained, leading to his exile to Mexico in 1923. Shortly thereafter, Haya de la Torre founded APRA, the American Popular Revolutionary Alliance. Despite being exiled, Haya de la Torre was incredibly successful at uniting the Peruvian Left—including Mariátegui and his companions—behind APRA's struggle against imperialism and for continental solidarity and economic nationalism. The direction of APRA, however, shifted dramatically in 1928 when Haya de la Torre announced his "Plan de México." Without any broad discussion of this proposal, Haya de la Torre turned the alliance into a political-military party oriented toward political power, be it through the election of Haya de la Torre to president or by violently seizing power. Mariátegui saw these political goals and the lack of discussion as evidence of Haya de la Torre's *caudillismo*. Haya de la Torre responded to Mariátegui's criticisms and accused him of being an ineffective intellectual whose socialism was a foreign ideology without any organic connection to the reality of Latin America. Although he did not believe the timing was quite right, Mariátegui decided to found the Peruvian Socialist Party to counter what he saw as APRA's misguided political strategies.[58]

Mariátegui's peculiar position in this debate, caught between APRA and the Communist International, cannot be understood without recognizing his emphasis on a mass-based united front. In "Punto de vista anti-imperialista" (Anti-Imperialist Point of View), a paper written by Mariátegui and presented by Julio Portocarrero in 1929 at the First Latin American Communist Conference in Buenos Aires, Mariátegui clearly articulates his disagreements with APRA and his alternative proposals. The fundamental premise of APRA, Mariátegui explains, is its anti-imperial orientation. Insofar as it was defined by revolutionary nationalism and populism, APRA conceived itself as the party of a Latin American race, of the progressive national bourgeoisie and the masses.

---

[58] Against the objections of the Communist International, Mariátegui preferred to call his party "socialist," as opposed to "communist," in order to avoid political persecution—he had been arrested in 1927 on the grounds that he was a Soviet spy, even though he had no official links with the International at that time—and to make the party more adequate to a mass base in Peru. After Mariátegui's death, the party's name was quickly changed to the Peruvian Communist Party.

Despite Haya de la Torre's rejection of the Soviet Union, this conception of the party effectively coincided with the Comintern's argument about the needs of the party in semi-colonial nations, in situations in which bourgeois-liberal tasks supposedly had to be achieved before the struggle for socialism could begin. Mariátegui holds that the "economic status" of Latin American nations "undoubtedly is semicolonial," but, in contrast to both APRA and the Comintern, Mariátegui asserts that the political implications must be different because "the national bourgeoisie," in Peru at least, considers "imperialism as the best source of profits" (*Anthology* 265–6). That is, the national bourgeoisie, even in its weakness, should not be considered a reliable ally. Mariátegui begins, in other words, by drawing a division within the nation, the group that APRA falsely believes to be united in its opposition to imperialism. As a political proposal, anti-imperialism is misguided because it mystifies and displaces the contradictions within Latin American social structures into a purely external opponent: it "does not annul antagonisms between classes, nor does it suppress different class interests" (268). APRA's political and economic goals largely coincide with what would become the dominant paradigm in Latin America in the mid-twentieth century, namely, national modernization and development projects. And it is perhaps no surprise that many of Peru's futurist poets were some of APRA's most fervent supporters, since, as Nicholas Brown argues, "peripheral vanguardism"—the attempt to overcome the limitations of the peripheral situation within the realm of art by beating the literary elite at its own game—is structurally equivalent to "nationalist import substitution"—the attempt to develop domestic industry and thus overcome dependency—which "is the more or less spontaneous strategy of the anti-imperialist bourgeoisie" (*Utopian* 186). Alternatively, Mariátegui makes a simple, yet profound, reversal of an APRA slogan: from "We are leftists (or socialists) because we are anti-imperialists" (*Anthology* 268) into "we are anti-imperialists because we are Marxists" (272). That is, the recognition of internal antagonisms, not the antagonism toward an external enemy, constitutes the point of departure for a mass-based united front. And, insofar as it is a front, not a party, the united front does not claim that its constitutive components—urban masses and indigenous peasants—are identical. Instead, the direction of the party follows from the unfolding of this non-identity in its organizational structure. This political project, for Mariátegui, does not involve a putatively given national identity standing against external forces, but the piecing together of different forces—urban workers and indigenous peasants, Latin American and international masses—on the basis of a fundamental rift running throughout nations and the global contemporary scene.

Victorio Cordovilla, the director of the first conference for the Communist International in Buenos Aires, was perhaps right to associate Mariátgui's use of the essay with uncertainty. However, by casting uncertainty only in the negative, Cordovilla missed the specifically political character of the *Siete ensayos* and Mariátegui's writings more broadly. The essays do not rest on a putatively scientific foundation of facts, on a view-from-nowhere achieved by abstracting from historical subjects participating in a form of social life, an objective analysis that would outline the necessary movement of history. Rather, the essay, because of its partial and provisional character, always remains open to criticism and receives completion only by passing onto the domain of political praxis. When Mariátegui famously speaks of socialism as a "heroic creation," it is not simply a voluntarist statement that ignores historical determination. Rather, it is his acknowledgment that the political project articulated in the *Siete ensayos* cannot be taken as a given, as an automatic process. Mariátegui's writings express the commitments that must be sustained if the inorganic character of Peruvian society is to be overcome, the possibility of a united front whose existence depends entirely on the efforts of those who compose it in their struggle to abolish the peripheral forms of inequality. This collective project, in other words, cannot exist without uncertainty, the very terrain of the essay. Rather than falsely overcome the uncertainty of historical action, the essays make that uncertainty into a motivational force driving the formation of an alliance of urban workers and indigenous peasants, of a unity held together by nothing other than a shared conception of what matters in Peruvian society.[59] The commitments of Mariátegui's *Siete ensayos* thus become compelling through the

---

[59] I am borrowing this idea of the "motivational force" of uncertainty from Martin Hägglund. In *This Life*, when explaining this idea of "motivational force," Hägglund writes, "In keeping faith with a form of life—whether expressed through the commitment to a person, a project, or a principle—I have to believe that the object of faith is precarious. My commitment to the continued life of someone or something is inseparable from my sense that it cannot be taken for granted" (50).

form of the essay, not simply at the level of explicit propositions. The interpretive arrangement brings to light the inorganic character of Peruvian social reality in such a way that the normative demand to transform that reality for the better follows immanently from its failure to form a cohesive, self-reproducing whole.

BIBLIOGRAPHY

Adorno, Theodor W. "The Actuality of Philosophy." *Telos*, vol. 31, 1977, pp. 120–32.

———. "The Essay as Form." *Notes to Literature, Volume One*, translated by Shierry Weber Nicholsen, Columbia University Press, 1991, pp. 3–36.

Aguirre, Carlos & Charles F. Walker. "Modernizing Lima (1895–1940)." *The Lima Reader: History, Culture, Politics*, edited by Carlos Aguirre & Charles F. Walker, Duke University Press, 2017, pp. 101–102.

Arteta, Álvaro Campuzano. *La modernidad imaginada: Arte y literatura en el pensamiento de José Carlos Mariátegui (1911–1930)*. Iberoamericana, 2017.

Brown, Nicholas. Brown, Nicholas. *Utopian Generations: The Political Horizon of Twentieth-Century Literature*. Princeton University Press, 2005.

Bürger, Peter. *Theory of the Avant-Garde*. Translated by Michael Shaw, University of Minnesota Press, 1984.

Ciccariello-Maher, George. *Decolonizing Dialectics*. Duke University Press, 2017.

Clayton, Michelle. "Mariátegui y la escena contemporánea." *José Carlos Mariátegui y los estudios latinoamericanos*, edited by Mabel Moraña & Guido Podestá, Instituto Internacional de Literatura Latinoamericana, 2009, pp. 231–254.

Cornejo Polar, Antonio. "Una heterogeneidad no dialéctica: Sujeto y discurso migrantes en el Perú moderno." *Revista Iberoamericana*, vol. 62, no. 176–177, 1996, pp. 837–844.

———. *La formación de la tradición literaria en el Perú*. Centro de Estudios y Publicaciones, 1989.

———. *Writing in the Air: Heterogeneity and the Persistence of Oral Tradition in Andean Literatures*. Translated by Lynda J. Jentsch, Duke University Press, 2013.

Coronado, Jorge. *The Andes Imagined: Indigenismo, Society, and Modernity*. University of Pittsburgh Press, 2009.

De Castro, Juan E. *The Spaces of Latin American Literature: Tradition, Globalization and Cultural Production*. Palgrave Macmillan, 2008.

———. *Bread and Beauty: The Cultural Politics of José Carlos Mariátegui*. Brill, 2020.

De Obaldia, Claire. *The Essayistic Spirit: Literature, Modern Criticism, and the Essay*. Clarendon Press, 1995.

Elmore, Peter. *Los muros invisibles: Lima y la modernidad en la novela del siglo XX*. Fondo Editorial de la Pontificia Universidad Católica del Perú, 2015.
Flores Galindo, Alberto. *La agonía de Mariátegui: La polémica con la Komintern*. Centro de Estudios y Promoción del Desarrollo, 1980.
———. *In Search of an Inca: Identity and Utopia in the Andes*. Translated by Carlos Aguirre, Charles F. Walker, Willie Hiatt, Cambridge University Press, 2010.
Gramsci, Antonio. *Selections from the Prison Notebooks of Antonio Gramsci*. International Publishers, 1971.
———. *Pre-Prison Writings*. Edited by Richard Bellamy, Cambridge University Press, 1994.
Hägglund, Martin. *This Life: Secular Faith and Spiritual Freedom*. Anchor Books, 2019.
Harootunian, Harry. *Marx after Marx: History and Time in the Expansion of Capitalism*. Columbia University Press, 2015.
Hohendahl, Peter Uwe. "The Scholar, the Intellectual, and the Essay: Weber, Lukács, Adorno, and Postwar Germany." *The German Quarterly*, vol. 70, no. 3, 1997, pp. 217–232.
Jameson, Fredric. "Three Names of The Dialectic." *Valences of The Dialectic*, Verso, 2009, pp. 3–70.
———. *Representing* Capital: *A Reading of Volume One*. Verso, 2011.
Kipfer, Stefan. "City, Country, Hegemony: Antonio Gramsci's Spatial Historicism." *Gramsci: Space, Nature, Politics*, edited by Michael Ekers, Gillian Hart, Stefan Kipfer & Alex Loftus, Wiley-Blackwell, 2013, pp. 83–103.
Klarén, Peter Flindell. *Peru: Society and Nationhood in the Andes*. Oxford University Press, 2000.
Kristal, Efrain. *The Andes Viewed from the City: Literary and Political Discourse on the Indian in Peru, 1848–1930*. P. Lang, 1987.
Larsen, Neil. *Determinations: Essays on Theory, Narrative and Nation in the Americas*. Verso, 2001.
Lauer, Mirko. *La polémica del vanguardismo, 1916–1928*. Fondo Editorial de la Universidad Nacional Mayor de San Marcos, 2001.
Lukács, György. "On the Nature and Form of the Essay: A Letter to Leo Popper." *Soul & Form*, trans. Anna Bostock, eds. John T Sanders & Katie Terezakis, Columbia University Press, 2010, pp. 16–34.
Mariátegui, José Carlos. *El artista y la época*. Biblioteca Amauta, 1959a.
———. *La escena contemporánea*. Biblioteca Amauta, 1959b.
———. *Signos y obras*. Biblioteca Amauta, 1959c.
———. *Temas de Nuestra América*. Biblioteca Amauta, 1960.
———. *Invitación a la vida heroica. José Carlos Mariátegui. Textos esenciales*. Edited by Alberto Flores Galindo & Ricardo Portocarrero Grados, Fondo Editorial del Congreso del Perú, 2005.

———. *Siete ensayos de interpretación de la realidad peruana*. Linkgua, 2009.
———. *José Carlos Mariátegui: An Anthology*. Edited by Harry E. Vanden & Marc Becker, Monthly Review Press, 2011.
———. "The Lord of the Miracles Procession." *The Lima Reader: History, Culture, Politics*, edited by Carlos Aguirre & Charles F. Walker, Duke University Press, 2017, pp. 115–121.
Mignolo, Walter. "Mariátegui and Gramsci in 'Latin' America: Between Revolution and Decoloniality." *The Postcolonial Gramsci*, edited by Neelam Srivastava and Baidik Bhattacharya, Routledge, 2012, pp. 191–217.
Montaigne, Michel de. *The Complete Essays*. Ed. M. A. Screech, Penguin, 1991.
Moore, Melisa. *José Carlos Mariátegui's Unfinished Revolution: Politics, Poetics, and Change in 1920s Peru*. Bucknell University Press, 2014.
Moraña, Mabel & Guido Podestá, eds. *José Carlos Mariátegui y los estudios latinoamericanos*. Instituto Internacional de Literatura Iberoamericana. Pittsburgh University, 2009.
Nuñez, Estuardo. *La experiencia europea de José Carlos Mariátegui*. Biblioteca Amauta, 1994.
Pinkard, Terry. "What Is Negative Dialectics?: Adorno's Reevaluation of Hegel." *A Companion to Adorno*, eds. Peter E. Gordon, Espen Hammer & Max Pensky, Blackwell, 2020, pp. 459–471.
Rama, Ángel. *Writing across Cultures: Narrative Transculturation in Latin America*. Translated by David Frye, Duke University Press, 2012.
Robinson, Josh. *Adorno's Poetics of Form*. SUNY Press, 2018.
Salazar Bondy, Sebastián. "The Mislaid Nostalgia." *The Lima Reader: History, Culture, Politics*, edited by Carlos Aguirre & Charles F. Walker, Duke University Press, 2017, pp. 149–152.
Schutte, Ofelia. *Cultural Identity and Social Liberation in Latin American Thought*. SUNY Press, 1993.
Stabb, Martin S. *In Quest of Identity: Patterns in the Spanish American Essay of Ideas, 1890–1960*. The University of North Carolina Press, 1967.
Tarcus, Horacio. *Mariátegui en la Argentina, o las políticas culturales de Samuel Glusberg*. Ediciones Cielo por Asalto, 2001.
Terán, Oscar. *Discutir Mariátegui*. Editorial Universidad Autónoma de Puebla, 1985.
Thomas, Peter D. *The Gramscian Moment: Philosophy, Hegemony and Marxism*. Haymarket Books, 2010.
Unruh, Vicky. "Mariátegui's Aesthetic Thought: A Critical Reading of the Avant-Gardes." *Latin American Research Review*, vol. 24, no. 3, 1989, pp. 45–69.

CHAPTER 4

"The Century of Phrases": Roberto Arlt's Negative Dialectic of Belief and Distrust

The content of spirit's speech about itself and its speech concerning itself thus inverts all concepts and realities. It is thus the universal deception of itself and others, and, for that very reason, the greatest truth is the shamelessness in stating this deceit.
Hegel, *Phenomenology of Spirit* ¶521

In the previous chapter, I argued that the Peruvian Marxist José Carlos Mariátegui resorts to the form of the essay because of, not in spite of, its uncertainty. For Mariátegui, the uncertainty of this inorganic form of writing is crucial because it makes explicit the fundamental disunity of Peruvian society, namely, the split between urban coast and rural sierra, and it conveys the motivation needed to construct a coherent social organization when such coherence cannot be taken as a given. Uncertainty also occupies a prominent place in the work of the Argentine novelist Roberto Arlt (1900–1942). But uncertainty in Arlt's novels does not motivate a political struggle for socialism; instead, it appears as the pervasive deceit and distrust of urban life.

Arlt directly addresses such distrust in "Por algo somos desconfiados" (We Are Suspicious for a Reason), a piece written in December 1929.[1] Sitting on the train or in the park, overhearing conversations and talking to friends, Arlt notices a recurring pattern of deceit in Buenos Aires. He comes across a "disheartened" young woman, crying in her hands and asking a painful question: "who can you believe?" (*Aguafuertes* 206). At the risk of coming across as "cynical," Arlt offers a brutal response: "you can't believe anyone" (206).

It is not, Arlt believes, that no one deserves our confidence because all people are irredeemably bad. Rather, "the majority of men have neutral spirits" (207). They live "at the mercy of any wind" and "at any moment they can become evil" (207). A neutral spirit cannot be trusted because it lacks constancy. When explaining this notion of a neutral spirit, Arlt refers to Oscar Wilde's quote that "the supreme vice is shallowness," but he finds an even more compelling suggestion in Wilde's additional comment: there is no "shallow vice" [vicio ligero] (207). Only a spark is needed for a powder keg to explode, and an apparently "superfluous thing" that we may have noticed about a friend, lover, or acquaintance, actually betrays their true character, or, better yet, lack of character. Since the neutral spirit inhabits an urban social order characterized by abrupt shifts in expectations, it can neither commit itself to any principles nor take others to be genuinely committed to the ideals they espouse.

Arlt thus presents a deeply cynical picture of Buenos Aires. Hypocrisy and betrayal form the basis of social life in the city, but their ubiquity does not lead Arlt to moralize on the need for honest social relations. He acknowledges that the situation is "horrible. But that's the way it is" (207). It is just "human nature," and "there is no social force that could change it" (207). Arlt admits that things were different in the countryside. Deceit was rare because everyone knew everyone else. The city, by contrast, is "a sort of masonry forest where a wild animal hides in every cavern and stalks its prey" (*Aguafuertes* 206).[2] As urbanization advances and

---

[1] "Por algo somos desconfiados" appeared in the daily column *Aguafuertes* that Roberto Arlt wrote for the newspaper *El Mundo*. Published over the course of almost a decade and a half, Arlt's *aguafuertes* cover a wide range of topics: language, poverty, crime, international, and domestic political events, to name just a few. Rumor has it that Arlt's column was so popular that the editor varied the days in which it was published in order to encourage readers to buy the newspaper every day.

[2] "La ciudad, en cambio, es una especie de bosque de mampostería donde en cada caverna está escondida una fiera que acecha la presa."

village life becomes a thing of the past, our fate is to inhabit a dissociated form of social life in cities where we will deceive and be deceived. Arlt's answer thus risks being "cynical" not only because it conveys a completely disenchanted picture of human sociality, viewing even apparently principled or noble actions as concealing a self-interested motive, but also because it abandons any attempt to reform these ills in favor of full participation in this corrupt, compromised world.[3] In order to inhabit such a duplicitous world in which things and other people are not as they appear, cynical thinking must simultaneously hold, as Peter Sloterdijk puts it, "two views of things, an official and an unofficial view, a veiled and a naked view, one from the viewpoint of heroes and one from the viewpoint of valets" (218). Everyone wears a mask, whether they know it or not, and cynicism reveals the base self-interest hidden underneath noble statements and actions. What we are seeing, Arlt writes, is the "twilight of compassion. That's the truth. We live more savagely than beasts themselves, soulless and cynical" (206). In short, "This is the *century of phrases*" (206, emphasis added).[4]

Writing a few years later in 1933, the Spanish philosopher José Ortega y Gasset identifies in "phrases" the manifestation of a crisis.[5] The triumph of a culture, he argues, generates its own dissolution insofar as the ideas and practices that make up the culture come to be taken as given, not as binding expressions of current needs. Language becomes a "phrase," that is, "what is not thought out every time, but which is simply said and repeated" (78).[6] Through this repetition, language remains apparently the

---

[3] According to Sharon Stanley's very useful analysis of cynicism, what makes modern cynicism distinct from pessimistic moralism is its peculiar combination of social diagnosis and stance toward action. She writes that "the cynic accepts the impossibility of truly virtuous and principled action in human society," but the cynic also concludes that "If virtue, authenticity, and principled action are beyond the reach of human beings, then we must abandon hope for any future transcendence of corruption and injustice. Therefore, the cynic often decides that he can only secure personal satisfaction through a mastery of the arts of deception and manipulation which constitute the foundation of society" (390).

[4] "Escribí una vez que, en esta época, a nosotros, los hombres, nos había tocado asistir al crepúsculo de la compasión. Esa es la verdad. Se vive con más fiereza que las mismas fieras, desalmadamente, cínicamente. ¿Mal del siglo? ¡Macanas! Yo creo que éste es el siglo de las frases."

[5] Ortega y Gasset had close connections with the writers and intellectuals associated with the magazine *Sur*. He gave lectures multiple times in Buenos Aires during the late 1920s and early 1930s. On Ortega y Gasset in Argentina, see Wells "It's Complicated."

[6] "Frase es lo que no se piensa cada vez, sino que simplemente se dice, se repite."

same, but it undergoes an inversion, acquiring arbitrary, often contradictory, meanings. As phrases, words no longer carry their conventional social force; nonetheless, they continue to be used. In this way, phrases may constitute a repertoire of virtuous and principled appearances that can be wielded without any commitment to their meaning. Phrases are used knowingly and cynically, but this only betrays what Ortega y Gasset calls "negative convictions," or, "the lack of feeling certain about anything important" (70).[7] In the absence of certainty, the "man of crisis has been left without a world, given over again to the chaos of pure circumstance, in a lamentable state of disorientation" (71).[8] Ortega y Gasset's "man of crisis" is thus Arlt's "neutral spirit," someone who cannot be trusted because he disingenuously assumes social roles and oscillates unpredictably from one extreme to another, from indifference to fury. Amidst an "overburdened culture" composed of phrases, providing only a semblance of orientation, this man of crisis develops, as we will see in Arlt's novels, a "desire for simplification" (Ortega y Gasset 79). In an "excess of despair," he might seek to return to nature and become "rebarbarized" (76). The crisis, in other words, consists not only in distrust but also in a desperate desire to believe. Cynicism carries out a sort of negative synthesis of these two attitudes, alternating between appearances and naked truth, between noble magnanimity and reductive baseness, without overcoming the contradiction.

In this chapter, I show that this negative dialectic lies at the heart of Robert Arlt's *Los siete locos* (The Seven Madmen, 1929) and *Los lanzallamas* (The Flamethrowers, 1931). As José Amícola has asserted, the "seven madmen" of Arlt's novels "are, at bottom, seven cynics" whose project consists of "deceiving the very authors of the mechanisms of deceit, that is, society" (22). This aspect of cynicism appears most prominently in connection with the Astrologer. In one of the main threads of *Los siete locos* and *Los lanzallamas* (henceforth, *LSL/LL*), the Astrologer attempts to organize a secret society funded by brothels. According to the plan, the secret society would sow confusion and violence, paving the way for a dictatorship, and then an enlightened minority would use "science and

---

[7] "Pues bien, la vida, como crisis, es estar el hombre en convicciones negativas. Esta situación es terrible. La convicción negativa, el no sentirse en lo cierto sobre nada importante, impide al hombre decidir lo que va a hacer con precisión, energía, confianza y entusiasmo sincero."

[8] "Y este hombre de la crisis se ha quedado sin mundo, entregado de nuevo al caos de la pura circunstancia—en lamentable desorientación."

power" to create "apocryphal miracles" for the masses who have lost their faith (124/144).[9] The Astrologer's ideas seem "mad," but, as I argue in the first section, it is precisely the combination of "madness" and "cynicism" that allows Arlt to grasp not only the crisis of authority in Argentine politics, wherein the clash between rural economic power and urban political power had reached an impasse, but also the pressure to stabilize that crisis through a cynical rationality in which the subject dupes the other to believe in its place. In the second section, I examine the anguish of Erdosain, a failed inventor who joins the Astrologer's secret society. Finding that his self has become an issue, Erdosain performs various experiments in *LSL/LL* to know himself, but these experiments only have the effect of deepening his humiliation. He experiences this humiliation in the tension between incompatible perspectives on himself: he simultaneously aggrandizes his actions and inventions as heroic works and reduces them to base motives. In this way, Erdosain embodies the humiliation of the urban middle class, those who are, in Óscar Masotta's words, "condemned to live as true ethical norms that they have not built, that practice has proven to be false, that stubbornly must be performed" (117). As such, the middle class constitutes "el reducto ético" (117), the last stronghold for the dominant normative commitments and their *reductio ad absurdum*. In other words, humiliation in *LSL/LL* follows from inhabiting a social world characterized by the profound misalignment of ideas and reality, and Erdosain, as the most acute expression of that contradiction, finds himself compelled to adopt a cynical attitude that consists not principally in duping the other to believe for him but rather in sustaining beliefs that he does not truly believe. Furthermore, I argue that cynicism is not simply what the novels are about; rather, the novels enact cynicism in their language and composition. Put differently, the realism of *LSL/LL* depends on modernist abstraction. Language appears to operate independently of reality, but this misalignment itself expresses the specific demands of that reality. On one level, the Astrologer's speeches carry out a cynical laceration of language, thereby making palpable the misalignment of ideas and reality in the political crisis of the 1920s and 1930s. On another level, Erdosain's simultaneously frenzied and indifferent language in *LSL/LL* expresses the reductive flattening of the city: the anguish and atomization

---

[9] "La mayoría vivirá mantenida escrupulosamente en la más absoluta ignorancia, circundada de milagros apócrifos y por lo tanto mucho más interesantes que los milagros históricos, y la minoría será la depositaria absoluta de la ciencia y del poder."

of urban life and the self-defeating character of his experiments to overcome these conditions. The formal composition of *LSL/LL*, in short, express the cynical tendencies of social life in Buenos Aires, making palpable the anomic consequences of a dissociated form of sociality.

In the final section of this chapter, I draw out the implications of this account of *LSL/LL* to argue that the connection between cynicism and the city makes Arlt's novels into a compelling account of the contradictions of peripheral capitalism. Arlt presents peripheral capitalism as a disoriented form of sociality in which individuals are compelled and forbidden to perform a specific course of action. It gives rise to an experience of anomie insofar as this situation invalidates the normative order it nonetheless imposes on its subjects. In effect, *LSL/LL* trace the process of adjustment whereby "out-of-place ideas," to use Roberto Schwarz's phrase, come to find a place in the periphery, indeed, must find a place given the imperatives of global capitalism.

This focus on the periphery distinguishes my argument from prevailing interpretations of Arlt's work. Traditional literary history in Argentina tends to construe Arlt as a social realist in contradistinction to the fantastical and metaphysical stories of Jorge Luis Borges.[10] More recently, critics have established the importance of popular culture and media for Arlt's work[11] and the connection he posits between money and falsification.[12] Other critics see subversive, even anarchist, resonances in the conspiratorial politics of Arlt's characters.[13] By contrast, this chapter, in line with the work of Fernando Rosenberg, finds that *LSL/LL* engage in compelling ways with the position of Argentina in the world-system.[14] But whereas Rosenberg argues that Arlt attempts to map a spatial zone outside the world-system, I insist that for Arlt the specificity of social reality in Argentina—namely, its anomie and cynicism—can only be made fully intelligible in light of the contradictions of capitalism. By enacting a negative dialectic of belief and distrust at the level of form and content, *LSL* and *LL* stage how peripheral capitalism generates crises, namely, untenable

---

[10] The magazine *Contorno*, edited by David and Ismael Viñas, established this influential account of Arlt's work in the 1950s. For a more recent take on Arlt as realist, see Anna Bjork Einarsdottir, "'El bacilo de Carlos Marx,' or, Roberto Arlt, the Leninist."
[11] See Beatriz Sarlo, *La modernidad periférica* and *The Technical Imagination*.
[12] See Ricardo Piglia, *Crítica y ficción* and "Roberto Arlt and the Fiction of Money."
[13] See Glen Close, *La imprenta enterrada*.
[14] See Rosenberg, *The Avant-Garde and Geopolitics in Latin America*, Chapter 3.

situations of anomie, and the stabilization of those crises by cynically adjusting ideas to the reality of brutal forms of inequality, by cynically confirming oppositions that ought to be overcome.

The Astrologer as "Neutral Man": Cynicism and Madness

In the appropriately titled chapter "La farsa" (The Farce) from *Los siete locos*, the Astrologer convenes a meeting of the various "chiefs" (*jefes*) that will head the revolutionary "cells" of his secret society. The attendants include: Erdosain, a failed inventor; the Melancholy Thug, a pimp who will aid in establishing brothels to fund the secret society; the Gold Prospector; a lawyer; and a Major. The others are surprised by the presence of the Major and astonished when he tells them that many in the army believe Argentina may "be fertile ground for a [military] dictatorship" (138/160).[15] The army, he explains, sees itself as "a superior state within an inferior society" (138/160).[16] The army looks in disgust at "the contest between the political parties," which "is no more than a squabble between salesmen vying to sell the nation to the highest bidder" (139/161).[17] The secret society, working through the army, could stop the degeneration of politics in Argentina by "creat[ing] a state of revolutionary agitation": "a kind of collective unrest, incapable of finding its true goal; everyone is on edge, their passions aroused," and when "the revolutionary agitation has reached its peak, that's the moment for us military people to step in" (140/162).[18] These pronouncements may have appeared shocking to the other members of the secret society and to readers in 1929, when *Los siete locos* was first published, but the declarations

[15] "Las ideas de 'dictadura' y los acontecimientos politicos militares de estos últimos tiempos, me refiero a España y a Chile, han hecho pensar en muchos de mis camarads que nuestro país podría ser también terreno próspero para una dictadura."
[16] "El ejército es un estado superior dentro de una sociedad inferior, ya que nosotros somos la fuerza específica del país."
[17] "No exajero, cuando digo que la lucha de los partidos politicos en nuestra patria, no es nada más que una riña entre comerciantes que quieren vender el país al mejor postor."
[18] "La 'inquietud revolucionaria' yo la definiría como un desasosiego colectivo que no se atreve a manifestar sus deseos, todos se sienten alterados, enardecidos, los periódicos fomentan la tormenta y la policía les ayuda deteniendo a inocentes, que por los sufrimientos padecidos se convierten en revolucionarios ... Ahora bien, cuando numerosas bombas hayan estallado por los rinconces de la ciudad y las proclamas sean leídas y la inquietud revolucionaria esté madura, entonces intervendremos nosotros, los militares."

would become uncanny on September 6, 1930. In the midst of the early years of the Great Depression, which exacerbated the underlying problems of Argentina's dependence on exports, the military overthrew president Hipólito Yrigoyen and seized power. The so-called conservative revolution of September 1930 would inaugurate an "infamous decade" during which authoritarian nationalism replaced liberal reforms. In 1931, when the second addition of *Los siete locos* was published, Arlt added a footnote for the Major's speech, commenting on the remarkable coincidence "that the declarations made by the army revolutionaries of the 6 September movement should coincide so precisely with the Major's, and that subsequent events should so closely follow his predictions" (139/161).[19] Critics remain struck by this "coincidence." In his excellent *Astrología y fascismo en la obra de Arlt*, José Amícola argues that the presence of the Major makes *Los siete locos* into a compelling account of the contradictions of the interwar political situation in Argentina. Amícola thus finds it regrettable that the Major becomes less prominent in the sequel, *Los lanzallamas*. "If Arlt had fully understood the reach of his intuitive suspicions," Amícola writes, "he would have positioned the Major in the sequel as the true antagonist and catalyst of the conflicts" (80). Amícola continues: "The Astrologer, with his admiration for the US, and the Major, in his more traditional line that silences the industrial factor within Argentine problems, would have corresponded to the real conflict of interests" that the military dictatorship "embodied" (80). While Amícola comprehensively reconstructs the many connections between *LSL/LL* and the political context in Argentina, I argue in this section that the realism of Arlt's novels does not lie in their direct correspondence with the empirical historical events. I insist that the most compelling expression of historical reality in *LSL/LL* can be found in its abstraction from immediacy, from a history that we claim to know independently of the novels. Although the Astrologer often echoes, or anticipates, the views of the military regime in the 1930s, his speeches make this authoritarian nationalism into one ingredient of a motley mixture of phrases associated with, among others, Mussolini, Lenin, Spengler, Nietzsche, and Henry Ford. As a "neutral

---

[19] "Esta novela fue escrita en los años 28 y 29 y editada por la editorial Rosso, en el mes de octubre de 1929. Sería irrisorio entonces, creer que las manifestaciones del Mayor han sido sugeridas por el movimiento revolucionario del 6 de Septiembre de 1930. Indudablemente, resulta curioso que las declaraciones de los revolucionarios del 6 de Septiembre coincidan con tanta exactitud con aquéllas que hace el Mayor y cuyo desarrollo confirman numerosos sucesos acaecidos después del 6 de septiembre."

man," the Astrologer does not represent a coherent political ideology; rather, he represents the tendency for language, under the conditions of a crisis of authority and negative convictions, to become phrases uttered without binding commitment. And yet, with this empty phraseology, the Astrologer can present himself as uniquely capable of stabilizing the intractable conflict of interests animating the crisis of authority. In this apparent independence or abstraction of language, LSL/LL do not simply resemble the events of Argentine history. More fundamentally, the novels identify the impasse according to which neither rural economic forces nor urban political forces could defeat the other and establish legitimate domination. It is this impasse that makes Buenos Aires a peripheral metropolis, a city simultaneously dependent on a moribund export economy and obsessively oriented toward modernity.

To understand the relationship of the novels to the political situation in interwar Argentina, we need a fuller account of the Astrologer's ideas and organizational strategy. As I mentioned above, brothels will fund the secret society, but the Astrologer needs money for the initial investment. Erdosain proposes that they kidnap his relative Barsut, steal his inheritance, and then kill him. With the first step of this plan accomplished, the Astrologer expounds to Barsut his diagnosis of modern society. In short, "humanity, masses all over the earth, have lost their faith" (122/142).[20] And "Once science has extinguished all faith, nobody will want to go on with a purely mechanical existence" (122/142).[21] As the masses sink into desperation, "an incurable plague will return to the earth ... the plague of suicide" (122/142).[22] Rational thought has proven incapable of giving meaning to life because "Man's happiness depends on a metaphysical lie" (123/142).[23] The Astrologer thus proposes "tak[ing] a step backwards" [volver para atrás] (123/143): inventing gods, fabricating miracles,

[20] "La humanidad, las multitudes de las enormes tierras han perdido la religion."
[21] "Nadie tendrá interés en conserver una existencia de carácter mecánico, porque la ciencia ha cercenado toda fe."
[22] "Y en el momento que se produzca tal fenómeno, reaparecerá sobre la tierra una peste incurable ... la peste del suicidio."
[23] "Y pensando, llegué a la conclusión de que esa era la enfermedad metafísica y terrible de todo hombre. La felicidad de la humanidad sólo puede apoyarse en la mentira metafísica ... privándole de esa mentira recae en las ilusiones de carácter económico ... y entonces me acordé que los únicos que podían devolverle a la humanidad el paraíso perdido, eran los dioses de carne y hueso: Rockfeller, Morgan, Ford ... y concebí un proyecto que puede parecer fantástico a una mente mediocre ... vi que el callejón sin salida de la realidad social tenía una única salida ... y era volver para atrás."

spreading mythical disasters. But the Astrologer recognizes that God is dead. "[T]he only ones who could restore man's lost paradise," he asserts, "were the flesh and blood gods: Rockefeller, Morgan, Ford" (123/142-3). In effect, these financial, industrial capitalists have become gods because they possess "a power which ... many mythologies attribute to a creator god"—that is, the power to "destroy the moon" (122/141, translation modified).[24] The existential crisis of modern life, according to the Astrologer, can only be resolved by resurrecting archaic myths, but since religion itself has lost its capacity to motivate and inspire faith, industry must inherit the task. Modern science thus appears both as the problem, the source of the disenchantment of the world, and the solution, the means for recreating a meaningful universe. This paradox, for the Astrologer, rather than posing a problem, constitutes the only "way out of the blind alley of social reality" [el callejón sin salida de la realidad social] (123/143). He aims to reconcile this opposition by dividing "this new society" into "two castes":

> [W]ith a gap between them ... or rather, an intellectual void of some thirty centuries between the two. The majority will live carefully kept in the most complete ignorance, surrounded by apocryphal miracles, which are far more interesting than the historical kind, while the minority will be the ones who have access to science and power. That is how happiness will be guaranteed for the majority, because the people of this caste will be in touch with the divine world, which today they are lacking. The minority will administer the herd's pleasures and miracles, and the golden age, the age in which angels roam along paths at twilight and gods are seen by moonlight, will come to pass. (124/144)[25]

---

[24] "Entonces me di cuenta que toda la antigüedad clásica, que los escritores de todos los tiempos, salvo usted que había escrito esta verdad sin saber explotarla, no habían concebido jamás que hombres como Ford, Rockefeller o Morgan fueran capaces de destruir la luna ... tuvieran ese poder ... poder que, como le digo, las mitologías sólo pudieron atribuir a un dios creador."

[25] "Mi idea es organizar una sociedad secreta, que no tan sólo propague mis ideas sino que sea una escuela de futuros reyes de hombres. Ya sé que usted me dirá que han existido numerosas sociedades secretas ... y es cierto ... todas desaparecieron porque carecían de bases sólidas, es decir, que se apoyaban en un sentimiento o en una idealidad política o religiosa, con esclusión de toda realidad inmediata. En cambio, nuestra sociedad se basará en un principio más sólido y moderno: el industrialism, es decir, que la logia tendrá un elemento de fantasía, si así quiere llamar a todo lo que le he dicho y otro elemento positivo: la industria, que dará como consecuencia el oro."

The Astrologer's plan thus represents a particularly striking version of what Jeffrey Herf calls "reactionary modernism," a proto-fascist current that rejected the philosophical and political heritage of the Enlightenment but affirmed "the most obvious manifestation of means-end rationality, that is, modern technology" (1).[26] Unlike conservatives, who posit an insurmountable gap between technology and culture, reactionary modernists attribute to modern technology the possibility of defending, and even intensifying, the traditional social order.[27] In this way, we might revise the Astrologer's previous statement: he proposes taking a step backward with one foot, while taking a step forward with the other foot.

The Astrologer's industrial mysticism prompts Barsut to ask if he is "a complete cynic, or a madman?" (128/148). The Astrologer admits that he is "both" (128/149).[28] The Astrologer invokes the historical precedent of secret societies composed of "incredible cynics, who believed in absolutely nothing," and, in an allusion to Mussolini, says, "We'll be bolsheviks, Catholics, fascists, atheists or militarists, depending on the level of initiation" (129/150).[29] The Astrologer is the master of what Bakhtin, in his analysis of Dostoevsky's *Notes from Underground*, calls the loophole, "the retention for oneself of the possibility for altering the ultimate, final meaning of one's own words" (233). In the hands of the mad cynic, words

---

[26] I should also note that this idea of a society divided into "two castes" separated by an "intellectual void of some thirty centuries" bears a strong resemblance to Shigalyovism in Dostoevsky's *Demons*. According to Shigalyov, the solution to "the social organization of the future society" lies in "the division of mankind into two unequal parts. One tenth is granted freedom of person and unlimited rights over the remaining nine tenths. These must lose their person and turn into something like a herd, and in unlimited obedience, through a series of regenerations, attain to primal innocence, something like the primeval paradise—though, by the way, they will have to work" (402–4).

[27] Herf's argument deals with interwar Germany, and he argues that the incongruous ideological combination of reactionary modernism was made possible by the combination of rapid, yet partial, industrialization of the German economy and the absence of a corresponding bourgeois revolution (5–6). We could draw an important connection here between these conditions in Germany and uneven development in Argentina.

[28] "'¿Pero usted es un cínico o un loco?' ... 'Las dos cosas.'"

[29] "Seremos bolcheviques, católicos, fascistas, ateos, militaristas en diversos grados de iniciación." José Amícola identifies the link between this quote and Mussolini's "Noi ci permettiamo il lusso d'essere aristocratici, conservatori e progressisti, reazionari e rivoluzionari, legalisti e illegalisti, a seconda delle circostanze di tempo, di luogo, d'ambiente nelle quali siamo costretti a vivere ed agire" (qtd. in Amícola 39). We ought to remember, as Amícola notes, "si el fascismo se adueñó de fórmulas y elementos superficiales del socialismo, no es válida la afirmación inversa" (40).

conveying political commitment become mere phrases repeated to organize an incoherent mass. The Astrologer's mad cynicism, in other words, lies not primarily in the distortion of universal principles to make them conform to a hidden, self-interested end, but more fundamentally in the complete identification with incompatible roles without any binding commitment. This is what makes the meeting of the secret society a "farce." The Astrologer wears masks, but the masks conceal emptiness and negativity, not an underlying identity. The farcical character of this reunion of madmen culminates when the Major, after delivering his speech on the failings of parliamentary democracy and the need for the military to intervene, admits that he has been playing a role, that "this was nothing more than a rehearsal, but some day we'll act out the comedy for real" (142/165, translation modified).[30] By taking off his mask, the Major reveals the secret society to be a comedy. But the organization becomes utterly farcical when the narrator adds a footnote that reverses the picture once again: "It was later discovered that the Major was a real rather than an imaginary officer" (142/165).[31] The secret society thus performs not only for the other, for the masses, but also for itself. By underlining this constitutive performativity, Arlt suggests that what motivates the Astrologer and his "chiefs" is not a coherent set of ideas but negative convictions, the disorienting lack of certainty regarding anything essential about oneself and the world. The cynic is normally understood as concealing an underlying identity and private interests by appealing to noble aims and universal ideals, but the Astrologer's mad cynicism exhibits a preoccupation with phraseology itself, with the formal articulation of words and ideas indifferent to the incompatibility of their content. Indeed, when the other chiefs begin to debate the ideological orientation of the secret society, the Astrologer insists that they must confront questions of "organization," not "ideas" (141/164).[32]

I will return to the Astrologer's ideas below when I address Erdosain's existential anguish, but the preceding discussion of the secret society shows how the novels abstract from ideological content to questions of

---

[30] "Este no fue nada más que un ensayo ... ya que representaremos la comedia en serio algún día." It is curious that Nick Caistor, the translator of *Los siete locos*, would decide to translate "comedia" as "drama."

[31] "Más tarde se comprobó que el Mayor no era un jefe apócrifo, sino auténtico, y que mintió al decir que estaba representando una comedia."

[32] "Ahora se trata de la organización comercial ... no de ideas." And, of course, by "commercial organization," the Astrologer means the use of brothels to fund the secret society.

form. In effect, this phraseology constitutes an attempt to represent a fundamentally antagonistic social order as if it had unifying interests. Due to the intractable conflict of interests, the idea of representing the interests of society as a whole loses credibility. And yet, it is the independence of representations from what they represent that gives language the peculiar ability to stabilize this volatile situation. In making this move toward abstraction, the novels identify the development of a profound historical contradiction in the structure of Argentine society. Phraseology, in other words, formally expresses the impasse that emerged when the remarkable success of the agricultural economy generated urban sectors that represented a threat to the export system but did not constitute an independent force sufficiently powerful to displace the oligarchical elite.

In the late nineteenth and early twentieth centuries, the Argentine economy experienced rapid growth through the export of agricultural raw materials and beef to industrializing economies in Europe and the United States. As Ernesto Laclau argues in an early essay, this arrangement—in which labor-intensive and even pre-capitalist modes of production persist in Latin America while industrialization rapidly advances in the center of the world economy—typically generates an average rate of profit whereby surplus-value produced in Latin America compensates for the rising organic composition of capital and the corresponding tendency for the rate of profit to fall in metropolitan centers. Argentina, however, held a peculiar position in the global economy. Although it was entirely dependent on exports, Laclau argues that the relatively high level of productivity of the land allowed Argentina to appropriate surplus-value produced elsewhere, a surplus that peripheral nations cannot normally capture because of their position in the international division of labor (292).[33] This surplus fueled the rapid expansion of Buenos Aires, which grew from about 400,000 inhabitants in 1887 to more than 2.5 million in 1936 (Gorelik, *La grilla* 13). Buenos Aires, known from the colonial period through the

---

[33] Laclau's argument draws on Marx's theory of rent. Against the neoclassical theory of rent as a form of income whose source is the land, Marx insists that labor is the singular source of value and rent refers to a particular distribution of surplus-value to landowners. Landed property presents an obstacle to the movement of capital and complicates the formation of an average rate of profit. Whereas the average rate of profit normally involves the transfer of surplus-value from industries with a lower organic composition capital (OCC) to industries with a higher OCC, landed property, because of the obstacles it poses, enables surplus-value to be captured in the form of rent by less capital-intensive industries, like agricultural production.

nineteenth century as "la gran aldea" (the great village), became a massive peripheral metropolis inhabited primarily by immigrants and children of immigrants, including Roberto Arlt and his parents.[34]

The new urban masses of this peripheral metropolis began to put pressure on the legitimacy of the old political system, which had been dominated by the rural oligarchy. That pressure attained political representation in the late 1910s when the Sáenz Peña Law established universal male suffrage, secret ballots, and compulsory voting. The law dramatically changed the political terrain in Argentina because the electoral participation of urban, popular sectors brought the Radical Party to power and effectively displaced the oligarchical elite from its previous position of political authority. But the Radical Party quickly found itself caught between the imperatives of the export economy and the demands of urban workers. Hipólito Yrigoyen, the first Radical president, came to power in 1916, and although he initially supported trade-union struggles, he ordered a brutal crackdown on workers when the chaos of the post-WWI moment undermined the export market.[35] Amidst a general strike in January 1919, anarchists and syndicalists faced the army and para-military groups in a bloody confrontation that left more than 100 militants dead. It would come to be known as the "tragic week" (la semana trágica). Labor agitation abated in the twenties with the temporary recovery of the export economy. In this more favorable context, Yrigoyen implemented what he called "distributive justice," using the gains from the export economy to improve the conditions of the nation's middle and working classes. But the program of "distributive justice" could not be sustained after the stock market crash in 1929. The conflicting demands coming from urban workers and the rural oligarchy resurfaced, and the economic system that had previously—in boom times, at least—allowed for reconciliation, now appeared utterly bankrupt.

However, if the export paradigm had been exhausted, the urban sectors were not sufficiently organized to displace the rural oligarchy and transform the economic foundations of Argentina. The export economy would remain the foundation of Argentina even if it offered diminishing returns. The balance of social forces thus created what Edwin Williamson calls a

---

[34] Arlt's father came from Prussia and his mother from Trieste.
[35] Luis Alberto Romero emphasizes the importance of the post-WWI crisis: "With the First World War—much more than the crisis of the 1930s—a stage in the history of the Argentine economy came to an end" (42).

"lop-sided society, in which political authority no longer coincided with economic power" (460). "There was," Williamson writes, "no way out of the deadlock caused by the divergence between the economic power of the *estanciero* élite and the electoral weight of the urban bloc" (460) because the middle class would waver back and forth from the working class to the oligarchy, supporting the former in periods of prosperity and siding with the latter in moments of economic uncertainty.[36] Given this economic arrangement and political composition, Buenos Aires constituted not a genuine metropolis but a peripheral formation that could not subordinate the countryside to its own industrial and social dynamics.

Arlt's *LSL* and *LL* convey the sense emerging at the time that these opposed forces had entered into a dramatic standstill, that this crisis would not be overcome by reconciling the opposition or with the triumph of one side over the other. Instead, the continuation of this impasse might bring about social breakdown. This "lop-sided society" had become, in the Astrologer's words, a "blind alley." Antonio Gramsci, writing in prison, describes such an impasse as a crisis "situation in which the forces in conflict balance each other in a catastrophic manner; that is to say, they balance each other in such a way that a continuation of the conflict can only terminate in their reciprocal destruction" (Gramsci, *Prison* 219). In these conditions, as the Major explains, the military sees its moment to intervene. The military takes itself to be independent of these opposed force, to be the "superior state within an inferior society," and thus uniquely capable of resolving the crisis, preventing the catastrophic outcome that would follow from the continuation of the conflict. As Gramsci puts it, if "neither A nor B defeats the other," eventually "they bleed each other mutually and then a third force C intervenes from outside, subjugating what is left of both A and B" (219). This, for Gramsci, is the formula for "Caesarism," a political phenomenon encompassing the rise of the Roman Emperor, Napoleon Bonaparte, Louis Bonaparte, and Mussolini.[37] In a crisis of authority, neither class can present its own interests as representing the interests of society as a whole. As a result, the established political institutions now appear fraudulent and lack credibility. Amidst this chaos,

---

[36] Indeed, this dynamic would recur throughout the twentieth century in Argentine politics.
[37] It should be mentioned that Gramsci distinguishes between "qualitative" and "quantitative" variants of Caesarism. Napoleon Bonaparte exemplifies the qualitative type insofar as he brings out a transformation of state structures, whereas his nephew, Louis Bonaparte, represents only a quantitative development of the political system.

"charismatic 'men of destiny'" (Gramsci 210) emerge to restore order by means that are far from orderly. Without a social transformation, the volatile situation can only be stabilized, and this stabilization must be carried out by a figure that appears to transcend the impasse and embody in itself the interests of society as a whole. But, given the fundamental nature of the conflict, this appearance cannot derive from a positive, independent position but only from the ability to perform incongruous roles.

Caesar, Bonaparte, Mussolini, and the Astrologer. In this company, the Astrologer does not appear subversive, as readers of Arlt have often taken him to be. He embodies political violence. For instance, he enlists Erdosain to design a mustard gas factory. But, like Caesar, Bonaparte, and Mussolini, he carries out political violence to reconstitute, not transform, the social order. Beatriz Sarlo describes the Arltian imagination, which is perhaps most fully expressed in the Astrologer, as "extremist," meaning that "one only gets out of a conflict through violence" (*Escritos* 226). But the Astrologer does not aim to "get out" of the conflict. It would be more accurate to say that he turns to violence to stabilize the conflict. He recognizes that, under the conditions of this crisis of authority, it is only through violence, only by changing everything, that everything can stay the same. Despite his often revolutionary language, he utilizes advanced, technological means to construct a "metaphysical life" and thus reconstitute existing social relations with all their brutality and inequality.[38]

The association of the Astrologer and Bonaparte also brings into focus the transformation of language into phrases.[39] In *The Eighteenth Brumaire of Louis Bonaparte*, Karl Marx famously writes that the "phrase transcended the content" of the French Revolution (*Surveys* 149). The rising bourgeoisie acted in the name of liberty, equality, and fraternity, but, given its class position, the bourgeoisie could not actualize these ideals. After the

---

[38] As the Gold Prospector recognizes, "everything is a sham, if we only think about it," and the Astrologer is "simply exchanging a trifling lie for one that's eloquent, enormous, transcendental" [Sí, todas las cosas son apariencias ... dése cuenta ... no hay hombre que no admita las pequeñas y estúpidas mentiras que rigen el funcionamiento de nuestra sociedad. ¿Cuál es el pecado del Astrólogo? Sustituir una mentira insignificante, por una mentira elocuente, enorme trascendental] (150/174).

[39] I should note that the Argentine Marxist José Aricó has questioned the validity of the term Bonapartism for an analysis of Latin America. Pointing to an encyclopedia article in which Marx compares Simón Bolívar to Bonaparte, Aricó suggests that this concept blinds Marx to the specificity of social conditions in Latin America. See Aricó, *Marx and Latin America*.

defeat in 1848 of the proletariat, which represented the possibility of making "the content transcend the phrase" (149), tragedy becomes farce. The nephew's Bonapartist state, Marx writes, "seem[s] to have attained a completely autonomous position" (238), that is, appears as the master of the bourgeoisie, rather than an expression of its class interests. In other words, representation itself becomes divorced from the reality it putatively represents.[40] When discussing the 1848 Constitution, for instance, Marx writes, "as long as the *name* of freedom was respected and only its actual implementation was prevented (in a legal way, it goes without saying), its constitutional existence remained intact and untouched however fatal the blows dealt to it in its actual existence" (160, emphasis in the original). Freedom, though codified in legal form, becomes a mere phrase whose repetition bears no inherent connection to the content, to its actualization in social life. The year 1848, we might say, marks the beginning of the "century of phrases," a historical period when "Men and events appear as Schlemihls in reverse, as shadows which have become detached from their bodies" (171). Of course, the ultimate expression of this phraseology is Louis Bonaparte himself. Bonaparte, the mere "caricature" (149) of his uncle, "conceives the historical life of nations and their state proceedings as comedy in the most vulgar sense, as a masquerade in which the grand costumes, words and postures merely serve as a cover for the most petty trickery" (197). When the Major asserts, "some day we'll act out the comedy for real," he follows the example of Bonaparte and makes this masquerade self-consciousness. In history-*cum*-farce and the secret society, language becomes phrases, and representations become independent of what they represent.

And yet, Arlt and Marx would also seem to agree on the relative impotence of unmasking. Ideology critique, traditionally conceived, shows how representations falsely describe a pre-existing reality. Once revealed as false, these ideological appearances should be rejected. Along these lines, we might say that *LSL/LL* attempt to disclose the lie at the heart of the secret society. If the masses were to see through the Astrologer's comedy,

---

[40] In this way, Marx could be seen as anticipating the modernist critique of representation. For this sort of interpretation, se Jeffrey Mehlman, *Revolution and Repetition: Marx/Hugo/Balzac*. Along these lines, Neil Larsen explores the parallels between Marx's *Eighteenth Brumaire* and Adorno's *Minima Moralia*, but he rejects Melhman's claim about Marx's critique of representation per se. Unlike Adorno, Marx does not make the historical crisis of representation into the basis of an argument for the political autonomy of art. See Larsen, *Modernism and Hegemony*, Chapter 1.

to see the "metaphysical lie" as a lie, they would not follow this charismatic leader. But Arlt and Marx insist that lies and absurd appearances have a practical power that outstrips our attitudes toward them. In the preface to the *Eighteenth Brumaire*, Marx asserts that Victor Hugo, in his "bitter and witty invective," naively assumes that it would be enough to demonstrate the absurdity of Louis Napoleon to defeat the farcical repetition of his uncle (144). But Hugo's parody of Bonaparte "amounts to the same thing as pointing out that money is no more than a piece of paper" (Karatani 10). We know that money is just a piece of paper, but it rules our lives nonetheless. Although Marx may at times suggest that the cultural superstructure constitutes a mere epiphenomenal appearance of the economic base, the *Eighteenth Brumaire* demonstrates that Marx's thought involves a richer form of critique that "accords equal attention to what events are and what they are named" (Petrey 455). That is, Marx neither reduces representations to mere effects of objective reality nor asserts the absolute independence of appearances. The Bonapartist state appears autonomous, but it also, in Marx's analysis, represents the small-holding peasants. Unlike the bourgeoisie and the proletariat, the peasantry does not constitute a class. "[T]he great mass of the French nation," Marx writes, "is formed by the simple addition of isomorphous magnitude" (*Surveys* 239), by combining isolated atoms. The peasantry, in one of Marx's more notorious formulations, are no more unified than "a sack of potatoes" (239). And yet, Bonaparte brings the peasantry into being as a class through the performative work of representation. The abundance of "theatrical language" in the *Eighteenth Brumaire* thus establishes "the double point that while nothing objective authorizes a successful performance, something objective can follow it" (Petrey 466).

This theatricality implies a distance from reality, but it also follows from the reality of a crisis of authority, from a situation in which opposed forces balance each other in a catastrophic manner. Louis Bonaparte may be a "caricature" of his uncle, but, Marx adds, this is "the caricature form he had to take in the middle of the nineteenth century" (149). Bonaparte had to take this "caricature form" because the crisis brings to the foreground the conflicting interests at the heart of the social order. Indeed, the crisis makes the interests incompatible within the existing framework. Under such conditions, only an individual, not a deliberate body like parliament, could appear to immediately represent not one group versus others but the interests of society as a whole. Only an individual could appear to stand above social antagonisms. If the crisis of authority negates the putatively universal principles that had bound individuals and classes together into an ostensibly cohesive social whole, then the charismatic individual can only restore order by means of phrases and performances. "[T]he adventurer," that is, Louis Bonaparte, "had to win, because he treated the comedy simply as a comedy" (198).

The Astrologer does not "win" in *LSL/LL*. The secret society never amounts to more than planning and crime, but the Astrologer treats the "comedy simply as a comedy," that is, he knows that the situation demands a charismatic caricature, a magnetic figure who can attract opposing forces by adopting a different mask for every situation. To recall the Astrologer's reference to Mussolini above, "We'll be bolsheviks, Catholics, fascists, atheists or militarists, depending on the level of initiation" (129/161). The line expresses the Astrologer's desire to dupe the others, and, by extension, the ability of the secret society to dupe the masses. But his cynicism does not conceal an underlying identity and interests. Rather than realize a private, veiled agenda, the mad cynic, by putting on a series of elaborate, incompatible masks, ends up carrying out a universal end that he does not fully understand. Indeed, Erdosain recognizes in *Los siete locos* that he and the Astrologer are a "mystery" to themselves: "That's the truth of it. He's as uncertain as I am about where he's heading. A secret society! For him, the whole of society is summed up in those words: a secret society!" (72/87).[41] This point about the secret society gets recapitulated in the crucial transition between the two novels. At the end of *Los siete locos*, Erdosain tells the Astrologer that he looks like Lenin and then abruptly leaves. The sequel, *Los lanzallamas*, opens with the Astrologer thinking to himself, "Yes ... but Lenin knew where he was going" (287).[42] In this way, the Astrologer is not any different from the other *locos* in the novels. None of them know where they are going. The *locos* are defined by "negative convictions," or, "the lack of feeling certain about anything important" (Ortega y Gasset 70). They find themselves thus "given over again to the chaos of pure circumstance, in a lamentable state of disorientation" (71). Indeed, the title of the opening chapter of *Los lanzallamas* indicates that the Astrologer is what Arlt calls a "neutral man," a man whose principles are meaningless because they can be

---

[41] "Él es, como yo un misterio para sí mismo. Esa es la verdad. Sabe tanto hacia donde va como yo. La Sociedad Secreta. Toda la sociedad se resume en él en estas palabras: Sociedad Secreta."
[42] "Sí ... pero Lenín sabía a dónde iba."

discarded at any moment. The Astrologer's revolutionary organization thus constitutes a *secret* society not because it maneuvers to carry out a "secret" agenda, but because its own motives and animating ideas remained obscure to itself. It seeks to dupe everyone, but it is the ultimate dupe.

But if all the characters in *LSL* and *LL* are "neutral," the Astrologer stands out because he knows that he is neutral and he knows how to use that knowledge. Arlt stages how the Astrologer uses this knowledge to stabilize his own uncertainty in the remarkable chapter "Presence of the Subconscious." Haunted by the "impending crime" of murdering Barsut, the Astrologer has been "transformed ... into a twin mechanism with two such different rhythms" (210/243).[43] One Astrologer exists in ordinary clock time, but he finds himself "parlay[zed]" by another Astrologer who inhabits "subconscious time" and "keep[s] his ideas to himself, leaving [the first Astrologer] as limp as a squeezed orange when it comes to thinking up the ideas [he] needs" (210/244).[44] Disoriented by a flow of ideas he can neither comprehend nor arrest, he needs "to project his thought on to something new outside himself that would break up the monotonous rhythm of his feelings and help him rediscover the presence of mind he had before the decision to kill Barsut" (214–5/249, translation modified).[45] He externalizes these ideas by tying a string around the necks of five puppets, hanging the string on a rope, and then giving the puppets the names of the members of the secret society: "Then a silent dialogue began, with the Astrologer asking the questions and receiving the replies inside him whenever he looked directly at one of the figures. His thoughts became surprisingly swift" (216/251, translation modified).[46] The scene underlines the Astrologer's drive to deceive others. But deception here should not be understood as a means to carry out a concealed, pre-existing plan.

---

[43] "La certidumbre de haberse convertido por la proximidad del crimen en un doble mecanismo con dos nociones del tiempo tan diferente y dos inercias tan desemejantes, lo apoltronaban sombrío en la obscuridad."

[44] "Será el tiempo de nerviosidad lo que me inutiliza, o el Astrólogo subconsciente que se reserva sus ideas y me deja exprimido como una naranja para concebir pensamientos que ahora me hacen falta."

[45] "Quería hacer saltar su pensamiento a una novedad exterior, que rompiendo el monorritmo de sus sensaciones le devolviera la presencia de ánimo que, anteriormente a la determinación de asesinar a Barsut, estaba en él."

[46] "Y así comenzo un diálogo silencioso cuyas preguntas partían de él, recibiendo en su interior la respuesta cuando fijaba la mirada en el fantoche interrogado. Su pensamiento tomó una celeridad sorprendente."

Instead, the scene dramatizes how his ideas emerge out of deception, out of his relations to others. He is "neutral" not in the sense that he constitutes an independent framework for others to realize their own ends. He stabilizes the contradictions of the secret society by dominating it, by becoming the only individual who can claim to represent the interests of the whole. As the Astrologer tells the others, evoking Louis XIV, "I am the society" (136/158).[47] He can be the society only insofar as his neutrality allows him to identify with whatever role he performs.

The realism of *LSL/LL* lies in this dialectical relation between uncertainty and performance, that is, in the connection the novels establish between the crisis of authority and abstraction. This realism, in other words, derives from the form of the novels, not from correspondence with empirical political events. As I mentioned above, Amícola argues that *Los lanzallamas* abandons the realist intuition of *Los siete locos* because the Major, as the representative of the military, recedes into the background. Although the sequel may appear less immediately realistic because of the absence of the Major, the sequel continues to develop the most compelling political dimension of the work, namely, the Astrologer's phraseology. In *Los lanzallamas* this phraseology culminates in a conversation between the Lawyer and the Astrologer. The Lawyer, an avowed communist, storms out of the reunion of the secret society in *Los siete locos* when the Major announces his plan for a military coup. In the sequel, he returns to the Astrologer's house to confront him about the ideological character of the secret society. The Astrologer now claims that he is a communist. In the initial meeting of the secret society, a communist revolution appears as a pretext for the military to seize power. But now he proposes that a military dictatorship is needed to create the conditions for communism. "The people turn communist out of hunger or out of an excess of oppression," the Astrologer tells the Lawyer, "not because of intellectual procedures," and "only the military can oppress and terrorize" the people (367–8).[48] What makes this exchange with the Lawyer important is not that the Astrologer finally reveals the true ideological content of his plans. Instead, this moment reaffirms that the significance of the Astrologer's plan lies in

[47] "la sociedad soy yo."
[48] "Es decir, que nosotros nunca podremos llevar el convencimiento y aceptación del comunismo, por procedimientos intelectuales al pueblo. Un pueblo se hace comunista por hambre, o por el exceso de opresión. Nosotros no tenemos poderes para provocar el hambre ... tampoco para provocar la opresión. Los únicos que pueden oprimir y tiranizar a un estado son los militares. Entonces auxiliamos a los militares a clavar las uñas en el poder."

its inconsistency, its "neutrality," and in the way that he makes this neutrality self-conscious. The Astrologer does not represent a departure from the logic regulating existing politics, but he knows better than most that normative commitments have lost their binding power. He takes as his inspiration, for instance, the dishonest means employed by Theodore Roosevelt to establish the Panama Canal. In a nation that apparently avows the principles of democracy, what, he asks the Lawyer, could be a bigger "cynical mockery of democratic procedures" (371)? By pointing to this historical example, among others, the Astrologer indicates that the truth of *LSL/LL* must be found not in any content—in the correspondence of his ideas with historical figures—but in the formal relationship between deceit and belief, in the abstraction of language from its content.

When we attend to how *LSL/LL* relate cynicism to this disorientation and lack of conviction, it becomes clear that the novels do not aim to expose lies as lies. The *locos* know that the ideas that the secret society would propagate are apocryphal. As the Gold Prospector tells Erdosain after the reunion of the secret society, "everything is a sham, if we only think about it," and the Astrologer is "simply exchanging a trifling lie for one that's eloquent, enormous, transcendental" (150/174). But the society does not merely lie to others. The society itself operates on the basis of lies. The Gold Prospector makes this comment about exchanging "a trifling lie for" an "elegant" lie after he admits to Erdosain that the story he told during the reunion about gold in Patagonia was just a story. Erdosain, momentarily exhilarated by the possibility of escaping the city to embark on an adventure in southern Argentina, becomes crestfallen, but he does not oppose the pervasiveness of deceit in the secret society. Instead, he "realized he was getting ever deeper into something which was bound to ruin his life in ways he could not even imagine, and this realization, coupled with his complete lack of enthusiasm for the Astrologer's plan, gave him the feeling of play-acting, of gratuitously creating this absurd situation" (119/137–8, translation modified).[49] Moreover, shortly after the conversation with the Gold Prospector, Erdosain visits the Espilas, a family who had fallen on hard times, and finds himself "stimulating ... fantasies" of becoming rich from his inane inventions (180). Erdosain knows he has

---

[49] "Comprendía que ahora iba en camino hacia un hundmiento del cual no se imaginaba de qué forma saldría maltrecha su vida, y esa incertidumbre así como su absoluta falta de entusiasmo por los proyectos del Astrólogo, le causaban la impresión de que estaba obrando en falso, creándo gratuitamente una situación absurda."

been duped and that he is performing an absurd role, but he proceeds anyways and dupes others in turn.

This sort of episode, which recurs again and again in *LSL* and *LL*, highlights a crucial aspect of the cynical rationality pervading the novels. Characters deceive not only to avoid being deceived but also to believe through the other. The Astrologer describes himself as a "cynic" who "believes in nothing," but we might also say that he is the most fervent believer. He needs a "majority ... carefully kept in the most complete ignorance, surrounded by apocryphal miracles" (124/155), to believe for him.[50] The cynical subject, in this way, disavows belief, keeping an ironic distance from the gullible masses, but, at the same time, this subject must unconsciously—or consciously, in the case of the secret society—sustain beliefs with which it does not identify. The enlightened minority of the secret society would see through the "metaphysical lies," but by dedicating all their efforts to constructing these myths, their actions appear effectively identical to those of the unenlightened majority.

When Arlt says "you can't believe anyone," he endorses a cynical distance from belief. But the novels suggest that such distance presupposes that others believe in your place. The secret society, in others, makes explicit the objective, disavowed structure of belief. Moreover, *LSL/LL* link this structure of belief to the political situation in Argentina, to a crisis of authority in which the dominant ideas have lost credibility due to the impasse between rural economic power and urban political power. In Buenos Aires, in this rapidly growing peripheral metropolis that cannot extricate itself from a dying export economy, neither social force can defeat the other and present its own ideas as universal. This crisis can only be stabilized, rather

---

[50] In *Cinismo e falência da crítica*, Vladimir Safatle discusses cynicism in relation to a situation that closely resembles the Astrologer's scheme of a society divided between a majority "surrounded by apocryphal miracles" and a minority with access to science and power. Emperor Julian, Safatle writes, "found himself facing the follow paradox: a committed and enlightened atheist, he, as emperor, must be the head of the official religion of the State" (85). This dual commitment also corresponded to a double audience: the skeptical elite and the masses. Julian thus found that he had to write for both audiences at the same time, ironizing religious belief for the former and endorsing religion for the latter. Safatle imagines a hypothetical modification to Julian's predicament, albeit one that does not change anything. If the elite were the entirety of the Empire, there would still be a "*subject-supposed-to-believe*, someone who always believes in my place, legitimizing the necessity of ideology" (86). That is, "all subjects would be enlightened, but *they would act as if they didn't know*, everyone would be an atheist, but they would objectively continue to kneel, even though such an act wasn't motivated by any belief in socially shared myths" (87).

than overcome, if subjects objectively sustain beliefs they know to be false. The mutual ruin of the opposed forces can be avoided only if words become phrases that acquire, through mere repetition, arbitrary meanings and, at the same time, maintain the ability to have social effects.

Porteño Misery, or the Reductive City

In this section, I turn from the Astrologer's "mad cynicism" to the anguish of Erdosain.

Erdosain represents, according to the Astrologer, "all those eccentrics" who "are so much wasted energy" because they "can't find their way in society" (130/151). "[T]he progress and misery of this century have knocked so many people off balance" (130),[51] and the Astrologer intends to make these "coffee-bar intellectuals," "backyard inventors," and "parish prophets" into "the cannon fodder of [the] secret society" (131). The Astrologer claims that when these madmen are "properly duped," they would be "capable of doing things that would make your hair stand on end" (131),[52] an assertion that he makes in the presence of Erdosain and with him clearly in mind. In light of these comments, we might conclude that Erdosain indicates a move away from cynicism. As a foil to the Astrologer's shameless deception, Erdosain appears as the dupe. But he also knows that the Astrologer aims to dupe him, and he goes along with the plan anyways. He thus highlights another aspect of cynicism: not the dependence of the subject on others to believe in its place, but the dissociation of the self into one part that believes and another that distrusts, one half that sees its actions in heroic terms and another half that reduces those same actions to base, mechanical impulses. Erdosain establishes the inseparability of this humiliating self-diremption and cynicism, and through his frenzied speech and the conception of the city as a reductive, flattening force, *LSL/LL* present this existential condition as the truth of social life in Buenos Aires, or what I will call "porteño misery."

---

[51] "Y lo que me alienta es saber que la civilización y la miseria del siglo han desequilibrado a muchos hombres. Estos locoides que no encuentran rumbos en la sociedad son fuerzas perdidas."

[52] "Estos imbéciles ... y yo se lo digo porque tengo experiencia ... bien engañados ... lo suficiente recalentados, son capaces de ejecutar actos que le pondrían a usted la piel de gallina. Literatos de mostrador. Inventores de barrio, profetas de parroquia, políticos de café y filósofos de centros recreativos serán la carne de cañón de nuestra sociedad."

Before entering into a detailed discussion of Erdosain, I will take a detour through a discussion of Fyodor Dostoevsky. "Arlt," according to the Uruguayan novelist Juan Carlos Onetti, "translated Dostoevsky into *lunfardo*" (375), the slang of Buenos Aires. Onetti recognized that *LSL/ LL* borrow heavily from the characters and themes of Dostoevsky's *Demons* (1872).[53] This novel, which was based on the "Nechaev affair,"[54] depicts the activities of a revolutionary secret society as it brings nihilistic destruction to a provincial town. Although I will periodically refer to specific connections between *LSL/LL* and *Demons*, my argument in this section does not deal with Dostoevsky's influence on Arlt.[55] Rather, I want to show, with the aid of Georg Lukács's 1943 essay on Dostoevsky, how Arlt connects Erdosain's existential anguish to Buenos Aires and urban life. In so doing, the nihilism exposed and indicted by Dostoevsky becomes a problem of cynicism. Arlt inherits the humiliation, morbid individualism, and desperate experiments of Dostoevsky's novels, but in *LSL/LL* they appear as aspects of a form of cynicism springing from the conditions of capitalism in the city.

With Georg Lukács's essay on Dostoevsky, we revisit the world-historical significance of 1848 and Louis Bonaparte's farcical coup. In the Marxist tradition, 1848 marks the completion of the "heroic phase" of the bourgeois revolutions. In the first half of the nineteenth century, the bourgeoisie carried out the historical mission of dismantling feudalism, but once it was confronted by the rising working class in 1848, it abandons its

---

[53] Despite the general significance of this insight, Onetti does not correctly identify the specific parallels. For instance, Onetti associates Stavrogin with the Astrologer, but Pyotr Verkhovensky seems much more plausible as an inspiration for the Astrologer.

[54] Sergey Nechaev started an infamous revolutionary organization in 1869. When Ivan Ivanov, a member of the group, objected to Nechaev's authoritarian leadership, Nechaev and others executed him. I should also mention that Nechaev, possibly with the collaboration of Bakunin, wrote the manifesto *Catechism of a Revolutionary*. For a well-documented discussion of Nechaev and Pyotr Verkhovensky in *Demons*, see Frank, Chapter 23.

[55] For a more detailed discussion of connections between the novels, see Flint. I also include an insightful comment from José Amícola. According to Amícola, it is not that Arlt shared Dostoevsky's hostility toward revolutionary movements. Then why, Amícola asks, does "Arlt move the action of the Russian novel to Buenos Aires in 1928? Arlt clearly was interested in making a parable about the facts of his own concrete reality: in the Argentina of dependent capitalism during the liberal republic, the agrarian oligarchy longs for the days of its hegemonic leadership (from which it had been partially displaced by a rising petty bourgeoisie and the immigrants that it itself had brought to the country) and now dedicates itself to conspiring with a new military strata that sees its moment approaching" (17–8).

commitment to universal values and cedes political power to a third force who arrives on the scene to reestablish order and secure the accumulation of capital. This historical narrative informs Lukács's assertion that "Raskolnikov is the Rastignac of the second half of the nineteenth century" (181). In Balzac's *Comédie humaine*, Rastignac represents "the unimpeded rise of talents in a democratic society," that is, "the rise of individuals" in the early stages of bourgeois society (182). He embodies the spirit of Napoleon (the uncle, that is) in "his way of overcoming obstacles" at a time when "the peculiar aims of the generation ... remained clear and socially concrete" (182). The failed revolutions of 1848, however, generate an atmosphere of "disillusionment" with the ideals of the Enlightenment and "its dreams of a renovation and reformation of bourgeois society" (182). The violent restoration of order thus disarticulates the individual ambitions of a character like Rastignac from any social context. The relation between the individual and the social becomes even more twisted and deformed in Russia because, as Lukács notes, its "contemporaneity" with post-1848 Europe exists "in a prerevolutionary period ... when the Russian 1789 was still in the distant future" (182). As a result, "the Napoleonic dreams of Russian youth were more violent, more passionate than those of their Western European contemporaries" (182). The fact that in Dostoevsky's time Russia had not yet gone through its own 1789 does not mean for Lukács that his characters represent a past that has been consigned to the dustbin of history. Rather, it is precisely Russia's "backwardness" that allows Dostoevsky to express in a compelling form the fundamental problems of the second half of the nineteenth century.

Among Dostoevsky's novels, *Demons* most explicitly addresses the political expression of the combination of disillusionment and revolutionary enthusiasm that, according to Lukács, characterizes post-1848 Russia. Dostoevsky frames these political sentiments in terms of a generational conflict between the liberals of the 1840s and the nihilists of the 1860s.[56] The novel stages this confrontation in the estranged relationship of Stefan

---

[56] By addressing the issue of generations, *Demons* advances Dostoevsky's critique of Turgenev's *Fathers and Sons*. In this novel, Turgenev, a contemporary of Dostoevsky, aims to overcome the hostility between the two generations and claim a deeper continuity between the liberals and the nihilists. Joseph Frank summarizes the generation conflict of *Demons* in the following way: "What had been, in the generation of the 1840s, an amiable, relatively harmless flirtation with European culture and intellectual fashions had turned vicious and deadly by the mid-1860s" (475).

Trofimovich, the effete intellectual with a repertoire of French sayings, and his son, Peter Verkhovensky, the ruthless manipulator who claims to represent a revolutionary organization in Switzerland. Despite the falling out between father and son, Dostoevsky insists on the former's responsibility for the latter. Nihilism appears in *Demons* as the logical conclusion of the rejection of orthodox Christianity and the obsession with the abstract values of the Enlightenment.[57]

And yet, for Lukács, it is in the existential realm, not in politics per se, that Dostoevsky poses the fundamental question of the late nineteenth century. Raskolnikov replaces the figure of Rastignac because he represents what happens to action when it has been emptied of social content and concrete aims. Subjecting himself to a "test" to see if has "the moral capacity to become a Napoleon," that is, the capacity "to step over men for the sake of great aims," Raskolnikov makes action into an "experiment" ("Dostoevsky" 183). In so doing, according to Lukács, Dostoevsky's characters, despite their eccentricities, or perhaps because of them, make explicit "one of the main human problems of the bourgeois and intellectual world of the nineteenth and twentieth centuries"—namely, to "know oneself once [and] for all, in depth, to the very bottom" (184). Whereas previously the subject would know itself through its actions in a social space, under the conditions of mature capitalism the subject asserts its distance from its various social roles. As "this individualism turns inward" (185), the intrinsic content of an action and its specific consequences become a mere means. Lukács finds a clear articulation of this notion of the experiment in a letter written by Stavrogin in *Demons*. Testing his "strength everywhere" in an effort to know himself, Stavrogin asks, "But what to apply my strength to—that's what I have never seen, nor do I see it now ... I am as capable now as ever before of wishing to do a good deed, and I take pleasure in that; along with it, I wish for evil and also feel

---

[57] Although Roberto Arlt draws heavily on *Demons*, he does not put generational issues at the forefront of *LSL/LL*. The past carries little weight in Arlt's novels, but we should note that Erdosain's relationship with his father constitutes perhaps the primal scene of his humiliation. In the chapter "Humiliation," Erdosain explains to Elsa and the Captain that his father "began the twisted task of humiliating" him [este feroz trabajo de humillación] (49/62). His father would tell Erdosain, "tomorrow I'm going to thrash you," leaving him to "sleep awfully, like a sick dog" [mañana te pegaré ... Y esa noche dormía, pero dormía mal, con un sueño de perro] (49/62). Arlt returns to this image throughout the novel, demonstrating the importance of the father on Erdosain's path, but neither Erdosain's father nor any other fathers enter as characters.

pleasure" (Dostoevsky 675). This "loss of direction in all instincts" (Lukács, "Dostoevsky" 186), not to mention the fact that this is Stavrogin's suicide letter, demonstrates that "the experiment is the desperate attempt to find firm ground within oneself," a "desperate attempt to pull down" the barrier "between the self and the world" (187). And yet, this desperation expresses for Lukács the genuine human desire to break through the "moral and psychic deformation of man which is caused by the evolution of capitalism" (194). Dostoevsky thus surpasses, according to Lukács, his naturalist contemporaries by staging the experiment not as the action of eccentric social types but as the fundamental problem of "individualism turned inward."

Arlt's debt to the Dostoevskian experiment becomes explicit in Erdosain's decision to kidnap and ransom Barsut. The plan begins to materialize after Barsut confesses that he informed the Sugar Company that Erdosain had stolen money from his employer and then slaps Erdosain for allowing his wife Elsa to leave with the Captain.[58] As Barsut wonders what Elsa could have possibly seen in her pathetic husband, Erdosain imagines Barsut "as his double, a phantom" who "was posing him precisely the same questions as [his consciousness] had done in the past" (64/79).[59] Disturbed by this intimacy, Erdosain experiences "a cold certainty: for him to live in peace, he would have to get rid of Barsut" (64/79).[60] When Erdosain explains this realization to the commentator, he describes the slap as "the stamp of a hydraulic press casting the outlines of a murder plot on to my consciousness" (65/80).[61] The plan amazes

---

[58] Barsut explains that he wanted Erdosain to be imprisoned, leaving Elsa to turn to him. It is not that Barsut loves Elsa. Rather, he "would have loved to humiliate her. Humiliate her just for the sake of it: to see [Erdosain] down and out so that she would be forced to go on her knees and beg [him] for help" [Pero me hubiera gustado humillarla, ¿sabés?, humillarla porque sí, verte a vos hundido para que ella me pidiera de rodillas que te ayudara] (62/77).

[59] "Erdosain lo sentía en sus inmediaciones no como a un hombre, sino precisamente como a un doble, un espectro de nariz huesuda y cabello de bronce que de pronto se había convertido en un pedazo de su conciencia, ya que como ésta en otras circunstancias, él ahora le dirigía las mismas preguntas."

[60] "Sí, era probable que para vivir tranquilo fuera necesario exterminarlo, y la 'idea' se reveló fríamente en él."

[61] "Aquella bofetada que aún me hacía sangrar la encía, como el cuño de una prensa hidráulica estampó en mi conciencia las líneas definitivas de un plan de muerte."

Erdosain for its geometric simplicity: "the combination of three straight lines, nothing more ... abducting Barsut, having him killed and then using the money to set up the secret society the Astrologer was dreaming of" (65/80).[62] The succeeding chapter, appropriately entitled "'Being' Thanks to a Crime," further explores the existential dimensions of this plan. As Erdosain travels to Temperley to explain the idea to the Astrologer, Erdosain conceives of himself as "the negation of life ... Something like non-being" (70/86).[63] That is, his existence amounts to nothing insofar as he takes no action, insofar as he passively allows his wife to leave and does not react when Barsut slaps him. He finds that "it is only thanks to crime that [he] can affirm [his] existence, just as it is only evil which affirms man's presence on earth" (71/87).[64] Accordingly, the purpose of the crime is not to take revenge on Barsut. Rather, Erdosain wants to discover if he has "the will to kill him," to learn "how [his] consciousness and [his] sensibility react to committing a crime" (70/85-6).[65] Having spent the initial chapters wondering what he is doing with his life, Erdosain commits himself to an experiment that he thinks will demonstrate once and for all who he is.

Moving backwards, we can see that the slap represents the culmination of a series of humiliating experiences undergone by Erdosain at the beginning of *Los siete locos*.[66] Erdosain must debase himself to obtain the money to cover his debts with the Sugar Company, pleading for someone take pity on him as this "damned feeling of anguish ... drags [him] down" (30/40).[67] The Melancholy Thug gives him the six hundred pesos and seven cents, but when Erdosain returns home, he finds Elsa waiting with the Captain, her bags packed, and ready to leave. When Barsut slaps Erdosain, he neither defends himself nor retaliates. The slap thus recalls

---

[62] "Un plan son tres líneas generales, tres admirables líneas rectas, nada más ... secuetrar a Barsut, hacerlo matar y con su dinero fundar la Sociedad Secreta como deseaba el Astrólogo."

[63] "Para todos soy la negación de la vida. Soy algo así como el no ser."

[64] "sólo el crimen puede afirmar mi existencia, como sólo el mal afirma la presencia del hombre sobre la tierra."

[65] "Y sin embargo quiero tener voluntad de matarlo ... Ver cómo soy a través de un crimen. Eso, eso mismo. Vero cómo se comporta mi conciencia y mi sensibilidad en la acción de un crimen."

[66] I should note that the plan to kidnap and ransom Barsut takes place after Erdosain has secured the money to settle his debt with the Sugar Company. That is, he is not driven to formulate the plan out of desperation, out of fear that he will be sent to prison. It is a matter of his existential self-conception, not survival.

[67] "Esa 'jodida' angustia la que lo arrastra."

Stavrogin's reaction, or lack of reaction, when Shatov hits him at the end of Part I of *Demons*. It may appear as if Erdosain and Stavrogin passively suffer humiliation, but Arlt follows Dostoevsky in portraying humiliation as something self-inflicted. As Erdosain states in an earlier chapter, he:

> knew only too well he was gratuitously offending and fouling his soul. As he deliberately delved into the mire, he suffered the same terror as someone who dreams they are falling into an abyss but knows they will not die. Sometimes he felt compelled to humiliate himself, like saints do when they kiss the wounds of plague-bearers; not out of compassion, but so that they will be more worthy of God's mercy, even though He is revolted at the way they are seeking heaven through such disgusting tests of faith. (7/12)[68]

Following the example of Christ, humiliation is supposed to make someone worthy of salvation. But Erdosain, on the premise that God finds such debasement revolting, negates the redemptive dimension of humiliation. Accordingly, humiliation must be categorically distinguished from humility. André Gide makes such a distinction in a series of lectures when he suggests that Dostoevsky's characters should be understood in terms of the opposition of pride and humility, with humiliation aligned to the former. Gide points to Stavrogin as the "strangest, most disturbing" illustration of the combination of pride and humiliation, someone who has "been profoundly warped by humiliation" and discovers "delight and satisfaction in the resultant degradation, loathsome though it be" (82). If humility entails "a surrender of pride," the deliberate sacrifice of the self, humiliation, by contrast, "serves to strengthen" pride (83). In light of this dynamic, we can see that Erdosain turns humiliation into another experiment that ought to reveal his inner nature, to disclose of what he is capable. Having suffered humiliation throughout his life, he internalizes it and directs it at others. In so doing, he seeks to affirm himself, but this pathological self-assertion will only lead to ruin and submission.

Arlt's profound debt to Dostoevsky lies not simply in specific character parallels or plot points but in this conception of groundlessness and

---

[68] "Sabía, ¡ah, qué bien lo sabía!, que estaba gratuitamente ofendiendo, ensuciando su alma. Y el terror que experimenta el hombre que en una pesadilla cae al abismo en que no morirá, padecíalo él mientras deliberadamente se iba enlodando. Porque a instantes su afán era de humillación, como el de los santos que besaban las llagas de los inmundos; no por compasión, sino para ser más indignos de la piedad de Dios, que se sentiría asqueado de verles buscar el cielo con pruebas tan repugnantes."

humiliation. Moreover, Arlt shares with Dostoevsky the view that the problem of "individualism turned inward" has an urban basis. According to Lukács, this is what makes Dostoevsky "the first and greatest poet of the modern capitalist metropolis" (189). Dostoevsky was not, of course, the first novelist to deal with urban themes, but he remains "unsurpassed— in drawing the mental deformations that are brought about as a social necessity by life in a modern city" (189). The city does not appear in Dostoevsky's novels as a mere background or in detailed descriptions of setting. Rather, he shows "how the deformations of [the characters'] moral ideals grow out of the social misery of the modern metropolis," how "their morbid individualism" and "desire for power over themselves and their neighbors" follows from the "insulting and humiliating of men in the city" (190, translation modified).[69] What makes urban life pathological, in Lukács's interpretation of Dostoevsky, is the "alienation of the individual from the broad stream of the life of the people" (191). Dostoevsky's characters often misrecognize the cause of their morbid existence, but this alienation constitutes the "primary phenomenon" of his novel, namely, "Petersburg misery" (191). As a pamphleteer, Dostoevsky attributes this misery or poverty to the corrupting influence of European intellectual life and calls for a return to Russian Orthodox Christianity. But Lukács holds that "Dostoevsky's characters go to the end of the socially necessary self-distortion unafraid" (194), and this self-sacrifice constitutes a "revolt" that "shines a light in the darkness of Petersburg misery, a light that illuminates the road to the future of mankind" (197). Although we find his answer inadequate, Dostoevsky's manner of posing the question expresses the salient spiritual need for the sorts of social bonds that are emphatically absent in urban life.

Moreover, in naming this phenomenon "Petersburg misery," Lukács evokes Marx's characterization of the German *misère* in the 1840s and thereby suggests that the problem of alienation must be understood in light of the uneven development of Russia. At the turn of the nineteenth century, radical German intellectuals believed they were carrying out a spiritual revolution with universal significance for humanity. But by the middle of the century, this inwardness proved to be inseparable from political passivity and private self-concern. Rather than blame the inertia of the German population on some putative moral failings, Marx attributes the

[69] In the quote, I have used "humiliating" instead of "injuring" to make explicit Lukács's reference to Dostoevsky's 1861 novel, *Humiliated and Insulted*.

German *misère* to political-economic unevenness, namely, to the slow and partial development of capitalism and to fact that they "shared in the restorations of modern nations without having shared in their revolutions" (*Portable* 116). German intellectuals thus become "*philosophical* contemporaries of the present without being its *historical* contemporaries" (Marx 118).[70] Confronting antiquated political structures, German intellectuals have not only been atomized; they also find themselves compelled to adapt to a social order in which the emancipatory content of their philosophical ideas has no place. Under such conditions, German philosophy oscillates erratically between opportunism and radical declarations of future potential.[71]

The consequences of this misalignment of ideas and reality figure prominently in the porteño misery of *LSL/LL*. As we saw in the previous section, the Astrologer cynically makes revolutionary ideas justify conditions of inequality and deception. And, as I mentioned above, Erdosain represents for the Astrologer "all those eccentrics" and "backyard inventors" who "are so much wasted energy" because they "can't find their way in society." Alienated from social life and the effort to transform it, Erdosain's radical ideas assume a destructive—indeed, self-destructive—character. He precipitously alternates between presenting his actions in heroic terms and reducing them to base, mechanical impulses.

Arlt articulates a compelling expression of porteño misery—the humiliating experience of atomization and of the misalignment of ideas and reality—in the language of *LSL/LL*, notably in Erdosain's frenzied speech.

---

[70] For an excellent account of the broad discussion among socialists of German misère in the first half of the nineteenth century, see Breckmann.

[71] This aspect of the Petersburg misery becomes more explicit in an essay Lukács wrote in 1922 on a previously unpublished chapter of *Demons*. (Dostoevsky's publisher refused to publish the chapter; it was discovered and then published in the early years of the Soviet Union.) Stavrogin, according to Lukács, "is the Russian intellectual who possesses strength and abilities (amounting in [him] to demoniac brilliance), but who is unable to make any use of these in the Russian reality. So these qualities, if they do not end in smoke, as in Tugenev's and Goncharov's heroes, must lead to aimless, senseless, unworthy and even ridiculous rimes. There now opens up the whole abyss of despair and life's aimlessness which turned the honest section of the Russian intelligentsia into revolutionaries so early. And we see with a shock that there was nothing left for these people, if they honestly sought a goal in life, except suicide, depravity or revolution. (Stavrogin chooses the first course.) And however passionately Dostoevsky resisted revolution as a pamphleteer, with whatever conviction he preaches a religious solution to these sufferings, he is the very person who convinces one most clearly of revolution's necessity" ("Stavrogin's Confession," 47–8).

Perhaps the best description of Erdosain's speech comes from the narrator, or, as he is known in the novels, "the commentator."[72] When Erdosain explains his realization of the plan to kidnap Barsut, the commentator introjects, describing how Erdosain would get "carried away" and "circle around his central 'idea' with a torrent of words. In the grip of a slow frenzy which as he spoke gave him the feeling of being extraordinary rather than a useless nobody, he had to exhaust every last possibility of expression" (66/81).[73] The "torrent of words" suggests the lack of adequate expression, but in this lack he finds the opportunity to prove himself once again. "It seemed," the commentator continues, "his whole vocation was to look into himself, to analyze what was going on inside him, as if the very accumulation of details could convince him he was really alive" (66/81).[74] The "torrent of words," that is, operates like a crime, or experiment, insofar as it constitutes a form of action for testing his sense of self, a free act designed to reveal who he really is. It is as if he tries to pull himself together with this frenzied speech, but it is the very effort of pulling himself together that tears him apart.

As Óscar Masotta explains in his remarkable *Sexo y traición en Roberto Arlt* (1965), Erdosain's frenzied, "interminable talk" becomes a matter of cynicism (76). Erdosain's language, despite its sincerity and effusiveness, exhibits "indifference" and "silence" (76). His speech and actions, as experiments, must be pure expressions of spontaneity, but indifference manifests itself in the sense that Erdosain seems to describe someone else, appears to explain a mechanical, almost industrial, process determining his actions, rather than confess to something for which he is responsible. As a result, Masotta writes, "determinism exists here only through the freedom that helps to realize it" (77). This is a cynicism in which the "absolute opacity of a mystified consciousness must coincide with its total lucidity"

---

[72] Not incidentally, the commentator explicitly enters the narrative, or begins to comment, when Erdosain is left by Elsa and slapped by Barsut. As we subsequently learn, Erdosain murders the Cross-Eyed Girl (la Bizca), a character in *Los lanzallamas*, and then takes refuge with the commentator, to whom he confesses his crimes for three days before committing suicide.

[73] "En el curso de esta historia he olvidado decir que cuando Erdosain se entusiasmaba, giraba en torno de la 'idea' eje con palabras numerosas. Necesitaba agotar todas las posibilidades de expression, poseído por ese frenesí lento que a través de las frases le daba a él la conciencia de ser un hombre extraordinario y no un desdichado."

[74] "No hacía otra cosa que examinarse, que analizar lo que en él ocurría, como si la suma de detalles pudiera darle la certidumbre de que vivía."

(77). The total lucidity appears in Erdosain's "accumulation of details" and the use of "every last possibility of expression" to describe what he does, but this lucidity coexists with opacity, with the appearance of his actions as belonging to an other. By turning inward "to analyze what was going on inside him," Erdosain does not appropriate his alienated actions; rather, he deepens his self-diremption. Insofar as Erdosain adopts this reflexive distance toward his own motivations, he embodies a cynicism that can be distinguished from that of the Astrologer. Whereas the Astrologer's mad cynicism consists in getting the other to believe in one's place, Erdosain's cynicism oscillates interminably between a self that believes and a self that distrusts, one half that is subject to determining forces and another half that reflexively recognizes such determination.

In addition to this frenzied speech, in which cynicism appears in the reflexive distance from his own motivations, Erdosain's language also articulates his existential condition through forms of urban organization. At the beginning of *Los siete locos*, Erdosain describes this condition as the "anguish zone." Wandering the streets in desperation, fearing he will be sent to jail if he cannot settle his accounts with the Sugar Company:

> He imagined this zone floating above cities, about two meters in the air, and pictured it graphically like an area of salt flats or deserts that are shown on maps by tiny dots, as dense as herring roe. This anguish zone was the product of mankind's suffering. It slid from one place to the next like a cloud of poison gas, seeping through walls, passing straight through buildings, without ever losing its flat horizontal shape; a two-dimensional anguish that left an after-taste of tears in throats it sliced like a guillotine. (5–6/10)[75]

As densely packed dots, the "anguish zone" unites the inhabitants in the city only in their atomization. It is as if the anguish zone were the result of condensing the city's oppressive height into a horizontal plane. Both amorphous and razor-sharp, it permeates domestic spaces and inflicts wounds. As it passes from "one place to the next like a cloud of poison

---

[75] "Erdosain se imaginaba que dicha zona existía sobre el nivel de las ciudades, a dos metros de altura, y se le representaba gráficamente bajo la forma de esas regiones de salinas o desiertos que en los mapas están revelados por óvalos de puntos tan espesos como las ovas de un arenque. Esta zona de angustia, era la consecuencia del sufrimiento de los hombres. Y como una nube de gas venenoso se trasladaba pesadamente de un punto a otro, penetrando murallas y atravesando los edificios, sin perder su forma plana y horizontal; angustia de dos dimensiones que guillotinando las gargantas dejaba en éstas un regusto de sollozo."

gas," indifferent to the individuality of the atoms it has created, it represents "the coldest, emptiest death of all, having no more meaning than chopping off a head of cabbage or swallowing a mouthful of water" (Hegel, *Phenomenology* 343/¶590). The "anguish zone" establishes a pattern of images of flattening in *LSL/LL*. In a quote referenced above, for instance, Arlt images that the idea to kidnap Barsut was stamped onto his mind by a hydraulic press. Erdosain also utilizes the image of a mill to depict how the city weighs on its inhabitants.[76] After his wife leaves him, Erdosain "felt himself crushed by a sense of pure dread. His life could not have been flatter if he had gone through the rollers of a sheet-metal mill" (56/70).[77] Although this sensation derives immediately from his wife's departure, the industrial metaphor of the mill links Erdosain's suffering to a broader pattern in the novel. Repeatedly, images of flattening in *LSL/LL* evoke the anguish and alienation of life in Buenos Aires, the porteño misery that levels and reduces Erdosain's grandiose ideas.

In the 1920s and 1930s, Buenos Aires was noted for its flatness. In *Radiografía de la pampa* (X-Ray of the Pampa, 1933), for instance, Ezequiel Martínez Estrada asserts that Buenos Aires "lacks a third dimension" (146).[78] If, Martínez Estrada writes, "New York is all front," all façade, Buenos Aires is "all roofs" (146). This extensive plain of roofs gives one the sense of gazing at the *pampa*, the plains surrounding the city's western edge. The flatness of Buenos Aires thus embodies for Martínez Estrada the absence of a clear distinction between city and countryside. And this lack of a difference between urban and rural poses a challenge to the idea that Argentina faces a choice between "civilization and barbarism," as Sarmiento put it in the nineteenth century. According to Sarmiento's interpretation, the rationality of the city was exemplified by the geometrical organization of the urban grid.[79] But the grid assumed a

---

[76] See Renaud 204.

[77] "Erdosain se sintió aplanado en una perfección de espanto. Se lo hubieran pasado por entre los rodillos de un laminador, más plana por entre los rodillos de un laminador, más plana no podría ser su vida."

[78] Skyscrapers would only begin to be built in the second half of the thirties, so at the time Buenos Aires was composed of relatively low houses and buildings.

[79] With his idea of "la ciudad ordenada" (the ordered city), Ángel Rama similarly grasped this association of the grid with rationality, pointing in particular to the Renaissance idea that the Americas constituted a blank slate onto which a rational urban order could be imposed, in contrast to chaotic medieval towns and their historical baggage. See Rama, *The Lettered City* 1–15.

radically different character when Buenos Aires ceased to be a clearly delimited colonial village and became a vastly expanding metropolis in the early twentieth century. "[T]hrough the grid," Adrián Gorelik explains, "the modern city ... realizes the threat of the pampa; its expansion cannot be seen as the culturalization of the plains, but rather as its metamorphosis" (*La grilla* 30).[80] Despite its initial link with reason and historical progress, the urban grid comes to appear as the culmination of irrationality, as a reversion to the state of nature.[81] Through geometrical imagery, *LSL/LL* stage this transformation of the grid from a source of order into a flattening anguish. The novels, in other words, dramatize the barbarization of the city.

In *LSL/LL* the continuity of city and countryside appears most prominently in Erdosain's copper rose, a rather inane invention that captures the attention of the other *locos*. Erdosain does not merely shape copper into a rose. Rather, he invents a procedure for turning the organic matter of the flower into a metal product by submerging the rose in a chemical bath. The result is a "flower contained[ing] a botanical life that had been consumed by the acids, but was its very soul" (180/210).[82] In its submission to a technologically mediated labor process, the copper rose negates organic life, but, at the same time, it reestablishes nature in its artificial "soul." The copper rose does not therefore represent either the triumph of industrialization, since it has been reduced to reproducing natural

---

[80] Gorelik also cites an observation from the Italian writer Massimo Bontempelli: "Buenos Aires is a piece of the pampa translated into city" (qtd. in Gorelik 30).

[81] Moreover, the grid, with its seemingly endless, straight streets, distinguished Buenos Aires from medieval European cities that were organically formed over centuries and displayed the accumulation of history. Jean-Paul Sartre, in an article on American cities, distinguished between the ahistorical geometry of American streets and the organic forms of European cities. European cities, he wrote, are "closed cities" whose "slanting, winding streets run head on against walls and houses; once you are inside the city, you can no longer see beyond it," but the American metropolis contains "long, straight unobstructed streets" (124). Sartre also argues that New York is a colonial city, a city divorced from history. Ernst Bloch makes nearly identical statements about Berlin. Bloch, for instance, wrote that Berlin was an "eternal colonial city ... a structure that, so to speak, always becomes and never is" (Bloch, *Literary Essays* 366). For Sartre, "New York is a colonial city, an outpost" (130). The "colonial" character of these cities, for Bloch and Sartre, has less to do with imperial domination and more to do with the speed with which they are erected, as if out of nowhere and in an empty space.

[82] "El temblor de la llama de la lámpara de acetileno hacía jugar una transparencia roja, como si la flor se animara de una botánica vida que ya estaba quemada por los ácidos y que constituía su alma."

forms, or the victory of nature, given that the organic has been dissolved in the chemical bath. Instead, it embodies a sort of negative synthesis that accommodates opposite valences and negates the validity of each. Writing four years later, Martínez Estrada echoes the description of Erdosain's copper rose in his characteristically pessimistic reinterpretation of Sarmiento's analysis of Argentina. Martínez Estrada insists that Sarmiento failed to understand that "civilization and barbarism were the same thing, like centripetal and centrifugal forces of a system in equilibrium. He did not see that the city was like the country and that *within the new bodies were reincarnated the souls of the dead*" (*X-Ray* 256, my emphasis). Given the underlying identity between Buenos Aires and the *pampa*, the way that the latter has been possessed by the former in, for instance, the copper rose, Martínez Estrada concludes that we cannot simply invert Sarmiento's formula, as nationalist intellectuals do when they privilege the countryside as the source of authentic national values over foreign influences in the city. Rather, the peripheral metropolis exhibits a kind of mutual contamination and reciprocal debasement of rural and urban.

Many of the *locos* in *LSL/LL*, like nationalists, construe the countryside as the negative of the city. More specifically, they imagine rural life as a dangerous refuge from the monotony and comfort of the city. During the meeting of the secret society, the Gold Prospector tells a story about the discovery of gold in Patagonia, but, as he later reveals to Erdosain, it is another lie. As a rehearsal of the comedy the secret society will later perform, the story offers rural adventure as a form of "salvation for mankind worn out as it is by the mechanization of our civilization" (151/175).[83] "Cities," the Gold Prospector asserts, "are the world's cancer" because they make men into "cowards who are sly and envious" (153/177).[84] Whereas these cowards "prefer comfort and entertainment," they can "put their souls to the test in the mountains or the empty plains" (152/177).[85] With the secret society, however, "anyone who does not feel at home in the city should head out for the wilderness," like the early

---

[83] "Lo que proyecta el Astrólogo es la salvación del alma de los hombres agotados por la mecanización de nuestra civilización."
[84] "Las ciudades son los cánceres del mundo. Aniquilan al hombre, lo moldean cobarde, astuto, envidioso y es la envidia la que afirma sus derechos sociales, la envidia y la cobardía."
[85] "En vez de irse a romper el alma a la montaña, y a los campos, prefieren las comodidades y los divertimentos a la heroica soledad del desierto."

Christians fleeing to the desert (153/177).[86] As Erdosain listens to the Gold Prospector, he regards himself as "one of those miserable cowards who live in the city," a coward whose overdeveloped intellectual life prevents him from living an authentic life of action and bravery (154/178).[87] At this point in the narrative, Erdosain, often using the very language that he has heard from the Gold Prospector and the Astrologer, begins to make the city into an explicit target for his humiliation and anguish. Initially immersed in the city, Erdosain begins to distance himself from Buenos Aires, making it into an object he could observe and control. This separation from and opposition to the city culminates when he announces, "You'll be ours, city" (235/274).[88] This scene recalls Rastignac's declaration at the end of Balzac's *Père Goriot*. In the context of Balzac's novel, Rastignac's assertion indicates that he will ascend the social ladder and it exemplifies the "rise of individual talents" that, as we saw above, Lukács's associates with Napoleon. But in *Los siete locos*, the assertion immediately appears ironic. He makes the statement after a "careless passer-by bumped into him and sent him flying against a wall" (234/274).[89] Moreover, we are also told that the Major has been following him to ensure that he does not abscond with Barsut's money, even though the Astrologer had insisted that he had complete faith in Erdosain. Erdosain's assertion to take the city thus becomes the patently desperate expression of a "tiger cub let loose in a brick jungle" (234/274).[90] The desperate attempt to rise above and dominate the city, substituting its mechanical existence with metaphysical lies about rural life, parallels the frenzied speech in which Erdosain assumes a reflexive distance from his own actions, as if they were unfolding mechanistically and without his will. And, once again, the novels suggest that this distance actualizes what it disavows, that the explicit denunciation of the city realizes the humiliation of urban life.

---

[86] "Pero ya está todo organizado y no cabe otra cosa que decir: en nuestro siglo los que no se encuentran bien en la ciudad que se vayan al desierto." The countryside or the dessert would satisfy the "desire for simplification" that, as I mentioned above, Ortega y Gasset saw as the response to a culture in crisis. Turning away from thought and toward action, this solution entails a return to barbarism.

[87] "Yo soy menos personaje de drama que él, yo soy el hombre sórdido y cobarde de la ciudad."

[88] "Serás nuestra, ciudad."

[89] "De un encontronazo un faquín lo arrojó contra un muro."

[90] "Erdosain se detuvo espantado, apretó el dinero convulsivamente en su bolsillo y excitado, ferozmente alegre como un tigrecito suelto en un bosque de ladrillo, escupió a la fachada de una casa de modas, diciendo."

Since this hatred for the city does not culminate in the nihilistic destruction of its object, it would be more accurate to see it in terms of a cynical reconciliation. This cynicism comes into focus when, shortly before Erdosain evokes Rastignac, he imagines that the secret society will constitute an "aristocracy of cynics" (234/273).[91] Erdosain echoes the Astrologer's line about the need for a metaphysical lie, for "heroes" who will "offer mankind tremendous miracles" (234–5/273–4).[92] These "heroes" would accomplish great deeds, sacrificing their own particular interests for the good of humanity. But the specificity of Erdosain's thoughts here, in contrast to the Astrologer, should be understood in relation to his confession at the beginning of *Los siete locos*: "Yes, I am a lackey. I have the soul of a true lackey [*lacayo*]" (7/12).[93] Erdosain repeatedly imagines himself as a servant, degrading himself by serving an unworthy master. Whereas the Astrologer sees himself as the "manager of madmen" (131/152),[94] Erdosain embodies, to return to Sloterdijk's characterization of cynicism, both "the viewpoint of the heroes" and that of the "valets" (218). Sloterdijk alludes here to Hegel's famous quip that "No man is a hero to his valet, but not because that man is not a hero, but rather because the latter is—a valet" (*Phenomenology* 385/¶665).[95] From the point of view of the valet, the hero appears "as someone who eats, drinks, gets dressed, in general in the singularity of the hero's needs and ideas" (385). The valet, that is, reduces the world-historical significance of the hero's actions, and the normative dimension of social life as such, to the particularity of private desires and self-interest. Erdosain sees through the pretentions of the hero; he recognizes the metaphysical lie as a lie. But, as a cynic, he also sustains the position of mastery by believing in the lie. He thus internalizes what for the Astrologer is the other, the "backyard

---

[91] "Una aristocracia de cínicos, bandoleros sobresaturados de civilización y escepticismo, se adueñaban del poder, con él a la cabeza."
[92] "Héroes de todas las épocas sobrevivían en él. Ulises, Demetrio, Aníbal, Loyola, Napoleón, Lenín, Mussolini, cruzaban ante sus ojos como grandes ruedas ardientes, y se perdían en un declive de la tierra solitaria bajo un crepúsculo que ya no era terrestre ... Seremos como dioses. Donaremos a los hombres milagros estupendos, deliciosas bellezas, divinas mentiras, les regalaremos la convicción de un future tan extraordinario, que todas las promesas de los sacerdotes serán pálidas frente a la realidad del prodigio apócrifo."
[93] "Sí, soy un lacayo. Tengo el alma de un verdadero lacayo."
[94] "Manager de locos."
[95] For an excellent discussion of the hero and the valet in terms of the genealogical reduction of reasons to causes, see Brandom. And for a more radical take on Brandom's normative Hegelianism, see Brassier.

inventors" who would be "capable of doing things that would make your hair stand on end" if they are "properly duped."

The cynicism of Erdosain, which consists in both upholding and demystifying noble aims, in avowing universal values while simultaneously seeing those values as a façade for self-interested motives, appears inseparable from humiliation. As soon as he formulates a noble vision, he debases himself, reducing it to a mere animal impulse. For Óscar Masotta, Erdosain's humiliation has a definite basis in class relations; it is the "the humiliation" of "belonging to the middle class" (53). In Masotta's analysis, humiliation is the defining characteristic of the middle class because they have been "condemned to live as true ethical norms that they have not built, that practice has proven to be false, that stubbornly must be performed" (117). In other words, the middle class finds itself sustaining both the point of view of the hero—the dominant normative commitments of the social order—and the point of view of the valet—the demystifying critique that reveals the base impulses underlying those commitments. The middle class constitutes both the last line of defense for the dominant ethical norms and the point at which those values betray their emptiness, their failure to bind individuals together into a cohesive social whole. Masotta argues that Erdosain embodies the "truth of the class" because he raises this humiliation to self-consciousness, because, "as a result of this knowledge and the bad faith of others," he feels compelled "to adopt a cynical attitude" (54–55). His humiliation lays bare the asocial form of this social order because he cynically sustains the dominant norms without identifying with them, because he shows how apparently universal principles end up justifying naked economic self-interest.

Extending Masotta's brilliant interpretation, I want to insist on the connection of this combination of cynicism and humiliation to the city. Indeed, it is, for Arlt, precisely this combination that constitutes porteño misery. *LSL/LL* give expression to this misery because they establish a palpable connection between humiliation and salient aspects of social life in the city. The novels show how the metropolis embodies the profound social consequences of the shift from what Marx calls in the *Grundrisse* "[r]elations of personal dependence" to "personal independence founded on *objective* dependence" (158). The latter predominates in rural communities and pre-capitalist towns. But, as Georg Simmel describes in his classic essay "The Metropolis and Mental Life" (1903), these "deeply felt and emotional relationships" and "the steady rhythm of uninterrupted habituations" (410) collapse in the big city. The metropolis, Simmel writes, "has always been the seat of the money economy" (411). Accordingly, the metropolis dissolves the emotional ties and traditional values that previously bound production and consumption in a transparent whole. Now production takes place "for the market, that is, for entirely unknown purchasers" (411).[96] Insofar as emotional bonds have been replaced by commodity production and exchange, the individual adopts an intellectual and calculating orientation, a purely "matter-of-fact attitude in dealing with men and things" (411). Due to the abstraction involved in exchanging everything for a monetary equivalent, objects appear "in an evenly flat and gray tone" (414). The individual here adopts an indifferent, blasé attitude toward things because their inherent qualities vanish as they acquire exchange-value. This attitude corresponds to the point of view of the lackey insofar as they both reduce, or *flatten*, all values to self-interested economic transactions. This world of commodity production and exchange thus constitutes the necessary premise of the individual's unprecedented independence in the city. But this independence would perhaps "more correctly [be] called indifference" (Marx, *Grundrisse* 163) insofar as it leads to an attitude of "reserve" toward unknown others (Simmel 418).[97] Distrust emerges necessarily from the breakdown of traditional relations of dependence and the development of a peculiarly asocial form of social life, one in which we must constantly calculate in our dealings with others, in which we must expect deception and humiliation because others systematically take advantage of our vulnerability. We can't trust anyone, but we cannot not trust. Moreover, *LSL/LL* outline how this indifference and distrust become directed at the self. When Erdosain describes his own actions in neutral terms and expresses his desire to be simultaneously a lackey and a hero, we see that we cannot trust ourselves, but we also cannot not trust ourselves.

---

[96] The Astrologer's secret society is also the seat of the money economy. As he explains to Barsut, "Money will be what binds" the secret society "together" [El dinero será la soldadura y el lastre que le concederá a las ideas el peso y la violencia necesaria para arrastrar a los hombres] (126/145). And, as I have argued, the secret society represents the deepening of, not departure from, the logic of the narrative and the existing social world.

[97] Simmel modifies this sense of indifference: "For the reciprocal reserve and indifference and the intellectual life conditions of large circles are never felt more strongly by the individual in their impact upon his independence than in the thickest crowd of the big city. This is because the bodily proximity and narrowness of space makes the mental distance only the more visible. It is obviously only the obverse of this freedom if, under certain circumstances, one nowhere feels as lonely and lost as in the metropolitan crowd" (418).

If Erdosain's indifference toward his own actions should be seen in light of the blasé attitude in the metropolis, the seat of the money economy, his splitting into incompatible perspectives—that of the hero and that of the lackey—becomes intelligible in terms of commodity exchange, the very medium of social relations in the city and capitalism. Alfred Sohn-Rethel insists that the dual character of the commodity, as use-value and exchange-value, does not only refer to the properties of the commodity but also must be understood in terms of the separation of those activities directed at use and those oriented toward exchange. In a social world regulated by commodity production, these activities "must take place separately at different times" (24). Exchange is thus abstract because the act of exchange "excludes the action of use," and Sohn-Rethel crucially adds that "while exchange banishes use from the actions of people, it does not banish it from their minds" (28). In exchange, "the action and the thinking of people part company" in the sense that "*the action is social*," but "*the minds are private*" (29). This "parting company" of social action and private mind, I would argue, constitutes the socio-historical presupposition of Erdosain's humiliation. His desire to be simultaneously a hero and a lackey expresses the way in which we, by participating in commodity exchange, sustain dominant social relations even as we privately recognize the falsity of their claims to equality and freedom. Erdosain makes this divorce of social action and private mind self-conscious most notably in his cynical speech: the frenzied attempts to know himself in speech actually deepens his self-laceration. These incompatible perspectives should precipitate a crisis demanding resolution, but Arlt indicates how cynicism stabilizes the contradictory imperatives of commodity production and exchange in capitalism. By holding simultaneously the points of view of the hero and of the lackey, cynicism appears as the only way to inhabit an anomic form of social life characterized by the misalignment of ideas and reality when the possibility of overcoming those contradictions has apparently disappeared.

The Infringement Is the Norm; The Norm Is an Infringement

Óscar Masotta notes that Arlt, like Dostoevsky, "knew very well that there was nothing more intimate than the relation that ties the executioner to the victim, the subject being humiliated to the subject doing the humiliating" (43). Arlt's characters are more likely to identify with the aggressor and betray their peers than develop bonds of solidarity based on the common humiliation of belonging to the middle class. As we saw above, Erdosain sees himself in Barsut, but because he finds his own existence repulsing, he feels compelled to destroy this mirror image. Accordingly, even though the *locos* form a secret society, they represent, according to Masotta, an "impossible community" (51). This "impossible community," Masotta writes, "constitutes the inverted image of society" (51). By inverted, Masotta does not mean alternative. Rather, as the inversion of what society claims to be, the "impossible community" constitutes the truth of the social world. In such a community, we see not only the hypocrisy of social life—mutual distrust and deception—but also the self-defeating character of the rejection of such hypocrisy insofar as the humiliated subject sustains his bond to the executioner—that is, the dominant social order—and betrays the other. In this final section, I want to show how Arlt's "inverted image of society" grasps salient aspects of social life under peripheral capitalism. Critics have often seen in Arlt the expression of popular Argentine culture, but his novels take seriously something that the national problematic cannot fully admit, namely, the anomic character of peripheral situation. While this anomie constitutes the truth of the peripheral social formation in Arlt's work, it must be understood in light of, not independently of, the imperatives of global capitalism.

We might begin to grasp the specificity of the impossibility of community in Arlt by contrasting it with the work of one of his contemporaries, namely, Raúl Scalabrini Ortiz. In his essay *El hombre que está solo y espera* (The Man Who Waits Alone, 1931), Scalabrini Ortiz articulates a nationalist interpretation of the problem of atomization. He writes that the *porteño*, whose center of gravity he locates at the intersection of the streets Corrientes and Esmeralda in downtown Buenos Aires, "cannot be deduced" (40). That is: "Neither his financial hierarchy, nor the lineage of his descendants, nor the character of his friends allow one to infer his ideas or feelings. There are conservative workers and revolutionary plutocrats" (40). *Porteños* find themselves unmoored, bound by neither tradition nor social structure, thus allowing for unprecedented combinations. The Astrologer's secret society would be one example of such incongruity. Scalabrini Ortiz insists that a profound sense of disorientation has emerged among the new urban masses in Buenos Aires, a population formed not only on the basis of migration from the countryside but also on immigration from Europe. Immigration reached its peak in 1914, when half of the population in Argentina was foreign-born. That percentage was even higher in Buenos Aires. Unsurprisingly, these immigrants, including Arlt's parents, lacked a strong sense of national identity. Since the inhabitants of Buenos Aires were not unified in an imaginary national community, were not bound together by a feeling of likeness, Scalabrini Ortiz suggests that nationality could be formulated on the basis of a common opposition to imperialists and *vendepatrias*, the oligarchy with ties to the British. While Arlt agrees with Scalabrini Ortiz that social relations in Argentina are marked by negative convictions and disorientation, by a misalignment of ideas and reality, Arlt's novels do not provide orientation in national terms. Indeed, they do not seem to provide any positive orientation at all. In refusing the nationalist problematic, Arlt does not adopt a cosmopolitan perspective at the expense of the specificity of the national situation. Rather, *LSL/LL* express the truth of Argentine society in the 1920s and 1930s—and the truth of the peripheral form of capitalism—because they tarry with the negative, because they take seriously the impossibility of community as a problem that cannot simply be overcome with nationalist anti-imperialism.

By taking the way of despair, Arlt identifies the contradictions of this form of social life. The central contradiction, according to Masotta's analysis of Arlt, lies in the way that the reaction to humiliation gets directed not at the executioner but at others who also suffer humiliation. With this betrayal, self-assertion becomes indistinguishable from self-submission to the forces of domination and exploitation. The social world of *LSL/LL*, in other words, involves a dialectical relation in which the transgression of the rules regulating social life actually sustains those rules. In the words of Roberto Schwarz, "as well as being an infringement, the infringement is the norm, and the norm, as well as being a norm, is an infringement" (*Master* 25). For Schwarz, this relationship between norm and infringement describes both the formal rhythm of the prose in Machado de Assis's *The Posthumous Memoirs of Brás Cubas* and the apparent peculiarity that nineteenth-century Brazil was integrated into global capitalism precisely on the basis of its slave economy. The Brazilian elite embraced the normative commitments of liberal, bourgeois society, but the realities of slavery blatantly contradicted, or infringed on, these ideas. The infringement becomes the norm insofar as these ideas undergo an adjustment to the new context, justifying, rather than denouncing, an incompatible reality.

If this constitutes a dialectical relationship, it might be more appropriate to call it, following Paulo Arantes, a "negative dialectic." In Arantes's account, this "permanent reversibility of norm and infringement"

(*Sentimento* 93) appears alongside "the modern birth of the independent subject, the quasi-liberatory moment of indeterminacy between an *ancien régime* in agony and the not-yet established new bourgeois order" (95). The negative dialectic, in other words, characterizes the normative disintegration of a form of social life, a breakdown that prepares for the institution of a new social order. But in Brazil the form of social life reproduces itself through unresolved crisis. Instead of marking a world-historical transition from traditional to modern society, the negative dialectic now derives from a "practical foundation in the 'duality' ... of the national formation" (*Sentimento* 93). This dialectic is negative because it "articulates the 'two Brazils,'" the colonial and the modern, "without synthesis" or overcoming (93). "[E]verything happens," Arantes suggests, "as if in Brazil the Enlightenment switched its signal: separated from its reformist impulse, ... it was reduced to *an inventory of modern appearances* on offer for the dissipation of a cultured man" (98, my emphasis). Arantes insists that this reduction of enlightened ideas to appearances does not constitute a mere infringement of the normativity of modern capitalism. "If, on the one hand, the periphery does not reproduce itself according to the rules of the center," then we might say, "on the other hand, this exception to the rule is not a mere exception, but its opposite: it expresses a precise truth about the rule. That is, *it reveals the link between the norm and the exception*" (Caux & Catalani 131).[98] The periphery, in other words, discloses the truth of global capitalism precisely through its incessant, inconclusive inversion of the norms regulating the economic system.

In light of Arantes's comments, we can see the misalignment of ideas and reality in *LSL/LL* as an expression of the peripheral situation. But, whereas the coordinates of this misalignment in Schwarz's analysis of Machado de Assis align with the contradiction between the slave economy and the liberal ideology cynically adopted by the Brazilian elite, in *LSL/LL* the misalignment has been internalized by disoriented, *déclassé* intellectuals. The Astrologer's speeches, to paraphrase Schwarz on Brás Cubas, have "recourse to the stock" of radical "appearances," but these appearances are "subordinated to a principle contrary to" them insofar as the ideas are "soon abandoned for others and thus discredited" (*Master* 23). The Astrologer's ideas do not pass the test of reality, so to speak, and yet it is precisely this failure that indexes their adequacy to the peripheral context.

---

[98] Along these lines, Kefala writes: "Arlt's novel is primarily a cogniscape of the enlightened society turned inside out" (101).

Insofar as appearances appear as appearances, not as an expression of an underlying essence, they express a context in which explicit norms must be accompanied by a contrary set of rules regulating actual social relations.

The specificity of Arlt's negative dialectic as an expression of peripheral capitalism can be found in the *aguafuerte* "El arte de juntar puchos" (The Art of Collecting Cigarette Butts, 1931). In this piece, which forms the basis of a chapter in *Los lanzallamas*, Roberto Arlt discusses how desperate *porteños* devised inventive strategies to deal with the harsh economic realities of the interwar period. Arlt quotes a man he met in a café:

> This city lacks nothing in misery and poverty to match European cities. The only thing that distinguishes us from over there are *appearances*. Because, tell me: "Who, seeing my look, this cheap tie, my cheap boots, my cheap suit, my cheap hat, which all together give me the *appearance* of a decent person, could suspect that many nights, at twelve or one in the morning, I go out to gather cigarette butts in the streets so I have something to smoke the next day?" (*Aguafuertes* 239, my emphasis)[99]

The acquaintance begins by asserting that Buenos Aires has caught up to the European metropolis. But these cities have become equals in terms of misery, not modernization. And yet, he insists that the *porteño* clings more desperately to the fading appearance of distinction than the inhabitants of London, Berlin, and Paris. Each individual article of clothing indexes his poverty, but he knows how to arrange them to give "the appearance of a decent person." Additionally, this acquaintance continues to smoke by recovering the scraps of bourgeois society, by searching for butts in wealthy neighborhoods where a rich *porteño* might take a drag or two before causally throwing the cigarette onto the street. In the peripheral metropolis, appearances do not reliably index social standing. As Scalabrini Ortiz puts it, the porteño cannot be deduced. But this makes appearances all the more important.

When appearances become essential despite their unreliability, the situation demands a cynical attitude of suspicion and belief, a stance that in

---

[99] "A esta ciudad ya nada le falta en miseria y pobreza para igualarse a las ciudades europeas. Lo único que nos diferencia de allá son las apariencias. Porque, decime: ¿Quién viendo mi pinta, esta corbata regalada, mis botines regalados, mi traje regalado, mi sombrero regalado, que en conjunto contribuyen a darme la apariencia de una persona decente, puede sospechar que yo, muchas noches, a las doce o la una, salgo a juntar puchos por las calles para tener con qué fumar al otro día?"

Arlt's work derives from the unstable position of the middle class but also expresses the truth of the situation itself. For Masotta, middle-class existence, aspiring to the status of the wealthy but always at the risk of proletarianization, generates the uneasy feeling of "the inner void of what it does not have," that "what is hidden threatens at every moment to come to light" (88). Citing Claude Lanzmann, Masotta describes how the employee "who typically receives his salary in an envelope, keeps a secret, keeping quiet about the amount or exaggerating it" (89). No matter the circumstances, he must "keep up appearances" by, for instance, dedicating "a major part of what he earns to dressing with decency" (90). Decent appearances, in other words, conceal the vulnerability of middle-class existence in the social world of Arlt's novels, but the independence of appearances is also demanded by those precarious conditions. This discordant coexistence of what should be overcome indicates the anomic character of peripheral capitalism: not the absence of norms, but a dual normative structure in which inhabiting this form of social life means being obligated and prohibited to follow a specific course of action, being compelled at the same time to transgress and sustain normative commitments.

I would argue that *LSL/LL* give the most striking expression to this anomie in the recurring instances of suicide. As I mentioned above, the Astrologer claims: "Once science has extinguished all faith, nobody will want to go on with a purely mechanical existence ... an incurable plague will return to the earth ... the plague of suicide" (142/153).[100] Arturo Haffner, we learn, acquires the nickname "the Melancholy Thug" because he attempted suicide. Most prominently, suicide follows Erdosain throughout the novels. In the penultimate chapter of *Los siete locos*, Erdosain falls asleep at a café, and when the waiter wakes him up, he discovers that another man at the café, apparently asleep, had committed suicide. This man, Erdosain learns, left his wife and children to live with another woman, but he ends up killing her and sitting with her dead corpse in a hotel room for five hours before leaving and then taking his own life. The Astrologer claims that Erdosain must have hallucinated the story because he could find no evidence of the incident in the newspapers. Either way, the suicide anticipates Erdosain's own fate in *Los lanzallamas*. After killing La Bizca and spending three days recounting events to the commentator,

---

[100] "Nadie tendrá interés en conservar una existencia de carácter mecánico, porque la ciencia ha cercenado toda fe. Y en el momento que se produzca tal fenómeno, reaparecerá sobre la tierra una peste incurable ... la peste del suicidio."

Erdosain boards a train and shoots himself in the chest. These instances of suicide in *LSL/LL* differ from the role suicide plays in Dostoevsky's *Demons*, the putative model for Arlt's novels. In *Demons*, Kirillov asserts that he will become God through suicide. "If there is God," Kirillov tells Pyotr Stepanovich, "then the will is all his, and I cannot get out of his will. If not, the will is all mine, and it is my duty to proclaim self-will," and suicide, killing oneself "without any reason," constitutes "the fullest point of [his] self-will" (617). Suicide, in other words, constitutes the ultimate experiment. This sort of conception of suicide, indeed, can be found in *LSL/LL*, for instance, when Erdosain tells Hipólita: "Look, if you … if you were to ask me to kill myself here and now, I'd do it with pleasure" (192/224).[101] Erdosain makes this proposal after Hipólita has explained that she became a prostitute to free herself from her body. The idea of killing himself for her seems to similarly express a desire to overcome his base existence: not only the humiliation of his life but also the criminal activities he has undertaken with the Astrologer. But if suicide continues to be an expression of self-will in *LSL/LL*, it would be more accurate to say that the novels bring to light what Lukács calls "the loss of all direction in instincts" underlying suicide, thereby establishing the inseparability of self-assertion and self-submission. It is perhaps no coincidence that the chapter in which Erdosain discovers the suicide in the café is also the moment he makes his Rastignac declaration to conquer the city while getting shoved on the street and tailed by the Major.

Indeed, we could almost read *LSL/LL* as a fictional account of what Émile Durkheim called "anomic suicide." In his foundational work *Suicide: A Study in Sociology* (1897), Durkheim articulates this conception of anomie to distinguish a peculiar social phenomenon of suicide from other types: altruistic, egoistic, and fatalistic.[102] Anomie, in this framework, grasps the erosion of the shared norms regulating social relations and individual conduct, the breakdown of solidarity in its mechanical and organic forms. In other words, anomie corresponds to what Masotta calls the

---

[101] "Mirá, si vos … si usted me pidiera ahora que me matara, lo haría encantado."

[102] Durkheim offers the following helpful summary: "Egoistic suicide results from man's no longer finding a basis for existence in life; altruistic suicide, because this basis for existence appears to man situated beyond life itself. The third sort of suicide, the existence of which has just been shown, results from man's activity's lacking regulation and his consequent suffering" (219). Durkheim pays less attention to fatalistic suicide, but it should be understood as the opposite of anomic suicide—that is, instead of the lack of regulation, fatalism involves an excess of regulation.

"impossibility of community" in Arlt's novels. It might seem as if anomie were synonymous with the expansion of individualistic demands in conflict with social exigencies, but Durkheim takes pains to analytically separate egoistic suicide and anomic suicide. Indeed, anomie means, as Lukács describes it in the Dostoevsky essay, that individuality becomes problematic. The weakening of shared norms generates anguish and indeterminacy, a paralyzing uncertainty about what is expected of us and what course of action to take. In an anomic context—for instance, a moment of rapid social change—the normative sense of limits dissolves and we are plunged into the "insatiable and bottomless abyss" of "unlimited desires" (208). "[W]hen one walks toward no goal," Durkheim writes, "one does not advance" (208). Unlimited desire, in other words, produces "infinity sickness," a perpetual dissatisfaction with finite existence: "Reality seems valueless by comparison with the dreams of fevered imaginations" (216–7). This restless drive for infinity, rendering reality meaningless, characterizes for Durkheim the capitalist mode of production. Durkheim holds that capitalism institutes a form of organic solidarity in which social integration proceeds through the dependence of each upon all in the division of labor, but he also recognizes the tendency in capitalism to dissolve the binding power of social norms because of its ceaseless demand to overcome every barrier in the pursuit of profit. We have all become utterly dependent on others for our well-being, but because money "deceives us into believing that we depend on ourselves only," every normative limitation appears as an "intolerable" limitation and every concrete commitment seems meaningless (214). Economic crises, in general, produce anomie because the normative framework of expectations suddenly fails to regulate social life as it had before. But in capitalism, Durkheim asserts, that "state of crisis and anomie is constant and, so to speak, normal" (216).

Durkheim's comments about the relation between capitalism and anomie may appear restricted to "advanced" economies, where the tendencies of capitalism have fully developed, but we actually find this aspect laid bare in the periphery. In his remarkable essay "A fratura brasileira do mundo" (The Brazilian Fracture of the World, 2001), to which I will return in the conclusion, Arantes argues that "the absolute prevalence (and transparency) of economic reason" in the formation of Brazilian society calls into question the very idea of it constituting a "society," strictly speaking (*Zero* 59). Recalling how the Brazilian national formation was forged as a colony producing for the European market, Arantes quotes the economist Celso Furtado: "economic criteria were superimposed on everything. Few times in human history has a social formation been conditioned in the genesis of its form so completely by economic factors" (59). Based in "brute economic exploitation," the result, Arantes claims, now citing the Brazilian historian Caio Prado Junior, has been the "lack of a moral nexus," the absence of normative institutions that "maintain individuals linked and united in a society and integrate them into a cohesive, compact whole" (59). If, as Arantes insists, anomie characterizes the Brazilian social formation—and, I would argue, the Argentine situation—in its very core, then we have to set aside the idea of anomie as a temporary loss of norms and take seriously Durkheim's suggestion that it may become a chronic, normal state of affairs. In this case, it would be more accurate to speak not of normlessness but of what Vladimir Safatle calls a "dual normative structure." For Safatle, the "rationalization of peripheral countries" generates "a sort of dual normative structure in which the enunciated law is always accompanied by another implicit set of rules the regulates the actual processes of interaction in the social field" (*Cinismo* 78). In such a situation, social norms do not simply disappear; appeals to normative criteria continue to be made. But the "normative expectations that aspire to universal validity" somehow come to coexist with the demand to overcome every normative limit (139). These normative criteria thereby become, as in the case of Arlt's acquaintance gathering cigarette butts, the appearances that must be maintained even though they have no bearing on the realities of brutal inequality and the limitless demands of capital accumulation.

As we have seen in this chapter, Arlt's novels suggest that, as Safatle puts it, "the paradoxical synthesis" of this dual normative structure "can only be made through cynicism" (*Cinismo* 139). While Arlt shared with some of his Argentine contemporaries a sense of the atomization and alienation of urban life, they suspected that these issues could be resolved through the construction of a national identity. They, in other words, wanted to give the urban masses something to believe. In this way, these nationalist intellectuals formally resemble the Astrologer. But Arlt, because of his distance from the national question, was able to take the problems of urban life seriously, that is, to see the full extent of the issue without rushing to a positive solution. In his weekly column, he held that we cannot believe anything. But the novels show, more crucially, that he grasped how distrust depends on an underlying belief and vice versa. It is this negative dialectic of belief and distrust, one constantly inverting into the other without overcoming the opposition, that makes his characters so cynical. And this is what makes *LSL/LL* such a compelling depiction of the peripheral situation. "In the metropolis," Arantes writes, "everyone does it, but strictly speaking they know nothing, whereas in the periphery everyone knows very well what they are doing" (*Zero* 109). But, we might add, they do not necessarily grasp the significance of what they are doing. The novels, by contrast, grasp the truth of this situation by articulating this negative dialectic of belief and distrust in their formal composition. The Astrologer does not believe in "metaphysical lies"; he cynically manipulates such belief. But he does not know where he is going. Ultimately, his activities indicate an ardent, albeit confused, belief in the existing state of affairs, a belief that has been disavowed and attributed to others. Erdosain, by contrast, passionately feels the need to believe, to perform an experiment that would prove to himself who he is. But his experiments only aggravate his humiliation, splitting his subjectivity into, on the one hand, a putative hero who would accomplish great works and, on the other hand, a lackey who would know the base motivations for such actions. Cynicism in *LSL/LL* thus does not appear as the subversive unmaking of false expressions of decency; rather, it is disclosed as a way to "stabilize a situation that, in other circumstances, would be a typical and unsustainable situation of crisis and anomie" (Safalte, *Cinismo* 14).

Bibliography

Amícola, José. *Astrología y fascismo en la obra de Arlt*. Beatriz Viterbo Editorial, 1994.
Aricó, José. *Marx and Latin America*. Translated by David Broder, Brill, 2014.
Arantes, Paulo. *Sentimento da dialética na experiência intelectual brasileira: dialética e dualidade segundo Antonio Candido e Roberto Schwarz*. Paz e Terra, 1992.
———. *Zero à esquerda*. Conrad Editoria do Brasil, 2004.
Arlt, Roberto. *Las aguafuertes porteñas de Roberto Arlt: Publicadas en "El Mundo", 1928-1933*. Edited by Daniel C. Scroggins, Ediciones Culturales Argentinas, 1981.
———. *Aguafuertes porteñas*. Editorial Losada, 2008.
———. *Los siete locos. Los lanzallamas*. Edited by Mario Goloboff, Colección Archivos, 2000.
———. *The Seven Madmen*. Translated by Nick Caistor, New York Review of Books, 2015.
Bakhtin, Mikhail. *Problems of Dostoevsky's Poetics*. Translated by R. W. Rostel, Ardis, 1973.
Bloch, Ernst. *Literary Essays*. Translated by Andrew Joron, edited by Werner Hamacher & David E. Wellbery, Stanford University Press, 1998.

Brandom, Robert. "Reason, Genealogy, and the Hermeneutics of Magnanimity." Townsend Lecture. University of California, Berkeley, November 21, 2012. University of California, Berkeley. Lecture.

Brassier, Ray. "Dialectics Between Suspicion and Trust." *Stasis* 4, no. 2 (2016): 98–113.

Breckman, Warren. "Diagnosing the 'German Misery': Radicalism and the Problem of National Character, 1830–1848." *Between Reform and Revolution: German Socialism and Communism from 1840 to 1900*, edited by David E. Barclay & Eric D. Weitz, Berghahn Books, 1998, pp. 33–62.

Caux, Luiz Philipe de & Felipe Catalani. "A passagem do dois ao zero: dualidade e desintegração no pensamento dialético brasileiro (Paulo Arantes, leitor de Roberto Schwarz." *Revista do Instituto de Estudos Brasileiros*, vol. 74, 2019, pp. 119–146.

Close, Glen. *La imprenta enterrada: Baroja, Arlt y el imaginario anarquista*. Beatriz Viterbo Editora, 2000.

Cunningham, David. "The Concept of the Metropolis: Philosophy and Urban Form." *Radical Philosophy*, vol. 133, 2005, 13–25.

Davis, Mike. *Planet of Slums*. Verso, 2006.

Demaría, Laura. *Buenos Aires y las provincias: Relatos para desarmar*. Beatriz Viterbo Editora, 2014.

Dostoevsky, Fyodor. *Demons*. Translated by Richard Pevear & Larissa Volokhonsky, Vintage, 1994.

Durkheim, Émile. *Suicide: A Study in Sociology*, translated by John A. Spaulding & George Simpson, Routledge, 2002.

Einarsdottir, A. B. "'El bacilo de Carlos Marx,' or, Roberto Arlt, the Leninist." *A Contracorriente: Una Revista De Estudios Latinoamericanos*, vol. 18, no. 2, pp. 92–123.

Flint, J. M. "Politics and Society in the Novels of Roberto Arlt." *Ibero-amerikanishces Archiv*, 2, no. 2 (1976): 155–163.

Frank, Joseph. *Dostoevsky: The Miraculous Years, 1865–1871*, Princeton University Press, 1995.

Gorelik, Adrián. *La grilla y el parque: Espacio público y cultura urbana en Buenos Aires, 1887–1936*. Universidad Nacional de Quilmes, 1998.

———. "Images for a Mythological Foundation: Notes on Horacio Coppola's Photographs of Buenos Aires." *Journal of Latin American Cultural Studies*, vol. 24, no. 2, 2015, pp. 109–121.

Gramsci, Antonio. *Selections from the Prison Notebooks of Antonio Gramsci*. International Publishers, 1971.

Hegel, G. W. F. *The Phenomenology of Spirit*. Translated by Terry Pinkard, Cambridge University Press, 2018.

Herf, Jeffrey. *Reactionary Modernism: Technology, Culture, and Politics in Weimar and the Third Reich*. Cambridge University Press, 1984.

Jünger, Ernst. *On Pain*. Translated by David C. Durst, Telos Press, 2008.
Karatani, Kojin. *History and Repetition*. Edited by Seji M. Lippit, Columbia University Press, 2011.
Kefala, Eleni. *Buenos Aires Across the Arts: Five and One Theses on Modernity, 1921–1939*. University of Pittsburgh Press, 2022.
Laclau, Ernesto. "Modos de producción, sistemas económicos y población excedente, aproximación histórica a los casos argentino y chileno." *Revista Latinoamericana de Sociología*, vol. 69, no. 2, 1970, pp. 276–316.
Larsen, Neil. *Modernism and Hegemony: A Materialist Critique of Aesthetic Agencies*. University of Minnesota Press, 1990.
Leland, Christopher T. *The Last Happy Men: The Generation of 1922, Fiction, and the Argentine Reality*. Syracuse University Press, 1986.
Lukács, Georg. "Dostoevsky." *Marxism and Human Liberation: Essays on History, Culture and Revolution by Georg Lukács*, edited by E. San Juan, Jr., Delta, 1973, pp. 179–197.
———. "Stavrogin's Confession." *Reviews and Articles from* Die rote Fahne, translated by Peter Palmer, Merlin Press, 1988, pp. 44–48.
Martínez Estrada, Ezequiel. *Radiografía de la pampa*. Edited by Leo Pollmann, Colección Archivos, 1996.
———. *La cabeza de Goliat. Microscopía de Buenos Aires*. Editorial Losada, 1994.
Marx, Karl. *The Portable Karl Marx*. Edited by Eugene Kamenka, Penguin, 1983.
———. *Capital: A Critique of Political Economy, Volume I*. Translated by Ben Fowkes, Penguin, 1990.
———. *Grundrisse: Foundations of the Critique of Political Economy*. Translated by Martin Nicholaus, Penguin, 1993.
———. *Surveys from Exile: Political Writings*. Verso, 2010.
Masiello, Francine. *Lenguaje e ideología: Las escuelas argentinas de vanguardia*. Hachette, 1986.
Masotta, Óscar. *Sexo y traición en Roberto Arlt*. Eterna Cadencia Editora, 2014.
Mehlman, Jeffrey. *Revolution and Repetition: Marx/Hugo/Balzac*. University of California Press, 1977.
Onetti, Juan Carlos. "Semblanza de un genio rioplatense." *Nueva novela latinoamericana*. Ed. J. Lafforgue. Vol. II. (Buenos Aires: Paidos, 1972): pp. 363–377.
Ortega y Gasset, José. *Obras completas de José Ortega y Gasset: Tomo V, 1933–1941*. Revista de Occidente, 1964.
Petrey, Sandy. "The Reality of Representation: Between Marx and Balzac." *Critical Inquiry*, vol. 14, no. 3, 1988, pp. 448–468.
Piglia, Ricardo. *Crítica y ficción*. Anagrama, 1986.
———. *Artificial Respiration*. Translated by Daniel Balderston, Duke University Press, 1994.

———. "Roberto Arlt and the Fiction of Money." *Journal of Latin American Cultural Studies*, vol. 8, no. 1, 1999, pp. 13–16.
Postone, Moishe. *Time, Labor and Social Domination: A Reinterpretation of Marx's Critical Theory*. Cambridge University Press, 1996.
———. "An Interview with Moishe Postone: That Capital Has Limits Does Not Mean That It Will Collapse." *Crisis & Critique*, vol. 3, no. 1, 2016, pp. 501–515.
Prebisch, Alberto. "Una ciudad de América." *Sur*, vol. 1, no. 2, 1931, pp. 216–220.
Prieto, Adolfo. "La fantasía y lo fantástico en Roberto Arlt." *Boletín de Literaturas Hispánicas*, vol. 5, 1963, pp. 5–18.
Prieto, Julio. *La escritura errante: Ilegibilidad y políticas del estilo en Latinoamérica*. Iberoamericana, 2016.
Rama, Ángel. *The Lettered City*. Translated by John Charles Chasteen, Duke University Press, 1996.
———. *Writing across Cultures: Narrative Transculturation in Latin America*. Translated by David Frye, Duke University Press, 2012.
Read, Justin. "Topofilia Porteña: Imaging Buenos Aires and Modernity in (and around) the Journal *Sur*." *Spectacle and Topophilia: Reading Early Modern and Postmodern Hispanic Cultures*. Ed. David R. Castillo & Bradley J. Nelson. Nashville: Vanderbilt University Press, 2012. 113–136.
Renaud, Maryse. "La ciudad babilónica o los entretelones del mundo urbano en *Los siete locos* y *Los lanzallamas*." *La selva en el damero: Espacio literario y espacio urbano en América Latina*, edited by Rosalba Campra, Giardini Editori, 1989, pp. 195–213.
Rock, David. *Authoritarian Argentina: The Nationalist Movement, Its History and Its Impact*. University of California Press, 1993.
Romero, Luis Alberto. *A History of Argentina in the Twentieth Century*. Translated by James P. Brennan, The Pennsylvania State University Press, 2013.
Rosenberg, Fernando J. *The Avant-Garde and Geopolitics in Latin America*. University of Pittsburgh Press, 2006.
Safatle, Vladimir. *Cinismo e falência da crítica*. Boitempo Editorial, 2008.
———. *Dar corpo ao impossível: O sentido da dialética a partir de Theodor Adorno*. Autêntica, 2019.
Sarlo, Beatriz. *Una modernidad periférica: Buenos Aires, 1920 y 1930*. Ediciones Nueva Visión, 1988.
———. *Imaginación técnica: Sueños modernos de la cultura argentina*. Ediciones Nueva Visión, 1992a.
———. "Arlt: ciudad real, ciudad imaginaria, ciudad reformada." *Punto de vista*, vol. 42, 1992b, pp. 15–21.
———. *Jorge Luis Borges: A Writer on the Edge*. Edited by John King, Verso, 1993.

———. "The Modern City: Buenos Aires, The Peripheral Metropolis." *Through the Kaleidoscope: The Experience of Modernity in Latin America*, edited by Vivian Schelling, Verso, 2000, pp. 108–124.

———. *Escritos sobre literatura argentina*. Siglo Veintiuno Editores, 2007.

Sartre, Jean-Paul. *Literary and Philosophical Essays*. Translated by Annette Michelson, Collier Books, 1962.

Scalabrini Ortiz, Raúl. *El hombre que está solo y espera*. Editorial Plus Ultra, 1964.

Schwarz, Roberto. *Misplaced Ideas: Essays on Brazilian Culture*. Translated by John Gledson, Verso, 1992.

———. *A Master on the Periphery of Capitalism: Machado de Assis*. Translated by John Gledson, Duke University Press, 2001.

———. *Two Girls and Other Essays*, translated by John Gledson, Verso Books, 2012.

Simmel, Georg. *The Sociology of Georg Simmel*. Trans. Kurt H. Wolff, The Free Press, 1950.

Sloterdijk, Peter. *Critique of Cynical Reason*. Translated by Michael Eldred, University of Minnesota Press, 1987.

Stanley, Sharon. "Retreat from Politics: The Cynic in Modern Times." *Polity*, vol. 39, no. 3, 2007: 384–407.

Sohn-Rethel, Alfred. *Intellectual and Manual Labor: A Critique of Epistemology*. Macmillan, 1978.

Wells, Robert. "It's Complicated—Ortega y Gasset's Relationship with Argentina." *Transatlantic Studies: Latin America, Iberia, and Africa*. Edited by Cecilia Enjuto-Rangel, Sebastiaan Faber, Pedro García-Caro & Robert Patrick Newcomb, Liverpool University Press, 2019, pp. 418–31.

Williamson, Edwin. *The Penguin History of Latin America*. Penguin Books, 1992.

CHAPTER 5

"There's Only One Crisis. The Sexual Crisis": Modernist Dissociation and the Reserve Army in Patrícia Galvão's *Parque Industrial*

Horríveis as cidades!
Vaidades e mais vaidades ...
Nada de asas! Nada de poesia! Nada de alegria!
Oh! os tumultuários das ausências!
Paulicéia—a grande boca de mil dentes;
e os jorros dentre a língua trissulca
de pus e de mais pus de distinção ...
Giram homens fracos, baixos, magros ...
Serpentinas de entes frementes a se desenrolar ...

Mário de Andrade, "Os cortejos"

As I have been arguing throughout *Modernism in the Peripheral Metropolis*, peripheral social formations do not contingently enter into a crisis; rather, they are what they are on the basis of crisis. The peripheral situation reproduces itself through brutal forms of social disunity, through the integration of opposed normative commitments that would normally need to be overcome to prevent collapse. This thesis, however, does not imply that a crisis of international capitalism appears as a matter of indifference for

© The Author(s), under exclusive license to Springer Nature Switzerland AG 2023
T. Mulder, *Modernism in the Peripheral Metropolis*, New Comparisons in World Literature,
https://doi.org/10.1007/978-3-031-34055-0_5

Latin America. Rather, my argument suggests that a crisis like the Great Depression—to which we turn in this chapter through the work of the Brazilian Patrícia Galvão—presents itself in the periphery as the actualization of contradictions in the organizing principles of society, not as inexplicable event that comes "out of nowhere." Accordingly, when the stock market crashed in 1929, it represented not the spectacular, unexpected collapse of the system, but rather, in Tulio Halperín Donghi's words, "a rude anticlimax to half a century of economic expansion composed of discrete local cycles of boom and bust (many of which had reached the end of their prosperity well before 1930)" (169). In Latin America, the crash did not suddenly throw into question a system that had been functioning normally. Instead, it definitively confirmed that the export system had failed to fulfill its promise of development.

To explain how the crash resonated among Latin American intellectuals, Antonio Candido in "Literatura e subdesenvolvimento" (Literature and Underdevelopment, 1970) characterizes the perspective emerging in the 1930s as a shift from the idea of "the new country" to a consciousness of underdevelopment. The first, formed in the euphoria of the boom of the export era, displays an "interest in the exotic," the veneration of the "grandiose," and, most fundamentally, it marveled at the "possibilities" that seemed to be in store for such a new country (35). But when the bubble of possibilities deflated over the course of the twenties and thirties, intellectuals became increasingly preoccupied with current conditions of underdevelopment: "the reality of the poor lands, the archaic technologies, the astonishing misery of the people, the paralyzing lack of culture" (37). Where the idea of the new country sees promise, the consciousness of underdevelopment finds frustration. Out of this frustration, Candido asserts, writers developed a "combative" attitude and made "a decision to struggle" (37). These writers could no longer assume that the problems facing Latin America would resolve themselves as the continent realized its potential in due time. Literature, in this new structure of feeling, would thus need to abandon its contemplative detachment from social concerns and commit itself to an ideological, political project. Moreover, as the reference to "poor lands" suggests, Candido finds that this shift manifests itself in the meaning ascribed to nature. It is thus predominantly in the regionalist literature of the period, according to Candido, that this sense of political commitment finds expression. This regionalism, abandoning its previous affinity with the naturalist focus on the picturesque, becomes critical through its "consciousness of crisis, motivating the documentary and, with a feeling of urgency, political engagement" (53). The crisis of the thirties, in short, prompted not only commitment, but also a turn away from the cosmopolitan city toward the particularity of the region as manifested in the countryside.

We might infer that Candido formulates this compelling account of Latin American cultural production during the collapse of the export system because the outlines of such a framework can be found in the history of Brazilian *modernismo*. Critics typically understand Brazilian *modernismo* as moving from a "heroic" phase in the twenties to a "mature" stage in the thirties. Or, in an alternative formulation, the initially "aesthetic" project developed into an "ideological" undertaking.[1] *Modernismo*'s "heroic" or "aesthetic" moment began with the historic *Semana de Arte Moderna* (Modern Art Week) held in São Paulo during February of 1922. The *Semana* brought together various artists and writers—including Mário de Andrade, Oswald de Andrade, Tarsila do Amaral, Anita Malfatti, among others—who aimed to effect a break with the stultified atmosphere of Brazilian intellectual and cultural life. To accomplish this aim, they insisted on the need to synchronize Brazilian art with the avant-gardes in Europe and to rediscover the popular elements of national culture. In effect, Brazilian *modernismo* in the twenties embodied a belief in the compatibility of national-popular and cosmopolitan orientations for Latin American avant-garde art. However, with the onset of the economic crisis and changes in the political landscape, formal experimentation appeared inconsistent with what came to be the urgent goal of the thirties, namely, the affirmation of a mass-based national identity.[2] Mário de Andrade, for instance, expresses this view in his own history of the movement, *O movimento modernista* (The Modernist Movement, 1942), when he describes how the "intellectual orgy" of the twenties settled in the following decade into "a calmer, more modest and quotidian, more proletarian phase, so to

---

[1] For the characterization of Brazilian *modernismo* in terms of its "aesthetic" and "ideological" phases, see João Luiz Lafetá, *1930: a crítica e o modernismo*.
[2] As Carlos Jáuregui nicely puts it, the *modernista* "party came to an end with the crisis that followed the stock market crash of 1929, the coffee sector's loss of political hegemony and the ascent of populist nationalism to power represented by Getúlio Vargas" (40).

speak, of construction" (34, 43).[3] The paradigmatic literature of the thirties would thus not be the urban, cubist poetry of Mário de Andrade's *Paulicéia Desvairada* (1922) or Oswald de Andrade's cubo-expressionist manifestos, but rather the regionalist novels of Jorge Amado and Gracilano Ramos. The spirit of *modernismo* continued in these regionalist novels through the focus on folk elements of Brazilian culture, but realism appeared as a more adequate vehicle for revealing social conditions and expressing indignation at the underdevelopment of the country. Jorge Amado, for instance, affirms in a note at the beginning of his novel *Cacau* (Cocoa, 1933) that this story about quasi-slave conditions in the northeastern state of Bahía was told with "a minimum of literature and a maximum of honesty" (137). He ends the note with a question that provoked debate among Brazilian intellectuals and writers: "Will it be a proletarian novel?" (137).[4]

For Amado, this was a question. For Patrícia Galvão, it was a statement.[5] Her novel *Parque industrial* (Industrial Park), published in 1933, the same year as Amado's *Cacau*, contains the subtitle, "Proletarian Novel." Indeed, Galvão's novel was the first self-described proletarian novel in Brazil. Galvão, also known by her nickname Pagu, thus unmistakably joins the current of committed writers of the thirties. But whereas Amado and Ramos turned their attention to the rural northeast, Galvão's novel attempts to represent the brutal conditions for women workers in

[3] This characterization also parallels Sarah Wells's recent argument about late modernism in South America, albeit with a focus on media. Wells describes the shift in the following way: "In the first decades of the twentieth century, São Paulo had been positioned as the stage for the most triumphant of the Latin American avant-gardes, ripe with futurist promise. It would be up to those writing in the wake of this period to trace the residual oligarchical system that underpinned this modernizing thrust, to probe the underside of this futurity" ("Mass Culture" 56).

[4] Guedes argues that this question betrays an uncertainty and a desire for reconciliation, whereas *Parque industrial* exhibits fully developed contradictions: "O tom da dúvida talvez prenuncie o temperamento dessa escrita, que deseja a acolhida muito mais que o questionamento, ou a destruição e superação de qualquer coisa que seja. Nesse sentido, as tensões formais procuram ser evitadas. E as decisões narrativas parecem buscar, a todo momento, uma postura conciliatória. Há a presença de fala do homem simples, mas em discurso direto, delimitando seu lugar e não lhe permitiendo mesclar-se à fala culta do narrador. A inovação e o 'engamento' se fazem pela presença da voz proletária, no entanto, ela não está posta como problema" (108).

[5] For a comparison of Galvão and Amado and the regionalist novel more broadly, see João Carlos Ribeiro Junior, *Literatura e política no romance de Patrícia Galvão*, pp. 66–74.

industrial São Paulo.[6] Moreover, *Parque industrial* eschews the realism prevailing among the regionalists in favor of modernist montage and abstraction. According to Thelma Guedes, *Parque industrial* should be understood as an attempt to synthesize apparently incompatible formal techniques: "reportage, pamphlet, and literary experiment" (55).[7] By employing modernist techniques for documentary purposes, Galvão inherits and radicalizes the *modernista* commitment to synthesize formal experimentation and national-popular content. The viability of such a project would thus depend on the novel's ability to communicate with women workers in São Paulo, that is, the very subjects of Galvão's novel.

This was undoubtedly Galvão's intention in *Parque industrial*. Indeed, the novel can be read compellingly as an attempt to establish a relation with the masses by sidestepping and undermining the authoritarian populism of then-president Getúlio Vargas.[8] But, as I have argued throughout *Modernism in the Peripheral Metropolis*, if we focus on the work's relationship to a putatively national-popular audience, we fail to recognize that such a relationship poses a problem, not a solution, for modernist writers and artists. Given the brutal forms of inequality and illiteracy in the periphery, the modernist cannot rely on pre-existing conventions for communication. Instead, it is through the autonomy of the work—that is, its internal organization—that the work acknowledges and makes intelligible the historical forces at work in the dissociated forms of social life in the

[6] According to Jackson, "Unlike regional works, the urban social novel could not be 'saved' by picturesque description or by the folkloric or indigenous themes then highly valued in the creation of the idea of a national character" (126). Similarly, Randal Johnson, drawing on the work of José Miguel Wisnik, argues that "the modernists tended to adopt and stylize only those forms deriving from *rural* popular culture, which they idealized as the 'pure, hidden physiognomy of the nation.' They tended to reject the emerging *urban* popular culture, such as that of black or proletarian communities, which reflected the social contradictions of urban society" (200).

[7] Or, in Guedes's more elaborate formulation, "um realismo revolucionário não-edificante, sob a forma de romance experimental que, mais do que apoiar e tomar partido, assume a voz de um grupo social oprimido—mulheres operárias" (40). João Carlos Ribeiro Junior undertakes a similar approach when he states, "*Em uma obra com relevo panfletário, supomas que a análise revele as contradições daquilo que ela promove em relação com o material que ela configurou*" (17, emphasis in the original).

[8] Sarah Wells, for instance, argues persuasively that Galvão uses cinema to articulate a relation to the masses and thus offer up "the proletarian voice ... as an antidote to a phenomenon that is also emerging during the period, one connected to the struggle to represent the masses: that of populism in its emergent construction of politics as spectacle" ("Mass Culture" 68).

periphery. Accordingly, this chapter will emphasize, in the words of Roberto Schwarz, "the mimetic value of the *composition*, as against the descriptive value of the parts" (*Two Girls* 17). When we read *Parque industrial* in terms of form as a "profound synthesis of the movement of history … that cannot be grasped in the immediacy of events" (Schwarz 17), we find not only the documentation of exploitative conditions in São Paulo or the articulation of the revolutionary goals of women workers; we also find a modernist dissonance specifically attuned to those aspects of the Brazilian situation that would prove to be salient for peripheral capitalism more broadly.

Galvão's novel presents the brutal conditions of industrialization in São Paulo through a series of vignettes or snapshots of the lives of anonymous, seemingly dispensable, characters. I argue that the significance of these moments does not lie in their photographic or documentary immediacy. When we grasp the relationship of these parts of the novel to the whole, we find a formal pattern that makes these characters meaningful precisely because of their dispensability. In this way, *Parque industrial* is a novel about what Marx calls the industrial reserve army of the unemployed. The novel thus formally expresses how waged workers become dispensable when "a mass of human material" stands "ready for exploitation" (*Capital: Volume I* 784). Interestingly, Galvão connects the industrial reserve army to sex. Sexual relations in *Parque industrial* embody a logic of one-sided dispensability insofar as they are premised not on mutual recognition but on contradictory projects. Thus, in the opinion of one character, "there's only one crisis. The sexual crisis" (112).[9] I argue that the failure of sexual relations in *Parque industrial* amounts to a crisis—indeed, the only crisis—because it is ultimately a matter of social reproduction itself. In effect, the sexual crisis only becomes fully intelligible in light of the novel's formal dissociation of instances of production and consumption. This dissociation expresses how peripheral capitalism renders labor irrelevant as a source of consumption. To the extent that peripheral capitalism exploits labor without regard for its ability to reproduce itself, it depends for its existence on a massive industrial reserve army and ultimately sustains itself only by undermining its very ability to reproduce itself. The novel thus radically puts into question the assumption underlying both the idea of the "new country" and the "consciousness of underdevelopment," namely, that modernization, whether it takes

---

[9] "Para ela só há uma crise. A crise dos sexos que invade todo o bairro operário" (102).

place through a liberal export economy or a national-populist regime, will integrate subjects into a coherent social formation.[10] *Parque industrial* draws out the full implications of the "consciousness of underdevelopment" not by searching for a positive answer to the dilemma, a way to resolve the problems of Brazilian industrialization, but by articulating a negative critique of the blind process of capital accumulation that has given rise to our "planet of slums."[11]

SÃO PAULO AND GALVÃO'S RELEVANCE, HIGHS AND LOWS[12]

Given that *Parque industrial* is a self-declared proletarian novel, it is not surprising that the work opens with propaganda. But it does not begin by, for instance, telling the workers of the world to unite. Instead, the first line states: "*São Paulo is the greatest industrial center of South America*" (7, emphasis in the original).[13] The message appears "on the imperialist crown of the 'shrimp'" (7), or *bonde* (trolley), as it passes by textile workers in the

---

[10] Along these lines, Roberto Schwarz suggests that very idea of national formation has been "disqualified by the direction of history." "The nation," he writes, "will not be formed, its parts will detach themselves from one another, the 'advanced' sector of Brazilian society has already integrated itself into the most modern dynamics of the international order and left the rest behind." See Schwarz, *Sequências brasileiras*, p. 57.
[11] Marx insists that a conception of capitalism in its fully developed form reveals crucial aspects of its historical genesis. Galvão, writing in the 1930s, could not have seen the fully developed form of Brazilian industrialization, but she seems to have intuited what would in time prove to become its fatal contradictions. Accordingly, we might complement Marx's insight with Ruy Mauro Marini's assertion that "the insufficient development of a society, by highlighting a simple element, makes its more complex form, which integrates and subordinates that element, more comprehensible" (109).
[12] The title of this section alludes to Roberto Schwarz's essay "Brecht's Relevance—Highs and Lows." In this essay, Schwarz reflects on the meaning of Brechtian theater both for Brazilian culture in the twentieth century and in light of the current situation, namely the ongoing crisis of capitalism and the absence of an effective political opposition. Schwarz admits that we, situated in the present, cannot but hear Stalinist bureaucracy in the language of the militants in Brecht's *Saint Joan of the Stockyards*. And yet, "In everything it says regarding the nature of capital," Schwarz proposes, "the timeliness of *Saint Joan* could hardly be greater" (*Two Girls* 249). My reading of *Parque industrial* is similarly premised on the idea that "Today there seems more to be gained from the [novel's] configuration of" crisis, "and of its deepening, than from its positing of the revolutionary exit, limited to the determination to win, or perhaps even die, so that other workers will win later on" (259).
[13] "São Paulo é o maior Parque industrial da América do Sul: o pessoal da tecelagem soletra no cocoruto imperialista do 'camarão' que passa" (17).

proletarian neighborhood *Brás,* located to the east of the city center. One of these workers, an "Italian girl," challenges the attempt to claim this industrial productivity for the city of São Paulo. After she "throws an early morning 'banana'" (7),[14] that is, directs a vulgar hand gesture at the *bonde*, the Italian girl exclaims, "*Brás* is the greatest!" (7, translation modified).[15] This initial vignette concisely and powerfully establishes central elements of *Parque industrial.* It highlights class divisions within São Paulo by insisting that productivity belongs to labor, to those living in *Brás*.[16] It incorporates the popular, colloquial speech of those workers. And it emphasizes, in particular, the activity of poor women as they protest against their own exploitation. In short, this vignette announces the politics of the novel.

By staging a confrontation between *paulista* chauvinism and the working class at the beginning of *Parque industrial,* Galvão briefly refers to the contemporary political situation in Brazil. But she does this in order to displace those tensions in favor of class struggle. The novel portrays the development of a militant working class in *Brás.* This narrative thread culminates in an insurrection that is brutally put down by the forces of the state, leading to the death of various characters and the disintegration of the bonds of solidarity among the workers. At the time of writing the novel, in 1932, an insurrection swept over São Paulo, but it was not a revolutionary uprising of workers. Indeed, the workers played little to no part in this insurrection. Instead, the "*Paulista* War," as it has come to be known, called for a return to the constitutional order that President Getúlio Vargas had abandoned with his turn to authoritarian populism in 1930. The constitutional order of the First Republic (1889–1930) had given São Paulo unique political autonomy among the states of Brazil because it had become the economic engine of the nation. Therefore, the war was also an expression of a sense of *paulista* superiority that had been challenged by the rise of Vargas.

Galvão seems to have hoped that working-class politics could break the impasse between *paulista* chauvinism and the populism of Getúlio Vargas. But the Communist Party found itself outmaneuvered by Vargas's

---

[14] "A italianinha matinal dá uma banana pro bonde" (17).
[15] "Mais custa! O maior é o Brás!" (17).
[16] The *bonde* will also appear as a representative of a "global network of exploitation" (Wells, "Mass Culture" 58). "The capitalist 'shrimp' flings open its door to the victim who will shell out another two hundred *réis*, destined for Wall Street" (Galvão 16).

strategic incorporation of trade unions. Likewise, *Parque industrial* did not resonate among its intended audience, the textile workers in Brás. Although Galvão's novel may have failed to make itself directly relevant to the politics of 1930s Brazil because of its focus on class struggle, I will argue in this section that Galvão's attention to exploitation leads her to raise questions about the background conditions of peripheral capitalism, conditions that have become increasingly relevant since the publication of the novel. These questions come to light not when we subordinate the novel to an external end—namely, political struggle—but rather when we see how *Parque industrial* establishes its independence from the immediate political situation and institutes its own formal principles. Galvão suggests that the city itself expresses the brutal logic of the factory, most notably, its dependence on a mass of the unemployed workers in the background, on a reserve army whose existence makes it possible for waged workers to be exploited without regard for their ability to reproduce themselves. I insist that an understanding of this critique is premised on grasping the composition of the novel, namely, its formal pattern of anonymous, seemingly dispensable, characters.

To comprehend the political situation in 1930s Brazil and the long-term conditions that Galvão makes legible in *Parque industrial*, I will provide some context on the emergence of São Paulo as the economic engine of Brazil. A famous image from the time depicted São Paulo as a locomotive pulling twenty cars, the twenty cars being the other Brazilian states. São Paulo became this economic locomotive toward the end of the nineteenth century thanks to the coffee boom in the world market. In the initial phase of the export era, São Paulo remained a backwater relative to the capital, Rio de Janeiro, and to the regions in the northeast that produced sugar, Brazil's main export at the time. But by the time Vargas rose to power in 1930 and brought about the end of the First Republic, coffee accounted for 72.5% of all export revenue (Fausto 161). Coffee was cultivated in the rural areas of the state of São Paulo, and the money gained from its sale on the world market fueled investment in the city and rapid urban population growth. In the first half of the twentieth century, the population of São Paulo doubled every fifteen years: for instance, from 500,000 in 1917 to 1,000,000 in 1933 (Morse 279).

Like other peripheral metropoles in Latin America, São Paulo's spectacular urban growth did not primarily derive from its internal dynamics. São Paulo became what it is in virtue of its relation to the world market and to its own countryside.[17] The nascent industrial bourgeoisie in São Paulo, for instance, emerged out of the rural oligarchy. Moreover, with the nation being utterly dependent on a single export, when the price of coffee fluctuated on the world market, especially during and after WWI, workers were dismissed from the plantations and migrated en masse to the city. Taking place over various boom and bust cycles in the beginning of the twentieth century, this migration would become the basis of the urban proletariat for emerging textile industries. The textile industry actually began to rival coffee in the mid-1920s (Jackson 116), but this fact should not necessarily be seen as a sign of the strength of São Paulo's industrial development. More fundamentally, it indicates the crisis of the export model. To deal with the instability of coffee prices, the state instituted a "valorization" scheme to artificially elevate the price on the world market by stockpiling a surplus until demand recovered. This policy only aggravated the tendency toward overproduction in the 1910s and 1920s. But, in the words of Richard Morse, it was "[n]ot until the vast oversupply and collapse of 1929, when coffee was used as fuel for locomotives, [that] valorization [stood] clearly forth as characteristic of a central illusion of the urban mind" (207). São Paulo had become the nation's most dynamic, industrializing urban center, but the locomotive pulling along the other states remained dependent on coffee, and it was consuming itself to continue fueling the engine.

With the unraveling of the export economy, the political situation in Brazil became untenable and forces emerged to challenge São Paulo's hegemony. Prior to the stock market crash in 1929, the oligarchical system in early twentieth-century Brazil had stabilized itself through what was known as the *café com leite* politics, an alliance between coffee plantation owners in São Paulo and the ranching sector in Minas Gerais. According to this arrangement, the presidency would pass back and forth between political figures from the two departments. But this pattern was broken in

---

[17] We can see the rural basis of urban modernization in the class background of *modernismo*. The "coffee barons," whose fortunes were made and lost on the world market, were "well educated, widely traveled, and culturally refined with regard to contemporary styles and customs" (Johnson 194). "To reinforce that refinement," as Randal Johnson notes, the coffee barons "needed the association with new artistic currents" (194–195). In this context, the Brazilian *modernistas*, many of whom came from the oligarchy, could be supported as a way to shake up the parochial order and as a dynamic expression of the São Paulo's role in shaping the future of the nation.

1929 when the president of Brazil, the *paulista* Washington Luís, insisted on naming another *paulista* as his successor. This move exposed the fault lines of *café com leite* politics at a time when the economic basis of São Paulo's hegemony was put into question. With the assertion of *paulista* chauvinism against the backdrop of the blatant failure of the export system, discontent brewed among military officials, technocrats, liberal politicians, and industrialists. These social forces carried out a coup in 1930 that brought Getúlio Vargas to power, initiating a shift away from an arrangement favoring the coffee sector toward a form of national capitalism supported by the armed forces and an alliance of the industrial bourgeoisie with sections of the urban working class.

Ultimately, Vargas's "objective was to break up the *café com leite* alliance and so deprive São Paulo of its political dominance" (Williamson 416). Vargas appointed a lieutenant to impose new policies on São Paulo, and the *Paulista* War erupted on July 9, 1932 with the support of the coffee industry, the middle class, and industrialists. The federal army effectively isolated the *paulistas* by blockading their access to ports. "[U]nable to receive military supplies from abroad" and other departments, Morse explains, "São Paulo was thrown upon its own industrial park for war matériel" (247).[18] The city's industrial base, however, would not be sufficient to mount an effective defense. The *paulista* forces were outmatched by the federal army, and when the civil war ended in October, Vargas had effectively overcome the main threat to his authority. But Vargas did not disenfranchise the coffee sector and the elite of São Paulo. Instead, as he would do with organized labor, he integrated them into the newly centralized state. The Constitution of 1934, for instance, signaled the return to constitutional order, a key demand behind the *Paulista* War, but it also legitimated the Vargas regime and its authoritarian-populist state structures.

The *Paulista* War marks a decisive moment in the political history of twentieth-century Brazil, but Galvão emphatically disavows the historical significance of these contemporary events in her depiction of São Paulo. Galvão most obviously distances the novel from the immediate political situation by depicting an insurrection of revolutionary workers, not social forces clinging to a moribund economic system. But the more compelling

---

[18] The civil war thus impinged on the city's productive infrastructure, even though workers, like those in Galvão's *Parque industrial*, effectively played no part in the uprising.

aspect of *Parque industrial* lies in its formal expression of the suffering inherent in what was supposed to supplant the dependence on agricultural exports, namely, industrialization. To underline this theme, Galvão includes two epigraphs at the beginning of the novel. The first epigraph, taken from the "Industrial Statistics of the State of São Paulo" published in 1930, records the ups and downs of industrial output during the second and third decades of the twentieth century. Although the quote ends by noting a decline in output during the early stages of the Great Depression, it gives the overall impression that industrialization has been advancing rapidly in São Paulo. The second epigraph reveals the costs of such dazzling progress: "THE STATISTICS AND THE HISTORY OF THE HUMAN STRATUM THAT SUTAINS THE INDUSTRIAL PARK OF SÃO PAULO & SPEAKS THE LANGUAGE OF THIS BOOK, CAN BE FOUND, UNDER THE CAPITALIST REGIME, IN THE JAILS AND IN THE SLUM HOUSES, IN THE HOSPITALS & IN THE MORGUES" (5). *Parque industrial* attends to the human suffering that "sustains the industrial park," but this does not confine the work to immediate experience. Rather, as the juxtaposition of the epigraphs suggests, the novel seeks to articulate the underlying "human stratum" of a system of production whose effects have permeated the entire city.

Along these lines, we might be tempted to say that *Parque industrial* asks us to leave behind the "noisy sphere" of exchange, "where everything takes place on the surface and in full view of everyone," and enter "into the hidden abode of production" (Marx, *Capital: Volume I* 279). And yet, *Parque industrial* dedicates surprisingly little attention to the factory itself. Instead, by tracing the consequences of the labor process, rather than depicting it directly, the novel shows how the industrial logic of the factory imprints itself on every aspect of social life in *Brás*. It would thus be more fitting to say that *Parque industrial* connects the "hidden abode of production" to the capitalism's non-economic "background conditions of possibility," namely, the social-reproductive activities that "form capitalism's human subjects, sustaining them as embodied natural beings while also constituting them as social beings, forming their *habitus* and the cultural ethos in which they move" (Fraser 23). Galvão, in other words, seeks to bring to the foreground the background conditions on which capitalism depends, the conditions that, because they remain in the background, capitalism exploits without regard for their own needs.

In order to fully understand the relationship between foreground and background in *Parque industrial*, we must recognize it as a formal question. Galvão poses this question in the print she co-designed with Oswald de Andrade for the cover.[19]

[19] Galvão not only designed the cover. She, along with Oswald de Andrade, also made specific formatting choices for the text itself, using large font and leaving a substantial amount of space between each vignette. Although I will not discuss these decisions here, they could also be taken as evidence that Galvão was intentionally working through questions of foreground and background, or positive and negative space, in *Parque industrial*. On the choice to use a large font and amble space between the vignettes, Ribeiro Junior writes: "Sua feição gráfica original faz crer que o livro foi pensado para um leitor poco treinado, por isso deveria ser mais convidativo" (19). Also on the cover, see Catherine Bryan, "*Antropofagia* and Beyond."

With stark, expressionist contrasts,[20] the cover depicts a factory, a billowing smokestack, and electrical lines powering the new economic engine of São Paulo. The factory thus seems to occupy the foreground of the cover. But the medium of the print raises questions about the meaning of foreground and background, or perhaps more accurately, positive and negative space. In a print, everything becomes a matter of positive and negative space, a blunt choice between black and white without gray areas. Moreover, to make a print, positive and negative space must be inverted. Rather than concentrate one's creative energies on the subject or the figure of the picture, the printmaker leaves untouched what will become the foreground, carving away material in order to make negative space. The work of the printmaker, in other words, is restricted to the supporting space around the subject—that is, the factory—and yet, this work consists of taking away from the negative space to make the foreground stand out.

The issue of work in the print thus suggests, contrary to what I initially suggested, that background and foreground cannot simply be inverted. The reason why becomes clearer when we think about the meaning of positive and negative space. The former refers to the subject of a picture, the area of interest, whereas the latter refers to the area surrounding that area of interest. Galvão certainly aims to shift the area of interest away from quantitative measurements of industrial productivity to the qualitative lives of workers in *Brás*. But if we say that the positive and negative space can be inverted, or exchanged, we suggest that they exist in an external relation where each term has its identity independent of its connection with the other. This is not the case in *Parque industrial*. The background conditions in the novel—the social-reproductive activities that sustain the industrial park—remain in the background, but they have been thoroughly transformed, and deformed, by the logic of capital accumulation in the foreground. Workers are relegated to the background because they constitute a dispensable mass that can be exploited without regard for their needs. In other words, the positive space—that is, industrialization—becomes the area of interest at the expense of the area surrounding it. The

---

[20] Although Thelma Guedes does not explicitly discuss Galvão's use of the print, she offers comments on expressionism and woodcuts that rhyme with the interpretation I propose here. Guedes relates *Parque industrial* to the comments of the Brazilian Mário Pedrosa on the expressionist woodcuts of Käthe Kollwitz. Pedrosa, writing in 1933, the same year as the publication of *Parque industrial*, underlines how the simplicity of Kollwitz's woodcuts expresses the indignation of proletarian woman. According to Guedes, the same could be said of the literary techniques in Galvão's novel. See Guedes, pp. 99–106.

factory stands out because it takes away from the workers in the negative space. Or, more precisely, the factory occupies the foreground because the work is negative, the workers emptying themselves and externalizing their powers to compose a foreground. Accordingly, the lives of the workers in the novel remain negative even as they become the focus of the narrative. Right from the cover, *Parque industrial* sets itself the task of preserving, rather than overcoming, negativity in order to do justice to the suffering of the workers. In this way, the novel makes palpable the reality of commodity fetishism, which, as Marx insisted, is not an illusion that could be dispelled by bringing the background into the foreground, but a fundamental inversion or perversion in which "social relations between things" dictate the terms of human relations, making them thing-like (*Capital: Volume I* 166).[21]

Once the specific formal relation between foreground and background comes into view, the opening of *Parque industrial* assumes a different meaning. The novel makes the city into the "area of interest," but it simultaneously presents the city as the background, as a space that must be negated for the factory to become a positive foreground. Galvão thus undermines the idea, evoked by the "Italian girl" in the opening vignette, that the productive power of the industrial park could simply be reappropriated by the workers of *Brás*. This can be seen in the reversal that takes place after the Italian girl "defends" *Brás* against the imperialist *bonde*. The narrative shifts to a vignette presenting women workers on their way to the textile factory. The women discuss their dating lives, one claiming she will only marry a worker, another insisting that "One poor person is enough," and yet another raising doubts about the idea that the rich

---

[21] Along these lines, Ribeiro Junior argues that the novel opposes any futurist celebration of the machine, operating, instead, with "the reification of humans and the humanization of things" (47). Because the novel attempts to preserve, rather than overcome, the negativity of commodity fetishism, I would venture a perhaps surprising comparison between *Parque industrial* and Adorno's negative dialectics. Werner Bonefeld has persuasively argued that Adorno's negative dialectics should be understood not only as an immanent critique of conceptual identity-thinking but also as a "dialectics of a social world in the form of the economic object, one that is governed by the movement of economic quantities" (5). Although this economic world is "created and reproduced by the acting subjects themselves," it "asserts itself behind their backs" in such a way that "definite social relations vanish in their own social world only to reappear as, say, relations of price competitiveness" (5) or industrial statistics.

"seriously" date poor women (8).[22] The women remain nameless, and the narrative seems to deprive them of agency by focusing on parts of the body in lieu of the whole. The "[c]olored slippers," not the women, "drag along still sleepy and unhurried on Monday" (8).[23] The vignette implicitly links the fragmentation of the body to the factory as the narrative focus shifts from the women to the "powerful cry of the smokestack envelop[ing] the borough" (8).[24] At the level of the form and content of the story, it becomes apparent that the logic of the factory organizes the surrounding social space, the effects of which become visible in the conclusion of the vignette. The narration returns to the women metonymically, observing a "small red slipper without a sole" that has been "abandoned in the gutter" and then identifying the "shoeless foot ... cut on the shivers of a milk bottle" (8–9).[25] The tattered shoe lies outside the factory, suggesting that the reification of persons cannot be confined to work. Rather, it permeates the surrounding area. The vignette ends with a terse, arresting image: "Blood mixed with milk" (9).[26] With these shifts from characters to background and back to character, the city becomes more than external setting. The city, with its proletarian inhabitants, appears as the negative background for "a living body" (Guedes 119), for an industrial logic driven by the incessant needs of capital accumulation.[27] Accordingly, even though various proletarian characters claim the productivity of the factory as their own, the novel quickly establishes that the industrial park is governed by forces that outstrip human control and, in their indifference to individual and social needs, deform the lives of workers.

Parque industrial further portrays this world dominated by the commodity fetish through anonymous characters. By Jackson's count, the novel includes fifty-two characters (139), the vast majority of which are either unnamed or have a name but are only mentioned once. These anonymous characters could be called "flat" since *Parque industrial* does

---

[22] "'Sai azar! Pra pobre basta eu. Passar a vida inteira nesta merda!' 'Vocês pensam que os ricos namoram a gente a sério? Só pra debochar'" (18).
[23] "Os chinelos de cor se arrastam sonolentos ainda e sem pressa na segunda-feira" (17).
[24] "O grito possante da chaminé envolve o bairro" (18).
[25] "Uma chinelinha vermelha é largada sem contraforte na sarjeta. Um pé descalço se fere nos cacos de uma garrafa de leite" (18).
[26] "Sangue misturado com leite" (18).
[27] For a reading of *Parque industrial* that focuses on a different aspect of the city, see David William Foster's argument on the "feminization" of space. David William Foster, *São Paulo: Perspectives on the City and Cultural Production*, pp. 27–44.

not present them as having complex personalities, but they do not typically serve to drive the plot forward or "round out" the main characters. Arguably, even the protagonists in the novel are relatively flat. Along these lines, Ribeiro Junior suggests that *Parque industrial* could be conceived as a "*novel without heroes*" (37, emphasis in the original). But Galvão does not replace heroes with anonymous characters to give the novel documentary value. These characters have significance not in virtue of some immediate reference to extra-literary reality but rather through the role they play within the structure of the novel. As anonymous, they remain background characters even as the narrative brings them into the foreground. At the beginning of the novel, the textile workers discussing their weekend plans on the way to the factory, one of whom cuts her foot on a broken bottle of milk, matter not intrinsically but because they form a pattern in the novel that crystallizes the pressures of industrialization. Insofar as these characters bear only a contingent, not necessary, relation to the organization of the whole, they are presented as superfluous or dispensable. But it is precisely in their superfluous character that these characters express their necessity with respect to the formal principles of the novel. Through this formal dynamic of necessity and dispensability, the technique of anonymous characters makes legible the contingent relation of the worker to the labor process. The historian of São Paulo Richard Morse points to the same trend by drawing on reports from the Department of Labor in the 1920s. "In good times," he writes, "a worker found ready employment, but he could never," in the language of these reports, "'make himself necessary.' 'He is almost always superfluous, parasitic, tolerated'" (208). Insofar as *Parque industrial* establishes the necessity of the superfluous, it makes its formal composition into a social critique.

In other words, the modernist technique of anonymity renders palpable the Marxist concept of the industrial reserve army, which, as I will discuss below, Galvão uses for the title of the final section of the novel. Marx introduces this concept to articulate, contrary to the assumptions of classical political economy, the interdependence of the supply of labor and the accumulation of capital. "Capital," Marx writes, "acts on both sides at once," determining the demand for labor and regulating its supply by generating a surplus population of unemployed workers (*Capital: Volume 1* 793). The accumulation of capital depends on a certain level of unemployment, on a surplus population, insofar as "a mass of human material" must always be "ready for exploitation" in accordance with "capital's own changing valorization requirements" (784). The reserve army not only stands at the ready for the moment when capital enters a phase of expansion or shifts from one sector to another. It also increases the supply of labor and thereby drives down wages. As a result, Marx insists that wages are not just a function of the size of the working population. Rather, the reserve army serves as "the *background* against which the law of the demand and supply of labor does its work" (792, my emphasis). But Marx also argues that the industrial reserve army does not simply indicate a mass that has been thrown out of the labor process during a crisis only to be reincorporated at a later date nor those who have been recently proletarianized, compelled to migrate from the country to the industrializing urban centers where they will eventually find work. Most fundamentally, the reserve army expresses the underlying contradiction whereby the working class "produces both the accumulation of capital and the means by which it is itself made relatively superfluous; and it does this to an extent which is always increasing" (783). Industrialization systematically replaces human labor with machinery, increasing what Marx calls the organic composition of capital, and the demand for industrial labor "falls progressively with the growth of total social capital" (781). As I will discuss in more detail below, this tendency appeared to have been overcome, or at least suspended, in the industrializing core during the middle of the twentieth century. But *Parque industrial* embodies Galvão's intuition that industrialization in Brazil, despite its apparent promise at the time, would ultimately presuppose and produce a growing reserve army, would necessarily reproduce a situation in which, "even if their labor is no longer needed, [workers] cannot stop selling their capacity to labor" (Benanav & Clegg 1633). Just as the anonymous characters simultaneously appear superfluous and bear an internal relation to the meaning of the work, in Brazilian industrialization workers will appear simultaneously disposable and necessary for the accumulation of capital, reproducing a form of sociality that undermines its ability to reproduce itself.

If we subordinate *Parque industrial* to the context of 1930s Brazil, we must admit that the novel failed to have the immediate relevance desired by Galvão. The novel did not inspire the working class to revolutionary action, and the major political confrontation at the time took place not between the proletariat and the bourgeoisie, but between *paulista* chauvinists and authoritarian populists. But *Parque industrial* becomes surprisingly relevant when we recognize how the internal organization of the novel expresses the exploitation demanded by industrialization. The novel thus suggests that the opposition of political projects in Brazil must be understood within a broader dynamic that tends to render this antagonism irrelevant. The revolutionary working-class women and the *paulista* elite appear subordinate to the pervasive dynamic of industrialization as it manifests itself in a hostile city.[28] The novel, seen in light of the formal principles organizing the factory and urban space, thus casts doubt on the shared presupposition of both political projects, namely, the idea that Brazil's relative backwardness could be overcome through industrialization. In so doing, *Parque industrial* shatters the *"mirage of innocent progress"* (*Misplaced* 121) that Roberto Schwarz finds in the poetry of Galvão's then-husband, Oswald de Andrade. Through dispensable characters and a specific relationship between positive and negative space, Galvão's novel identifies the contradictions that prevent industrialization in Brazil from producing a coherent social synthesis.

---

[28] It is important to note that this hostile city does not stand in contrast to a positive depiction of rural life. Indeed, Galvão briefly alludes to the countryside in the context of the novel's only retrospective moment, providing background on Rosinha's (im)migrant journey from Eastern Europe to the "feudal plantation" in São Paulo "that had enslaved them to coffee bushes" (85). I provide here the full passage: "Rosinha Lituana disembarks surrounded by recruits in the enormous Immigration presidio. She had passed through that house ten years before as an immigrant, very young. She had come from Lithuania with her penniless parents. The postwar had made them immigrate like so many people. They were mixed with many others in the great brick house on Visconde de Parnahyba Street. The same as today. Without the gardens and window bars. Afterward they had been directed like merchandise to a feudal plantation that had enslaved them to coffee bushes" (84–85). "Rosinha Lituana desembarca cercada de tiras no presídio colossal da Imigração. Estivera naquela casa dez anos atrás imigrante, pequenina. Viera da Lituâna com os pais miseráveis. O depois da guerra os fizera imigrar, como tanta gente. Foram misturados com muitos outros no casarão de tijolos da rua Visconde de Parnaíba. O mesmo de hoje. Sem os jardins e sem as grades. Depois, tinham sido endereçados como escravos para a fazenda feudal que os escravizara aos pés de café" (80). The countryside does not represent in *Parque industrial* a different, better form of social organization; rather, it underlines the superfluous character of labor, being expelled from the plantations when the coffee bubble bursts. Rosinha, among many others, finds herself pushed into a city that is equally indifferent because it embodies the logic of the factory.

There Is No Sexual Revolution

If *Parque industrial* did not achieve Galvão's aim to communicate with the workers of São Paulo, it equally failed to be embraced within intellectual circles, including those in the Brazilian Communist Party. Galvão was a member of the Communist Party at the time of writing her self-described "proletarian novel," but the Party disapproved of what they called her "individualistic and sensationalist agitation" (qtd. in Jackson 120). They insisted that she drop her own name and use a pseudonym for the publication. The original cover thus carries the name "Mara Lobo." The novel fared no better among literary critics. Murilo Mendes, a *modernista* poet, questioned Galvão's pretension to write a "proletarian novel," as if she had genuinely experienced the life and struggles of the working class. In truth, according to Mendes, *Parque industrial* is an "impressionistic, petty-bourgeois reportage, made by a person with the desire to make the leap but does not take it" (qtd. in Bueno 166). But Mendes asserts in this scathing review that the problem is not simply that Galvão depicts the struggles of the working class from the point of view of a bourgeois observer rather than that of a participant. More fundamentally, she distorts the aims of proletarian politics by making them conform to her own personal ambitions: "It seems that the goal of the revolution, for the author, is to resolve the sexual question" (160). For Mendes, Galvão subordinates *Parque industrial*'s revolutionary narrative, revolving around the militant textile workers Rosinha Lituana[29] and Otavia, to her own demand for sexual revolution. Contrary to Mendes's conclusion, this section will insist that the novel's focus on "the sexual question" brings into focus the contradictory nature of peripheral industrialization. *Parque industrial* embodies neither the call to liberate sexual activity from repressive conventions nor the demand that sex be disarticulated from (re)production. Instead, the novel portrays the perverse realization of these demands in a context where sex appears indissolubly linked to the pressures of the industrial reserve army, to the precarious position of depending on the wage even when labor is not needed. In the wage-relation, workers and capitalists engage in conflicting projects with distinct ends: the former looking to attain money to acquire means of subsistence; the

---

[29] Given the explicit references to Rosa Luxemburg in the novel, it seems that the German-Polish Communist was the inspiration for the character Rosinha Lituana. Ribeiro Junior suggests that Rosinha could also be a reference to Rosa Brickman, a Communist in São Paulo with whom Galvão may have had contact (34).

latter driven to exploit as much surplus labor as possible from the worker. Moreover, the relation between worker and capitalist is contingent because the reserve army stands ready to replace any individual. The same could be said of sexual relations in *Parque industrial*. The novel depicts a "sexual crisis" insofar as sexual relations institute not mutual recognition but a sort of non-relation, not a fusion of parts into a whole but a division that indicates the peculiar character of social reproduction in the periphery.

When Mendes repudiates Galvão for subordinating working-class politics to the "sexual question," he may have formed this impression from the opening of the novel. As we discussed above, the initial vignettes in *Parque industrial* shift from an assertion of the productive power of *Brás* to textile workers discussing their dating lives, one claiming she will only marry a worker, another insisting that "One poor person is enough," and yet another raising doubts about the idea that the rich "seriously" date poor women (8). This conversation lacks the militancy that we find, for instance, when Rosinha talks to other workers about exploitation, but it clearly establishes that sexual relations cannot be extricated from class. Marriage between poor people appears in *Parque industrial* only indirectly through the implications for such a family structure. As one anonymous character exclaims in a union meeting, "We can't get to know our own children! We leave home at six in the morning. They are sleeping. We return at ten. They are sleeping" (22).[30] The pressures of poverty make it effectively impossible for women to raise children in the novel. But, as we will see, *Parque industrial* devotes greater attention to the final two possible relations discussed in the vignette: the desire to marry a bourgeois man to escape conditions of poverty and rich men using women from the popular district without commitments.

When bourgeois men have sex with poor women in *Parque industrial*, the novel portrays the relationship in terms of the broader pattern of precarious, dispensable work. Galvão often draws on industrial imagery to evoke the nature of such a situation. For instance, the son of a politician tells his friends about a poor woman he raped over the weekend. Asked if he gave her any money, he replies, "I gave her teeth marks" (66).[31] Elsewhere, the novel associates teeth with the textile factory, whose logic, as we have seen, structures the surrounding social space. Just as the teeth

---

[30] "Nós não podemos conhecer os nossos filhos! Saímos de casa às seis horas da manhã. Eles estão dormindo. Chegamos às dez horas. Eles estão dormindo" (30).
[31] "'Deste dinheiro a ela!' 'Dei dentadas ...'" (66).

of the machines incessantly turn yarn into woven products, the poor woman appears as raw material to be consumed by the rapacious bourgeoisie. Dispensability also figures centrally in the storyline of one of central characters: Corina. Her path intersects at various moments with Rosinha and Otavia, but Corina "finds [their] proselytism of others a drag. She thinks life is colossal!" (16). When Corina becomes pregnant, she assumes Arnaldo, her bourgeois boyfriend, will support her, ignoring Otavia's warning: "The only thing he does is seduce girls like you who are unaware of the abyss that separates us from him" (44). Corina loses her job because of the pregnancy, and Arnaldo abandons Corina, leaving her "like a rag in Anhangabahú" as his "roadster beeps Corina's illusion" (45). As I will discuss in more detail below, Corina, unable to find work, turns to prostitution, allowing Galvão to explicitly connect the industrial reserve army to questions of social reproduction.

Even when relationships between bourgeois men and poor women become marriages in *Parque industrial*, they are not "taken seriously." This issue surfaces in the pairing of Eleonora and Alfredo Rocha: the former, a girl from *Brás* who yearns to leave behind her working-class past; the latter, a renegade bourgeois intellectual who hopes the marriage would put him in closer contact with the "people." With their marriage, Eleonora "enters society ... the isolated citadel of Brazilian high feudalism" where the rich live "on the distilled sweat of the Industrial Park" (32). Alfredo takes her to a lavish party, expecting her "to have [her] first disappointment" (32), but she does not share his disgust with luxury.[32] At the end of this scene, when Alfredo insists that he will go to *Brás* for Carnival, Eleonora announces, "I'll never return to *Brás*" (34, translation modified). As the rift in the relationship deepens, Eleonora seduces Matilde, a former classmate from *Brás* who has fallen on hard times. We might expect to find in this non-heteronormative relationship between poor women a greater possibility for reciprocity and mutual understanding, but when Eleonora asks Matilde why she wasn't interested in her at school, Matilde responds, "You didn't have this apartment or these delicious drinks" (63). In effect, Matilde reflects back to Eleonora her own desire in marrying

---

[32] Laura Kanost rightly states that "the narration sees rich bodies as disgusting because they are gluttonous consumers of food, drink and sex" (97). However, I think we should also note that this disgust follows not from consumption itself, but rather from the juxtaposition of such consumption and the hunger of the workers.

Alfredo. Offended by the recognition that the roles have been reversed, Eleonora kicks Matilde out of the house. The marriage between Alfredo and Eleonora thus constitutes one of *Parque industrial*'s starkest indications that the sexual relation is a non-relation. Eleonora and Alfredo do not appear unified as parts of a common identity; rather, the bond of marriage becomes a temporary contract between individuals with their own private ends.

Galvão dramatizes this division and underlines the subsequent non-relation in the chapter entitled "Where Surplus-Value is Spent" (*Onde se gasta a mais-valia*). By juxtaposing scenes, Galvão underlines separation: Eleonora shops and meets friends for cocktails in a lavish apartment where "the bourgeoisie entertains itself" (50),[33] while Alfredo reads Marx at home. In the same chapter, Alfredo meets Otavia when she delivers a dress for Eleonora to their apartment. Alfredo expresses an interest in Otavia's "class," adding, "Personally you don't interest me" (49). On guard, Otavia remembers Corina and suspects that "All bourgeois are just alike" (49).[34] Otavia eventually overcomes this initial suspicion, and the two fall in love after Alfredo has fully abandoned his bourgeois lifestyle and become a comrade in the working-class struggle. But when the Party accuses Alfredo of Trotskyist sympathies, Otavia abandons him.[35] At times, Alfredo and Otavia seem to represent the novel's only positive instance of love and solidarity, but their union disintegrates in accordance with the principle that there is no sexual relation.[36] Sex in *Parque industrial* does not represent the possibility of two becoming one; it reveals the division within any putative unity insofar as the relationship is sustained by incompatible desires.

Sexual relations in Galvão's novel thus embody the logic of the industrial reserve army, namely, the tendency to expel workers from wage-labor, the social institution on which they depend to sustain themselves. Corina

---

[33] "A burguesia se diverte" (52).
[34] "Ela pensa em Corina. Todo burguês é assim mesmo" (51).
[35] It is often said that the character Alfredo Rocha was modeled on Oswald de Andrade, Galvão's husband at the time of writing *Parque industrial*. Oswald, like Alfredo, attempted to renounce his class background and join the Communist Party. But we could also say that Alfredo embodies something of Galvão's own tense relationship with the Party because, as Ribeiro Junior has convincingly proposed, the Party was skeptical of Galvão's efforts to become a worker, a transformation that Oswald never attempted (113).
[36] I am referring her to the principle that Lacan articulates in Seminar XI.

makes this connection explicit insofar as she turns to prostitution after being fired for her pregnancy. She hopes that "One more [client] and she'll have the money for her baby's crib" (53),[37] but the novel will deflate even this meager hope to care for her child. When Corina arrives at the hospital to deliver her baby, the nurses direct her to the "indigent ward," where "The indigent prepare their children for the future separation demanded by work" (56).[38] The "paying class," the novel informs the reader, is taken to a separate section of the birthing house because "The bourgeois children are nurtured from early on, linked by the economic umbilical cord" (56).[39] In Galvão jarring description of the birth, Corina "vomit[s] suddenly something alive, red," and the nurse "recoils" in horror (57).[40] The doctor "examines the bloody mass that cries, soiling the covers," and when Corina asks for her baby, they refuse to give her the children, saying, "It's a monster. Without skin. And it's alive!" (57).[41] "This woman," another voice concludes, "is rotten" (57).[42] Some critics have interpreted the reaction of the doctor and nurses as expressing racist disgust with a *mulatto* child. But the child's lack of skin suggests that this dissonance is more than a matter of prejudice.[43] The child simply cannot survive in such a state. An abrupt cut then takes the narrative to a prison, where Corina has been confined because, according to an unidentified voice, she has "killed her son!" (57).[44] Corina herself confesses to the crime, but we are given no other explanation than the elliptical comment that "No one knows that" she did it "because of money" (58).[45] Perhaps she killed the child because she didn't believe she could support it. Or perhaps the child died from a venereal disease that Corina contracted

---

[37] "Mais outro e terá dinheiro para o berço do filhinho" (54).
[38] "As indigentes preparam os filhos para a separação futura que o trabalho exige" (56).
[39] "As crianças burguesas se amparam desde cedo, ligadas pelo cordão umbilical econômico" (56).
[40] "Lá no fundo das pernas um buraco enorme se avoluma descomunalmente. Se rasga, negro. Aumenta. Como uma goela. Para vomitar, de repente, uma coisa viva, vermelha. A enfermeira recua. A parteira recua" (57).
[41] "Examina a massa ensangüentada que grita sujando a colcha ... 'É um monstro. Sem pele. E está vivo!'" (58).
[42] "Esta mulher está podre..." (58).
[43] "In the novel, Corina's baby does not survive because, despite being born, it does not have skin. It is monstrous! Thus, the intention of the novel seems to be exactly that: to present it as a monster" (Guedes 30).
[44] "É aquela mulata indigente que matou o filho!" (58).
[45] "Ninguém sabe que foi por causa de dinheiro" (59).

while working as a prostitute. Either way, the novel insists, in its own ambiguous way, that Corina has been made "rotten" by the need to sell her body.

After the dust of the workers' insurrection settles, the narrative returns to Corina. In this final chapter, aptly titled "Reserve Army," we find Corina once again in the world of prostitution, "waiting" in a restaurant "for a young man," but in reality, "waiting for a sandwich" (110).[46] Then, desperately searching for a place to rest, she enters a church and encounters Pepe, an old friend who also maintained his distance from radical politics. In the last vignette, Corina and Pepe, "clinging together, victims of the same unawareness, cast on the same shore of capitalist ventures, carry salted popcorn to the same bed" (114).[47]

Given the fate of Corina and this language of them being "victims" of "unawareness," various critics regard this conclusion as a lesson about depoliticization. In Ribeiro Junior's reading, for instance, the scene acutely expresses Galvão's "partisan moralism" because Corina "suffers the consequences of illusions with the bourgeois world" and "is punished literarily" (36). This implicit moralism also surfaces when critics refer to Corina and Pepe as "lumpen." Indeed, the final chapter of *Parque industrial* begins with an epigraph from Marx on the lumpenproletariat: "Exclusive of vagabonds, criminals, prostitutes, in a word, the 'dangerous' classes" (109).[48] But if we read the chapter in light of the notion of the "reserve army" rather than the "lumpenproletariat," the moralism disappears. Beyond the political narrative in the novel, character of Corina expresses a crisis of social reproduction itself. The narrator asserts that for the character Corina "there's only one crisis. The sexual crisis that spreads through the whole worker's district" (112).[49] Most immediately, this crisis seems to represent the scarcity of sex, a collapse in the effective demand for the commodity on which Corina depends to buy a sandwich. More fundamentally, the "sexual crisis" indicates that the reserve army can barely reproduce itself, much less another human being, because it has only a contingent relation to the wage-labor, the social institution on which it depends to obtain

---

[46] "Corina não espera o homem. Espera o sanduíche" (101).

[47] "Os dois, agarrados, vítimas da mesma inconsciência, atirados à mesma margem das combinações capitalistas, levam pipocas salgadas para a mesma cama" (104).

[48] "Sem falas dos vagabundos, dos criminosos e das prostitutas, isto é, do verdadeiro proletariado miserando" (100).

[49] "Para ela só há uma crise. A crise dos sexos que invade todo o bairro operário" (102).

means of subsistence. It is in this way that "money," as the figure for capitalist social relations, kills Corina's baby. *Parque industrial* flatly denies that reproductive activities can be accomplished independently of wage-labor.

By insisting on this connection between sex and the reserve army, Galvão challenges the prevailing version of feminism in Brazil at the time. *Parque industrial* satirizes this feminism in a scene populated by "the emancipated, the intellectuals and the feminists that the bourgeoisie of São Paulo produces" (68).[50] The bourgeois feminists celebrate the announcement that the "vote for women has been achieved!" (69).[51] Someone raises a question about the vote for women workers and receives a dismissive response: "They are illiterate. Excluded by nature" (70).[52] Under Vargas, women obtained the right to vote: first in 1931 to women who were financially independent or had permission from their husband, and then in 1932, the year of composition of *Parque industrial*, equal suffrage was given to literate men and women. But even if suffrage was granted to the illiterate poor women, it would not change the fact that there were illiterate poor women. In contrast to the Brazilian feminist movement's narrow focus on political rights, *Parque industrial* attends to what the Bolshevik Alexandra Kollontai called in *The Social Basis of the Woman Question* (1909) the "double weight upon women," their exploitation as workers and their oppression as women (177). Kollontai argues that the "apparently radical" demands of feminism—namely, equal rights—do not aim for "that fundamental transformation of the contemporary economic and social structure of society without which the liberation of women cannot be complete" (176). *Parque industrial* not only underlines the limitations of a merely politico-legal liberation of women. We might also say that the novel depicts the burdens of a sexual revolution without social revolution. The São Paulo of *Parque industrial* seems to be devoid of sexual repression, but in the context of Brazilian industrialization, in a context where workers are exploited without regard for their ability to reproduce themselves, sexual revolution looks like Corina, a "rotten" woman who can neither give birth nor sustain herself.

---

[50] "São as emancipadas, as intelectuais e as feministas que a burguesia de São Paulo produz" (68).
[51] "O voto para as mulheres está conseguido!" (69).
[52] "Essas são analfabetas. Excluídas por natureza" (69).

With this focus, the feminism of *Parque industrial* anticipates in certain ways the concerns of Social Reproduction Theory, or SRT. The Marxist feminists associated with SRT call for the need to theorize what Marx tends to take for granted in his critique of political economy, namely, the existence of individual laborers. Challenging the identification of capital exclusively with relations of production in the workplace, SRT has insisted on viewing the "relation between labor dispensed to produce commodities and labor dispensed to produce people as part of the systematic totality of capitalism" (Bhattacharya 2).[53] The latter labor, without which capital cannot reproduce itself, not only consists in the practices of birthing and rearing children, but also includes the activities necessary for sustaining community bonds. As Nancy Fraser argues, these "social-reproductive activities" serve as the "background conditions of possibility" on which the more strictly economic processes depend to function smoothly (23). Whereas reproductive labor held a central role in pre-capitalist social formations, capitalism systematically separates it from waged labor and relegates it to the domestic sphere. This leads to what Fraser calls a "peculiar relation of separation-*cum*-dependence-*cum*-disavowal," a relation with a "built-in source of potential instability" precisely because the economic foreground of capital, with its relentless imperative to accumulate, exploits and takes for granted the background on which it depends (24). As we have seen, the form and content of *Parque industrial* raise compelling questions about the relationship between capitalism's foreground and background. But Galvão also dramatically expresses SRT's insistence on the unity of waged labor and reproductive labor. These two kinds of labor appear identical in the figure of Corina precisely because she forms part of the industrial reserve army, that is, insofar as she holds only a contingent, precarious relation to the wage. Accordingly, it makes no sense to categorically separate social revolution and sexual relations, as Murilo Mendes assumes in his review of *Parque industrial*. There is only one crisis: the sexual crisis.

---

[53] SRT insists on distinguishing its unitary framework, where the labor producing commodities and the labor producing labor power can be theorized as aspects of the same system, from the more traditional dualist account. According to the dualist interpretation, capitalism constitutes a strictly economic system that is interconnected with, but autonomous from, relations of patriarchy and gendered oppression. The unitary framework of SRT, by contrast, aims to disclose how capitalism maintains itself only through the maintenance of relations of sexual exploitation and oppression.

To fully articulate the specific nature of social reproduction and its crisis in *Parque industrial*, we should reconstruct the different historical forms assumed by this peculiar relation of "separation-*cum*-dependence-*cum*-disavowal." Fraser distinguishes between the regime of liberal capitalism, stretching from the early nineteenth century to the interwar period, and the regime of state-managed capitalism in the middle of the twentieth century. In the former, capitalism "tended to leave workers to reproduce themselves 'autonomously,' outside the circuits of monetized value, as states looked on from the sidelines," thereby generating the ideal of "separate spheres"—that is, the male arena of work and the domestic, female realm (25). In the latter, social reproduction becomes internalized into capital through the welfare state and domestic consumption. *Parque industrial* stands at the threshold of this transition from the separate spheres of liberal capitalism to the integrated form of state-managed capitalism. But Galvão's novel, by bringing to light how this transition unfolds in the periphery, reveals the perverse truth of these historical regimes of social reproduction. *Parque industrial* shows how peripheral capitalism "leaves workers to reproduce themselves autonomously" not in response to demands for social protection but, as we will see in the final section, because their domestic consumption does not matter in an economy organized around production for the world market. Through its account of sexual relations, prostitution, and the death of Corina's baby, *Parque industrial* dramatizes how peripheral capitalism reproduces itself by presupposing and positing an industrial reserve army, a mass of unwaged workers who lack the means to reproduce themselves.

The Auto-Cannibalism of Peripheral Capitalism

Insofar as Galvão connects sex, social reproduction, and the reserve army, the sexual crisis in *Parque industrial* also encompasses the relation between consumption and production in peripheral capitalism. We might say that sexual revolution aims at liberating sex from (re)production, making it a purely consumptive activity. *Parque industrial* would then present us with the perversion of this sexual revolution. Under the conditions of the industrial reserve army, sex cannot be reproductive—for example, the death of Corina's baby. Moreover, the consumption of sex either does not exist—for example, Corina waiting for a customer—or becomes a mere means—for example, Corina needing a sandwich; bourgeois characters seeking sexual gratification from dispensable poor women. As a sexual non-relation, not simply the absence of sex, the sexual crisis expresses the specific way in which consumption and production form not a complimentary, reciprocal unity but rather an unstable whole whose parts hold incompatible ends. In short, I argue in this final section that the question of sexual relations allows Galvão to make legible the fundamental contradictions of peripheral capitalism that industrialization would seem to overcome but actually exacerbates.

Before entering into a more detailed interpretation of these issues in *Parque industrial*, we should acknowledge that Brazilian *modernismo* displays a keen interest in questions of production and consumption. Oswald de Andrade, in particular, foregrounds such questions when he attempts to synthesize a Brazilian national identity and outline the role of the artist in constructing such an identity. In his "Manifesto Pau-Brasil" (1924), Oswald calls on poets to produce poetry-for-export to reverse the one-sided flow of cultural good from the metropolis to the periphery. Oswald gives this artistic project a national symbol, *pau-brasil* or brazil-wood: the wood from which the country gets its name and the putative first export during the Portuguese colonial period. *Pau-brasil* thus represents the aspiration to overcome Brazil's position as a consumer of imported cultural goods. In 1928, perhaps intuiting the inadequacy of the figure of *pau-brasil*,[54] Oswald formulates a different relation between production and consumption in his "Manifesto Antropófago" (Cannibalist Manifesto). Turning now to the figure of the cannibal, Oswald suggests that a Brazilian identity would be formed in the process of consuming and digesting imported cultural goods.[55] *Antropofagia* thus radically rejects the

---

[54] Along these lines, Nicholas Brown insists on the need to distinguish "between two export economies: the first is the export of raw materials, the hallmark of a colonial economy, and the second is the export of finished products—the hallmark of a core economy … In this context the meaning apparently intended by the notion of 'poetry for export'—poetry being, of course, a 'finished product'—is undermined by the choice of brazil-wood as an emblem" (*Utopian* 186). But Brown also suggests that this emblem was "all too apt, for in a sense the referent of the manifesto, the real basis upon which Brazilian modernism was possible, is part of the old export economy: coffee, which did, for a time, 'nourish the initial stage of industrialization,' even as it constituted a limit on that process as well" (186).

[55] Any reader of the "Manifesto Antropófoga" will surely recognize that this idea of consuming and digesting imported cultural goods constitutes only one part of the multifaceted, almost incoherent, manifesto. Carlos Jáuregui thus reminds us that *Antropofagia* also "alludes to the erotic, to the insolence of parricide, to the absence of private property, and to the discursive challenge to morality, monogamy, Catholicism and the authority of cultural institutions" (40).

nationalist belief that all foreign cultural tendencies should be opposed in favor of national-popular traditions. At the same time, Oswald does not insist that the Brazilian artist ought to merely copy European literary and cultural forms. Instead, consumption appears here as a productive moment, synthesizing incongruous materials, appropriating the power of the digested body, and constructing a new identity. The "Law of the cannibal," Oswald writes, is "I am only concerned with that is not mine" (38), and what is not "mine" encompasses cosmopolitan tendencies and folk cultures. Corresponding to this positive program, *antropofagia* implies a remarkably insightful diagnosis of the "precise problem with dependency": namely, in Neil Larsen's words, that cultural goods, "in coming from without and being locally consumed they do not give rise to a circulation *within* the local space, and thus they simply confirm the larger, extrinsic circuit of the world market" (81). If dependency thus "describes a consumption that is severed from production" (81), poetry-for-export, by emphasizing production for consumption abroad, could not overcome dependency; it would only reproduce the mutual dissociation of these two moments of social reproduction. *Antropofagia*, by contrast, aims to overcome this dissociation by making consumption immediately productive.

Galvão, despite her close ties to *antropofagia*, including the bond of marriage to Oswald himself, presents consumption in a radically different light. Casting doubt on cannibalism as the "consumption-digestion-and-spitting-out of something new," *antropofagia* instead appears in *Parque industrial* as the "cannibalization/devouring of the working classes by the textile industry, and the terrible associated-opposite of consumptive cannibalism, that of the hunger-starvation-poverty of those same workers" (Bryan).[56] The ravenous machines in the factory monopolize consumption, leaving nothing for the poor workers to ingest. The factory appears as a looming maw, for instance, in the first chapter when we read: "In the great social penitentiary the looms rise and march noisily" (9).[57] The noisy looms become a threat in this vignette as a textile worker warns her exhausted coworker that her braids will get caught in the mechanism. "The Shop Manager drifts by, idly, scowling," concerned not with the dangerous working conditions but with the fact that the two women are

---

[56] Or, as Jackson puts it, "Cannibalism is the metaphor Pagu applies to social and industrial bodies" (145).
[57] "Na grande penitenciária social os teares se elevam e marcham esgoelando" (18).

"chatter[ing]" (9).[58] Rather than an act of consumption producing a subject, we find here an act of production consuming its subject.

The narrative then jumps abruptly from the factory to "the salons of the rich," where "lackey poets declaim: How lovely is thy loom!" (10).[59] Taken out of the context of a mechanized labor process and translated into a space of luxury consumption, the loom becomes an aestheticized, Parnassian trope. The juxtaposition of loom as aestheticized object and dangerous machine exemplifies how Galvão uses montage. Sarah Wells has persuasively argued for the influence of Eisensteinian montage on *Parque industrial*. She claims that "Galvão appears to be adopting Eisenstein's assertion that montage works through collision" ("Mass Culture" 63). Indeed, this "dialectical conception of history, in which the collision of two oppositional shots produces something new" (63), resonates with the novel's depiction of the formation of a self-conscious working class, culminating in a violent confrontation with the police in the penultimate chapter, "Rally at *Largo da Concordia*." But, as I have argued throughout this chapter, *Parque industrial*'s narrative about the formation of a revolutionary working class ought to be seen in terms of the novel's formal expression of the contradictions of peripheral capitalism. In this light, the modernist technique of montage makes palpable the non-relation of consumption and production, makes intelligible that they are inseparable but do not form a cohesive, organic whole.

In addition to informing the arrangement of vignettes with anonymous characters, this sort of montage also imbues social significance into the juxtaposition of the novel's various narrative threads. For instance, Galvão intercalates the chapter "Where Surplus Value Is Spent" (*Onde se gasta a mais-valia*) between Corina's initial turn to prostitution and her descent into utter desperation before giving birth to her "monstrous" child. As we saw above, "Where Surplus Value Is Spent" dramatizes the separation of Eleonora and Alfredo and introduces the latter to Otavia, setting the stage for their eventual relationship. The chapter makes class divisions weigh on sexual relations, both in the growing distance between the married couple and in Alfredo's avowed interest in Otavia solely for her class position. Also, it should be remembered that the encounter between Alfredo and Otavia occurs because she has come to the apartment to deliver a dress for Eleonora. The chapter thus frames the action in terms of exploitation, but

---

[58] "O chefe da oficina se aproxima, vagaroso, carrancudo" (19).
[59] "Nos salões dos ricos, os poetas lacios declamam: 'Como é lindo o teu tear!'" (19).

the emphasis falls not on the logic of accumulation per se—that is, investing surplus in order to expand production—but on luxury consumption. The "surplus value is spent" on textiles produced by workers in *Brás* for a domestic market.

This production for domestic consumption indicates an important development in national industrialization, albeit one that serves to reproduce, rather than eliminate, the brutal forms of inequality characteristic of peripheral capitalism. The chapter identifies an emergent form of production in Brazil that resembles the prevailing shape of the labor process in the metropolis insofar it gives rise to its own mode of circulation. As such, this type of production seems to represent the possibility of overcoming dependency, as we defined it above. But, as Ruy Mauro Marini argues, the "similarities of the dependent industrial economy with the classical industrial economy," which began to appear around the time of *Parque industrial*, "concealed profound differences, which capitalist development would accentuate rather than attenuate" (137). When "Latin America enters the stage of industrialization," Marini writes, "it will have to do so on the basis of the foundations created by the export economy" (135). Those foundations, as we have seen throughout *Modernism in the Peripheral Metropolis*, developed in an international division of labor according to which Latin American economies provided agricultural products for consumption in the core and raw materials for industrialization. In other words, production in Latin America is not only oriented toward export, toward an external demand; Marini also crucially shows how Latin America contributes to the emergence of a regime of accumulation in the metropolis "based more on increasing the productive capacity of labor than simply the exploitation of labor" even though the contribution of the periphery is based precisely on greater exploitation (114). In this international division of labor, a greater exploitation of labor occurs in Latin American economies in order to compensate for the transfer of surplus-value from the periphery to the metropolis. According to Marini, this greater exploitation assumes various forms, including increasing the intensity of the labor process and lengthening the working day, but it also derives from "reducing the worker's consumption beyond its natural limit" (124). Effectively, the dependent economy in Latin America rests on a situation in which "the worker is denied the conditions necessary to replenish the wear and tear of his labor power" (126). Given these conditions, with Latin American production attending to an external demand and generating profit on the basis of greater exploitation, not increasing productivity, "the individual consumption of the worker does not intervene in the realization of the product" (134). This situation distinguishes peripheral capitalism in a crucial way from classical industrial capitalism, since in the latter the worker assumes a dual role as producer and consumer. The individual consumption of the worker becomes a decisive element in the expansion of mass industrial production, especially, as we saw above, during the stage of what Fraser calls state-managed capitalism. But peripheral capitalism, by contrast, will tend to "exploit as much as possible the worker's labor-power, without worrying about creating the conditions to replace the worker, as long as it can be replaced by means of the incorporation of new arms into the process of production" (134). As long as, in other words, it can depend on a massive industrial reserve army, which Marini identifies with European migration to Brazil and indigenous labor in Mexico, among many other examples. Marini thus holds that the dissociation of production and consumption in peripheral capitalism, in contrast to the integrated circuit of capital based on the productivity of labor, gives rise to a "stratification of the internal market" or a "differentiation of spheres of circulation": a "low" sphere, which is based on internal production; and a "high" sphere, which is composed of non-workers and is "linked to external production through the import trade" (135). Within this arrangement, the former must be restricted, since its brutal exploitation is the source of profit, while the latter tends to expand as Latin American economies are more fully integrated into the world market. As industrialization develops in the periphery, the high sphere of circulation turns toward domestic production, giving the impression that the economy has begun to overcome dependency and institute its own integrated circuit. We see this possibility in "Where Surplus Value Is Spent" not only in the production of the dress for Eleonora but also symbolically in the budding romance between the radical bourgeois man and the poor revolutionary worker. But this relation also proves to be another non-relation. Although the high sphere of circulation approaches domestic production, the individual consumption of the worker continues to play no significant role in the realization of production. Latin American industrialization will thus continue to rely, according to Marini, on the greater exploitation of labor, not its increasing productivity. *Parque industrial* likewise suggests that Latin American industrial production may contribute to expanding consumption in the upper sphere of Eleonora and Alfredo, but it remains effectively "independent of the wage conditions proper to workers" (Marini 141). Galvão's novel thus gives formal expression to the intuition, based on the situation in São Paulo at the time, that the dissociation of production and consumption would continue to inform Brazilian industrialization and that such industrialization could only be achieved on the basis of a massive industrial reserve army, on the basis of superfluous individuals, like Corina, who are compelled to sell their labor even when there is no demand for it.

The negativity of this account of industrialization in *Parque industrial* only fully appears when we bracket the novel's pamphleteering tendencies and attend to the formal organization of the work. As a pamphlet, *Parque industrial* makes overt assertions about, for instance, the pernicious effect of Hollywood film. The narrator refers to Greta Garbo as a "prostitute feeding the imperialist pimp of America to distract the masses" (78).[60] The novel assumes a didactic role when, to use another example, Rosinha has been exiled for her political activities and she responds: "What does it matter! If in all the countries of the threatened capitalist world, there's a *Brás* ... Other men will remain. Other women will remain. *Brás* of Brazil. *Brás* of the whole world" (88).[61] In the context of the early 1930s, the opposition to American cultural imperialism and the call for international working-class solidarity had an urgent significance. These lines no longer carry the same force. But if we are no longer compelled by the novel's immediate political tendencies, what compels conviction now is its understanding of the dynamics of peripheral capitalism, an understanding that appears not in any overt assertion but in the implicit organization of the vignettes. Beyond the positive space of the factory and the prominence of the class-struggle narrative, the negative space depicts the brutal consequences of separating what should be unified, namely, production and consumption. Through this non-relation, *Parque industrial* constructs a dissonant, dissociated sociality, according to which women are sexually and economically exploited in one minute and dismissed in the next without regard for their needs to reproduce themselves or others. Seen in light of this formal configuration, we should not take Corina's statement in the final chapter that "there's only one crisis. The sexual crisis" (112) simply as an expression of Galvão's desire for sexual liberation. There is a crisis of sex not because, or not only because, of a lack of sexual pleasure. For Corina, a lack of sex also means a lack of the means for her subsistence.

---

[60] "Prostituta alimentando, para distrair as massas, o cáften imperialista da América" (76).
[61] "Que importa! Se em todos os países do mundo capitalista ameaçado há um Brás... Ourtos ficarão. Outras ficarão. Brás do Brasil. Brás de todo o mundo" (83).

The statement should also not be seen as a condemnation of her depoliticization, of her distance from the organized proletariat as she falls into the strata of the lumpen: the vagabonds, criminals, and prostitutes. Rather, the novel gives us the sense that this "one crisis" unifies the formally employed textile workers (Otavia and Rosinha) and the reserve army (Corina) because it encompasses not only sexuality but also the very activities through which society reproduces itself and makes itself into a coherent whole. It would seem utterly implausible to assert that a society could continue even while it systematically undermines its capacity for social reproduction, but *Parque industrial* makes such a jarring idea plausible through its formal presentation. It expresses the historical dissonance of "This law of capitalist society" that "would sound absurd to savages, or even to civilized colonists," a law that "calls to mind the boundless reproduction of animals individually weak and constantly hunted down" (Marx, *Capital: Volume 1* 797). And we may need to take such an absurd idea seriously if we are to confront the crisis of capitalism today.

BIBLIOGRAPHY

Amado, Jorge. *O país do carnaval-Cacau-Suor.* Lisbon: Livros do Brasil, 1984.
Andrade, Mário de. *O movimento modernista.* Rio de Janeiro: CEB, 1942.
Andrade, Oswald de. "Cannibalist Manifesto." *Latin American Literary Review* 19.38 (1991): 38–47.
Candido, Antonio. "Literature and Underdevelopment." *The Latin American Cultural Studies Reader,* edited by Ana Del Sarto, Alicia Ríos & Abril Trigo, Duke University Press, 2004, pp. 35–57.
Benanav, Aaron & John Clegg. "Crisis and Immiseration: Critical Theory Today." *The Sage Handbook of Frankfurt School Critical Theory.* Eds. Beverley Best, Werner Bonefeld & Chris O'Kane. London: Sage, 2018. 1629–1648.
Bhattacharya, Tithi. "Introduction: Mapping Social Reproduction Theory." *Social Reproduction Theory: Remapping Class, Recentering Oppression.* Ed. Tithi Bhattacharya. London: Pluto Press, 2017. 21–36. 1–20.
Bonefeld, Werner. *Critical Theory and the Critique of Political Economy: On Subversion and Negative Reason.* New York: Bloomsbury, 2014.
Brown, Nicholas. *Utopian Generations: The Political Horizon of Twentieth-Century Literature.* Princeton, NJ: Princeton University Press, 2005.
Bryan, Catherine M. "*Antropofagia* and Beyond: Patrícia Galvão's *Industrial Park* in the Age of *Savage* Capitalism." *Ciberletras* 16.
Bueno, Luís. *Uma historia do romance de 30.* São Paulo/Campinas: Edusp/Unicamp, 2006.

Fausto, Boris & Sergio Fausto. *A Concise History of Brazil, Second Edition*. Trans. Arthur Brakel. New York: Cambridge University Press, 2014.
Fraser, Nancy. "Crisis of Care? On the Social-Reproductive Contradictions of Contemporary Capitalism." *Social Reproduction Theory: Remapping Class, Recentering Oppression*. Ed. Tithi Bhattacharya. London: Pluto Press, 2017. 21–36.
Galvão, Patrícia. *Parque industrial*. São Paulo: EDUFUSCar, 1994.
———. *Industrial Park*. Trans. Elizabeth Jackson & K. David Jackson. Lincoln, NE: University of Nebraska Press, 1993.
Guedes, Thelma. *Pagu: literatura e revolução: um estudo sobre o romance* Parque industrial. São Paulo: Nankin Editorial, 2003.
Halperín Donghi, Tulio. *The Contemporary History of Latin America*. Translated by John Charles Chasteen, Duke University Press, 1993.
Jackson, David K. "Afterward." *Industrial Park*. Trans. Elizabeth Jackson & K. David Jackson. Lincoln, NE: University of Nebraska Press, 1993. 115–153.
Jáuregui, Carlos A. *Canibalia: Canibalismo, calibanismo, antropofagia cultural y consumo en América Latina*. Madrid: Iberoamericana/Vervuert, 2008.
Johnson, Randal. "Brazilian Modernism: An Idea Out of Place?" *Modernism and Its Margins: Reinscribing Cultural Modernity from Span and Latin America*. Eds. Anthony L. Geist & Josee B. Monleón. Routledge: New York, 1999. 186–214.
Kanost, Laura M. "Body Politics in Patrícia Galvão's *Parque industrial*." *Luso-Brazilian Review* 43.2 (2006): 90–102.
Kollontai, Alexandra. "The Social Basis of the Woman Question." *The Essential Feminist Reader*. Ed. Estelle B. Freedman. The Modern Library: New York, 2007. 175–181.
Lafetá, João Luiz. *1930: a crítica e o modernismo*. São Paulo: Duas Cidades/Editoria 34, 2000.
Larsen, Neil. *Modernism and Hegemony: A Materialist Critique of Aesthetic Agencies*. University of Minnesota Press, 1990.
Marini, Ruy Mauro. *América Latina, dependencia y globalización*. Ed. Carlos Eduardo Martins, CLASCO & Siglo del Hombre Editores, 2008.
Marx, Karl. *Capital: A Critique of Political Economy, Volume I*. Translated by Ben Fowkes, Penguin, 1990.
Morse, Richard M. *From Community to Metropolis: A Biography of São Paulo, Brazil*. New York: Octagon Books, 1974.
Ribeiro Junior, João Carlos. *Literatura e política no romance de Patrícia Galvão*. 2015. University of São Paulo.
Schwarz, Roberto. *Misplaced Ideas: Essays on Brazilian Culture*. Translated by John Gledson, Verso, 1992.
———. *Seqüências brasileiras: ensaisos*. São Paulo: Companhia das Letras, 1999.

———. *Two Girls and Other Essays*. London: Verso, 2013.
Skidmore, Thomas E. et al. *Modern Latin America*. New York: Oxford University Press, 2010.
Wells, Sarah Ann. "Mass Culture and the Laboratory of Late Modernism in Patrícia Galvão's *Parque industrial*." *Luso-Brazilian Review* 53.1 (2016): 55–76.
———. *Media Laboratories: Late Modernist Authorship in South America*. Evanston, IL: Northwestern University Press, 2017.
William Foster, David. *São Paulo: Perspectives on the City and Cultural Production*. Gainesville, FL: University Press of Florida, 2011.
Williamson, Edwin. *The Penguin History of Latin America*. Penguin Books, 1992.

CHAPTER 6

Conclusion: The Peripheralization of the Metropolis

Debajo de la ciudad, siempre había estado latente el descampado.
Pedro Mairal, El año del desierto

The writers and artists examined in *Modernism in the Peripheral Metropolis* discern the significance of the crisis of the 1920s and 1930s for Latin America in the changing relationship between the city and the countryside. The export era of the late nineteenth and early twentieth centuries marks the moment of Latin America's insertion into the international division of labor of industrial capitalism. Production in Latin America, given its peripheral position in the global economy, attends principally to the demands of the industrializing core, providing raw materials for an increasingly capital intensive mode of production and foodstuffs for its emerging urban working class. This arrangement, which generated unprecedented growth in Latin American economies around the turn of the twentieth century, fueled the development of major cities in the region insofar as urban areas mediated the relationship between the industrializing core and the agricultural periphery. This historical phase also generated the expectation that urbanization in Latin America could follow the path of major cities in Europe and the United States. Nevertheless, this pattern of growth was geographically uneven and subject to cyclical booms and

© The Author(s), under exclusive license to Springer Nature 213
Switzerland AG 2023
T. Mulder, *Modernism in the Peripheral Metropolis*, New
Comparisons in World Literature,
https://doi.org/10.1007/978-3-031-34055-0_6

busts. When the export paradigm finally became untenable in the interwar period, it was not clear what could replace the existing economic structure. The nascent domestic industries in Latin American cities could not become the new center of the economy because they depended on the failing agricultural system, which was spurring migration to urban areas. Cities thus continued to grow, now at an even faster rate, but industrialization in peripheral capitalism could neither absorb the newly available labor power in urban areas nor expand consumption to incorporate the working masses. Urbanization in Latin American thus produces unexpected issues: persistent, extreme inequality in Mexico; the inorganic character of Peruvian society; anomie and cynicism in Buenos Aires; and the crisis of social reproduction in São Paulo. But whatever specific direction it took, the fate of urbanization in Latin American evidently could not be extricated from the imperatives of the international division of labor. Insofar as Latin America contributes to an increasingly productive regime of accumulation through greater exploitation and a persistent industrial reserve army, major cities may have the appearance of a metropolis in Europe or the United States, but they would become neither magnets for wealth nor engines of the economy. Rather, by internalizing the relation between the core and the underdeveloped hinterlands, they become a peripheral metropolis, an incongruous social formation in which rural and urban mutually contaminate and invalidate one another. They become, to return to Ezequiel Martínez Estrada's image with which I opened the book, the disproportionate head of a malnourished body.

The task for the modernists I have discussed involves elaborating a compelling formal composition that expresses this intuition about the uncertain direction of Latin American urbanization. These artists and writers take up modernist techniques not simply to convey the immediate experience of disintegration in the present but rather to grasp the crisis as a totality without assuming a standpoint outside the crisis. We have seen this crisis appear in many ways, for instance, in the relationship between noise and silence in Maples Arce's *Urbe*, in the inorganic form of Mariátegui's essays, in the phraseology of the Astrologer in Arlt's novels, and in the superfluous characters of Galvão's *Parque industrial*. The dissonance of their works thus discloses the contradictory historical reality and brutal forms of inequality characteristic of the peripheral. But this dissonance only becomes palpable and intelligible within the autonomous organization of the work. In light of the autonomy of the work, the incongruities of the peripheral situation appear fundamentally dependent on one another. Moreover, the assertion of autonomy suggests that this dissonance should not exist. The modernist work's dialectic of dissonance and autonomy, in other words, indicates that social life in the periphery integrates incompatible commitments that should be overcome for genuine unity or reciprocity to exist. The ongoing significance of modernist form in Latin America, I argue, lies in this ability to tarry with the underlying contradictions that animate a crisis rather than see it as either mere confusion or a completed phase of instability. This significance remains because the crisis has not been overcome. In Latin America, crisis does not indicate a transitional moment but a persistent impasse stabilizing contradictions that should precipitate a social transformation. As this crisis deepened throughout the twentieth century and into the twenty-first, it has generated slums overflowing with a surplus humanity that capitalist production cannot absorb. It might seem, Mike Davis writes, that these slums are "just volcanoes waiting to erupt" in demands for better living conditions, but the "Darwinian competition" that regulates our social lives perhaps makes it more likely that, "as increasing numbers of poor people compete for the same informal scraps," the slums will increasingly become sites of "self-annihilating communal violence" (201). The crisis, we might say, does not represent a sudden rupture; rather, it indicates a distressing compulsion to repeat in contemporary urbanization.

In light of this catastrophic historical repetition, it begins to make sense that one of the most compelling contemporary Latin American novels on the city actually centers on the vanishing of the city. Pedro Mairal's *El año el desierto* (The Year of the Dessert, 2005) follows the path of María Valdéz Neylan over the course of a year from the center of Buenos Aires to the *pampa*. Initially working as a receptionist for a financial firm, she becomes a maid and a prostitute before joining an indigenous tribe. In effect, this story of a year in María's life recounts the history of Argentina in reverse order. In Mairal's novel, the reversal is prompted by "la intemperie," an indeterminate force that progressively takes over Buenos Aires. The backward movement through Argentine history, in other words, coincides with a spatial invasion of the countryside into the city. At the end of the novel, María returns to Buenos Aires and sees that the Garay Tower, once the triumphant marker of modern capitalist civilization, has become "a giant tombstone in the middle of a pasture" (292).[1] She discovers that her former bosses have become cannibals, and as she disembarks on a boat for Ireland the tower vanishes: "all that could be seen was an increasingly thin strip of land on the horizon without any reference points" (300).[2] A novel about a metropolis collapsing into the disorienting flatness of the pampa would not immediately seem to speak to the current situation of hypertrophic urbanization in Latin America, but Mairal's *El año del desierto* articulates the historical and contemporary significance of the crisis.

The beginning of *El año del desierto* deliberately evokes the atmosphere of crisis in December 2001, when Argentina, having defaulted on its loan payments,[3] imposed limits on the amount of money that could be withdrawn from national banks. At the same time, by having this crisis precipitate a movement backwards through the history of Argentina, Mairal's novel presents the current crisis not as an exceptional event but as a moment in a continuous, albeit contradictory, historical process. When the wealthy take refuge from *la intemperie* by enclosing themselves in the Garay Tower, the novel captures the horrifying spatial organization of contemporary urban poverty in which the elite effectively avoid any contact with inequality on the streets. But *El año del desierto* also places the present moment in an inverted version of history when, for instance, the *Hotel de Inmigrantes* becomes the *Hotel de Emigrantes*. The immigrants once arriving in Argentina to seek a better life now become migrants fleeing the city. As Nicolás Campisi has observed, this historical rewind recalls Martínez Estrada's theory of an underlying continuity in the history of Argentina (4). As I discussed in the introduction, Martínez Estrada rejected the idea of a fundamental opposition between civilization and barbarism, seeing the two instead as equilibrating forces in a self-perpetuating system. But Mairal's novel does not portray the present as simply the repetition of Argentina's perpetual pathology. Rather, in the words of Zac Zimmer, *El año del desierto* "articulates an emergent catastrophe with the long-term nightmare of history" (375). The barbarism in Mairal's novel not only echoes the native, untamed savagery

---

[1] "El edificio parecía una gran lápida en medio del pastizal."

[2] "No se veía la torre por ningún lado, solo se veía una franja de tierra en el horizonte, sin puntos de referencia, cada vez más delgada."

[3] Fittingly, debt and structural adjustment programs have been a major factor in making Latin American cities into urban spaces characterized by informal economies, precarious work, and the lack of necessary services.

feared by Sarmiento but also grasps what Robert Kurz calls "second barbarism," the ruthless demands placed on sociality itself to sustain commodity production through its ongoing crisis. As Emilio Sauri has argued, *El año del desierto* succeeds in portraying the horror of this barbarism because its effects have been etched into the history of Latin America.[4] The collapse of Buenos Aires in Mairal's novel becomes such a compelling staging of the contemporary crisis not because the city represents the decisive victory of civilization over barbarism but because its brings to light the inseparability of barbarism and civilization in the history of the peripheral metropolis.

I have claimed that the figures examined in *Modernism in the Peripheral Metropolis*, by taking seriously the unanticipated problems of city life in Latin America, can be seen as writing a pre-history for contemporary urbanization in the region. But we might go further and suggest that the specificity of the peripheral metropolis in Latin America indicates the forces shaping the future of global capitalism as a whole. Along these lines, the Brazilian philosopher Paulo Arantes has discussed the tendency among commentators to refer to "Brazilianization" when describing the forms of polarization, extreme inequality, and economic insecurity that have become increasingly prevalent in the Global North. Duality, as we have seen, lies at the heart of the experience of peripheral capitalism, but globalization, Arantes writes, "dualizes cities, making them increasingly resemble Brazil's 'divided cities'" (*Zero* 45). In the Global North and South, the city "ceases to be the material framework for society" and now "host[s] a type of spatial organization that exacerbates the ongoing social desolidarization" (48). It is not just that Brazilian cities have anticipated the sort of racial and class divisions, the stark juxtapositions of wealth and poverty, that increasingly mark the cities of the core of capitalism. "Beyond the classical conflict of interests between antagonistic social groups," the "current explosion of inequalities," according to Arantes's analysis, signifies the "collapse of the *social bond* itself" (55). This barbarism emerges out of the heart of capitalist civilization, out of the imperative to reconstitute the dissociated form of sociality presupposed by accumulation. The insights of Arantes's essay, originally published in 2001, have only been

---

[4] See Sauri, *Imperial Decay: Literature and the End of Modernization in the Americas*, forthcoming.

confirmed in the subsequent twenty years of cascading crises. In effect, Arantes argues that the apparent Brazilianization of the world indicates "a new historical simultaneity" between the core and the periphery "produced in the moment of collapse—this being understood not as a cyclical crisis but as a crisis in the production of value triggered by a crisis of labor" (Caux & Catalaini 139). As I have suggested throughout the book, this crisis begins to make itself palpable in Latin American cities in the 1920s and 1930s. Accordingly, we could take the peripheral metropolis as an ominous image of the current peripheralization of the metropolis.

The artists and writers discussed in *Modernism in the Peripheral Metropolis* sense that urbanization in Latin America had begun to generate unexpected issues, but they also recognize that the specificity of those issues only become fully intelligible in light of the imperatives of global capitalism. Similarly, when we attend to the specific conditions of urbanization in Latin America today, we can grasp tendencies at work in capitalism as a whole, namely, those forces driving the peripheralization of the metropolis. We are currently witnessing in the Global North and the Global South, albeit more blatantly in the latter, the increasingly morbid attempts to stabilize the contradictions of capitalism. We are observing, in other words, what Albena Azmanova has called the "crisis of crisis." If a crisis represents "a brief moment of extreme challenge that marks a turning point in an entity's existence," then we can identify "three solutions to a crisis: death, returning to the precrisis situation, or transitioning to a new state" (Azmanova 15). But the current crisis of capitalism seems to be characterized by the absence of all three options. "Capitalism is not on the edge of its collapse," Azmanova writes, "but it is surely on edge" (15). This apparently unprecedented situation from the perspective of the Global North, however, looks quite familiar when we look at Latin America in the 1920s and 1930s. This resonance has not been lost on Pedro Mairal. By evoking the historical forces discussed in *Modernism in the Peripheral Metropolis*, Mairal's novel conveys the truth of the present moment in terms of this long history of the crisis of crisis. Rather than simply depicting the revenge of the savage countryside against the civilized city, *El año del desierto* expresses the barbarism that emerges when sociality itself must be sacrificed for the sake of capital accumulation. In striking ways, Mairal's novel tarries, like other works examined in *Modernism in the Peripheral Metropolis*, with the contradictions animating the present and imagines what it is like to inhabit the crisis without normalizing it or ignoring its constitutive uncertainty. That is, the dissonance of *El año del desierto* lies not in the depiction of collapse per se but in the possibility for a crisis to sustain itself and deepen the power of capital over all aspects of social life.[5]

Bibliography

Arantes, Paulo. *Zero à esquerda*. Conrad Editoria do Brasil, 2004.
Azmanova, Albena. *Capitalism on Edge: How Fighting Precarity Can Achieve Radical Change Without Crisis or Utopia*. Columbia University Press, 2020.
Campisi, Nicolás. "El retorno de lo contemporáneo: crisis e historicidad en El año del desierto de Pedro Mairal." *Cuadernos LÍRICO*, vol. 20, 2019.
Caux, Luiz Philipe de & Felipe Catalani. "A passagem do dois ao zero: dualidade e desintegração no pensamento dialético brasileiro (Paulo Arantes, leitor de Roberto Schwarz." *Revista do Instituto de Estudos Brasileiros*, vol. 74, 2019, pp. 119–146.
Davis, Mike. *Planet of Slums*. Verso, 2006.
Mairal, Pedro. *El año del desierto*. Eds. Susal Hallstead & Juan Pablo Dabove, Stockcero, 2012.
Mau, Søren. *Mute Compulsion: A Marxist Theory of the Economic Power of Capital*. Verso, 2023.
Sauri, Emilio. *Imperial Decay: Literature and the End of Modernization in the Americas*. Northwestern University Press, Forthcoming.
Zimmer, Zac. "A Year in Rewind, and Five Centuries of Continuity: *El año del desierto*'s Dialectical Image." *MLN*, vol. 128, 2013, pp. 373–383.

---

[5] On crisis as a source of power, see Mau, pp. 308–311.

Index[1]

A
Adorno, Theodor Wiesengrund, 19, 19n31, 21n34, 68, 69, 74, 87n12, 89, 89n15, 90n16, 94, 135n40, 189n21
architecture, 69
art as social production, 74
dissonance, 21n34, 94
Álvarez Bravo, Manuel, 35–38, 36n56, 41
"*Los agachados*," 35–37, 36n56, 39
Amado, Jorge, 178, 178n5
Amícola, José, 122, 126, 129n29, 139, 143n55
Andrade, Mário de, 177, 178
Andrade, Oswaldo de, 38, 177, 178, 187, 187n19, 193, 197n35, 203
Anomie, 6, 27, 30, 42, 43, 124, 125, 161, 165–169, 214

Arantes, Paulo, 12, 21, 97n26, 162, 163, 167–169, 217, 218
"A fratura brasileira do mundo," 167
Architecture
 Juan O'Gorman, 50, 51, 67, 67n31, 68
 Mexico City, 63
 neo-colonial vs. functionalist, 62
 Theodor Adorno, 69
Arlt, Roberto, 5, 13–18, 16n27, 16n28, 20–22, 25, 25n41, 43, 119–169, 214
 "El arte de juntar puchos," 164
 "Por algo somos desconfiados," 120, 120n1
anomie, 43, 124
appearances, 163
Buenos Aires, 17, 43, 143n55

---

[1] Note: Page numbers followed by 'n' refer to notes.

© The Author(s), under exclusive license to Springer Nature Switzerland AG 2023
T. Mulder, *Modernism in the Peripheral Metropolis*, New Comparisons in World Literature,
https://doi.org/10.1007/978-3-031-34055-0

Arlt, Roberto (*cont.*)
 cynicism, 25, 43, 124
 Dostoevsky, 143, 143n55, 148, 149, 160
 humiliation, 143, 148
 Los lanzallamas, 25, 122, 126, 137, 139, 151n72, 164, 165
 Los siete locos, 25, 122, 125, 126, 130n30, 137, 139, 147, 152, 156, 157, 165
 modernism, 13, 15
 phraseology, 139, 214
 preface to *Los lanzallamas*, 16
 realism, 126
 suicide, 165
Autonomy, 13, 19–21, 35–37, 41, 42, 53, 55, 58, 65, 66, 68, 69, 74, 77, 90, 111, 135n40, 179, 182, 215

B
Benjamin, Walter, 24n38, 95
Bloch, Ernst, 12n19, 154n81
Bolaño, Roberto, 53, 53n4
Borges, Jorge Luis, 7, 15, 16, 124
Brown, Nicholas, 20, 38n57, 114, 203n54
Buenos Aires
 civilization and barbarism, 2, 3
 flatness, 153
 history, 2, 21n35
 immigration, 161
 Martínez Estrada, 3, 4, 22, 153
 politics, 81, 133
 poverty, 164
 urban grid, 153, 154

C
Candido, Antonio, 17, 97n26, 176, 177
 "Literature and Underdevelopment," 176

Coppola, Horacio, 6–8, 6n9, 8n10, 41
Crisis, 3, 4n7, 5, 6, 13, 15, 18, 22, 26–28, 27n45, 30, 31, 33, 35, 37, 39–44, 40n60, 83, 84, 88, 90, 91, 94, 95, 97, 100, 101, 104, 105, 109, 121–123, 127, 128, 132n35, 133, 134, 135n40, 136, 139, 141, 156n86, 160, 163, 167, 169, 175–209, 213–219

D
Davis, Mike, 33, 33n52, 59, 60, 215
Dissonance, 13, 17, 20, 21, 21n34, 35–44, 90, 97, 98, 180, 198, 209, 214, 215, 219
Dostoevsky, Fyodor, 129, 129n26, 143–146, 143n55, 144n56, 148, 149, 149n69, 150n71, 160, 166, 167
 Demons, 129n26, 143–145, 143n54, 144n56, 145n57, 148, 150n71, 166
Durkheim, Émile, 166–168, 166n102

E
Essay
 Georg Lukács, 86, 86n10, 87, 87n12, 143, 150n71
 José Carlos Mariátegui, 43, 81–116, 119, 214
 in Latin America, 84, 85, 86n9
 Montaigne, 88
 Theodor Adorno, 89, 89n15, 90n16, 94
Export, 22, 27n45, 28–31, 28n46, 28n47, 41, 102, 103, 105–107, 126, 127, 131, 132, 141, 176, 177, 181, 183–186, 203, 203n54, 206, 213, 214

F
Flores Galindo, Alberto, 81, 83n5, 105, 106, 110
Fraser, Nancy, 186, 201, 202, 207
Futurism, 51, 54n5

G
Galvão, Patrícia, 5, 31, 43, 44, 175–209, 214
  cover of Parque industrial, 189
  feminism, 200
  modernism, 5, 43, 175–209
  Parque industrial, 31, 43, 175–209, 214
  proletarian novel, 43, 178, 181, 194
  reserve army of the unemployed, 180
  sex, 180, 202
  social reproduction, 196, 202
Gramsci, Antonio, 107, 107n44, 107n49, 112, 112n55, 112n56, 133, 133n37, 134
  Caesarism, 133, 133n37
  José Carlos Mariátegui, 107n44, 112
Greenberg, Clement, 18

H
Haya de la Torre, Víctor Raúl, 84, 110, 112–114, 112n57
Hegel, G. W. F., 26, 26n42, 26n43, 27, 27n44, 27n45, 30, 39, 40, 41n61, 153, 157
  rabble, 26, 26n42, 26n43, 27, 27n45, 30

I
Inequality, 6, 17, 19, 20, 25–27, 30, 36, 39, 42, 51–53, 58, 61, 69, 72, 72n38, 76, 77, 84, 97, 98, 104, 110–112, 115, 125, 134, 150, 168, 179, 206, 214, 216, 217

J
Jameson, Fredric, 66n30, 93, 93n22

K
Kollontai, Alexandra, 200

L
Larsen, Neil, 97n27, 135n40, 204
Lima
  coast and sierra, 8, 83, 84, 94, 98, 100, 109, 110, 112
  history, 12, 108
  indigenismo, 104, 105
  José Carlos Mariátegui on, 43, 83n2, 91, 96n24, 99, 101, 102
  modernization, 101, 102, 105, 106
Lukács, Georg, 38–41, 40n59, 40n60, 86, 86n10, 87, 87n12, 143–146, 149, 156, 166, 167
  "Dostoevsky," 143, 146, 149, 167
  essay, 86, 86n10, 87, 87n12, 143, 150n71
  realism, 39, 40

M
Mairal, Pedro, 215–218
  El año del desierto, 216–219
Maples Arce, Manuel, 5, 5n8, 42, 49–77, 214
  "Actual No. 1," 50n1, 53, 54, 54n5
  futurism, 51, 54n5
  Mexican Revolution, 42, 49–77
  Urbe, 53–58, 56n9, 214

Mariátegui, José Carlos, 5, 8n11,
  10n15, 12n19, 24, 43, 81–116,
  81n1, 83n2, 83n3, 83n5, 97n27,
  97n28, 101n33, 103n38,
  103n40, 104n41, 107n44,
  109n53, 112n57, 113n58,
  119, 214
 anti-imperialism, 114
 Antonio Gramsci, 107, 107n44, 133
 Blaise Cendrars, 95
 city, 5, 43, 83, 84, 96n24, 98–105,
  101n33, 102n34, 107n44,
  109n53, 120, 121
 coast and sierra, 83, 84, 94, 98,
  100, 104, 109, 110, 112
 communist international, 81, 113,
  113n58, 115
 the essay, 43, 82–98, 83n5, 86n9,
  86n10, 97n27, 109, 110,
  115, 116
 gamonalismo, 106–108, 112
 indigenismo, 83n5, 104, 105
 industrialization, 108
 inorganic, 83–98, 102, 106,
  108–116, 119, 214
 intellectual meridian debate, 110
 La escena contemporánea, 84,
  91, 94–96
 Pedro Henríquez Ureña, 97
 politics, 43, 55, 58, 81–116
 *Siete ensayos de interpretación de la
  realidad peruana*, 81, 84
Marini, Ruy Mauro, 31, 31n50, 32,
 32n51, 181n11, 206, 207
Martínez Estrada, Ezequiel, 1–5,
 6n9, 8, 21–23, 41, 153, 155,
 214, 216
 Buenos Aires, 2–6, 6n9, 8, 21, 22,
  43, 81, 81n1, 83n5, 101, 102,
  111, 120, 153–155
 La cabeza de Goliat, 1–3, 5, 6n9
 Radiografía de la pampa, 2, 153

Marx, Karl, 24, 25, 26n43, 30, 31n50,
 38n58, 53n4, 131n33, 134–136,
 134n39, 135n40, 149, 158, 159,
 180, 181n11, 186, 189, 191,
 192, 197, 199, 201, 209
 commodity fetishism, 189, 189n21
 *The Eighteenth Brumaire of Louis
  Bonaparte*, 134
 German *misère*, 149, 150, 150n70
 reserve army of the
  unemployed, 30, 180
Masotta, Óscar, 123, 151, 158,
 160–162, 165, 166
Mexico City
 architecture, 63, 65
 and the Mexican Revolution,
  42, 49–77
 migration, 21n35, 59
Migration, 6, 10, 12, 21n35, 30, 33,
 59, 161, 184, 207, 214
Modernism, 5n8, 10n15, 12–21, 23,
 23n36, 35, 37, 40, 41, 50–52,
 76, 77n48, 93n21, 104n41,
 129n27, 178n3, 203n54
 realism, 35–44
Modernismo (Brazil), 5n8, 43, 177,
 177n2, 203
Modotti, Tina, 5, 35–38, 41, 42, 49–77
 and Edward Weston, 70
 "La elegancia," 35–37
 and Leon Trotsky, 73
 "Mella's Typewriter," 73–76
 "Workers' Parade," 71, 71n34, 72
Montaigne, 88

O
O'Gorman, Juan, 5, 42, 49–77
 critique of functionalism, 53, 68
 functionalism, 50, 63–69, 64n26
 and Le Corbusier, 50, 64–67,
  64n26, 64n27, 66n30

Oquendo de Amat, Carlos, 8,
    8n11, 10, 11
  5 metros de poemas, 8–10, 8n11
Ortega y Gasset, José, 121, 121n5,
    122, 137, 156n86

P

Peripheral metropolis, 1–44, 58, 60,
    102, 102n35, 109, 127, 132,
    141, 155, 164, 214, 217, 218
Photography, 38, 42, 53, 69–77

R

Rama, Ángel, 13–15, 14n22, 19,
    50–52, 104, 104n41, 153n79
  "Las dos vanguardias
    latinoamericanas," 13, 50
Reserve army of the unemployed, 180
Rivera, Diego, 13, 51, 65, 68, 111
Rodó, José Enrique, 85, 86, 86n8
Romero, José Luis, 27–30, 105

S

Safatle, Vladimir, 42, 141n50, 168
Salazar Bondy, Sebastián, 105
São Paulo, 21n35, 22, 38n58, 43,
    177, 178n3, 179–194, 184n17,
    193n28, 194n29, 200, 208, 214
  coffee, 183–185, 184n17, 193n28
  Getúlio Vargas, 179, 185
  history, 185
  industrialization, 44, 180, 181, 186,
    188, 200, 208
  Paulista War, 182, 185
  politics, 43, 184, 185, 194, 195

Sarlo, Beatriz, 16, 21n35, 134
Sarmiento, Domingo Faustino, 2, 153,
    155, 217
Sartre, Jean Paul, 154n81
Scalabrini Ortiz, Raúl, 161,
    162, 164
Schwarz, Roberto, 17, 25, 38,
    38n57, 38n58, 39, 52, 124,
    162, 163, 180, 181n10,
    181n12, 193
Simmel, Georg, 24, 24n37,
    24n38, 24n39, 25, 25n40,
    25n41, 40n60, 158, 159,
    159n97
  "The Metropolis and Mental
    Life," 24, 158
Sloterdijk, Peter, 121, 157
Sohn-Rethel, Alfred, 160
Strand, Paul, 37, 76

T

Trotsky, Leon, 73–75, 73n40,
    73n41, 75n45
  Literature and Revolution, 73

V

Vargas, Getúlio, 177n2, 179, 182,
    183, 185, 200
Vasconcelos, José, 50n2, 62, 63,
    63n24, 65n29
Vela, Arqueles, 52, 58, 59

W

Warwick Research Collective, 12
Williams, Raymond, 23, 23n36

Printed in the USA
CPSIA information can be obtained
at www.ICGtesting.com
LVHW011955160324
774517LV00004B/417